THE CHARLES

by

ARTHUR BERNON TOURTELLOT

Illustrated by

ERNEST J. DONNELLY

FARRAR & RINEHART
INCORPORATED

New York   *Toronto*

FOR

E. M. H. T.

IN MEMORY

Contents

Part One

The Paradise of
Those Parts

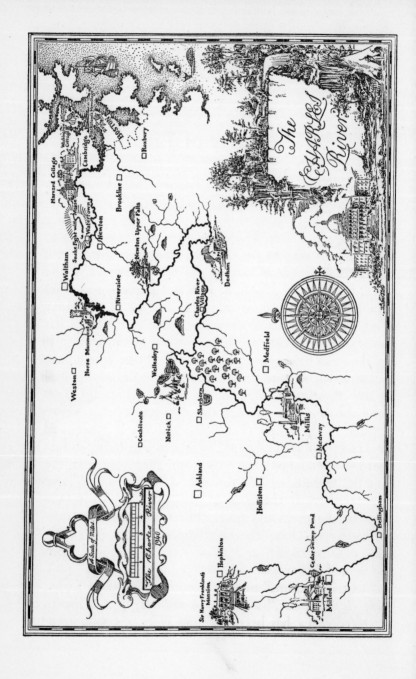

The CHARLES River

Scale of Miles
The Charles River
1940

Harvard College
Cambridge
BOSTON
Roxbury
Waltham
Snake Fight with Moses
Watertown
Newton
Newton Upper Falls
Brookline
Riverside
Norse Manuments
Weston
Charles River Village
Dedham
Wellesley
Medfield
Cochituate
Natick
Sherborn
Millis
Medway
Ashland
Holliston
Hopkinton
Cedar Swamp Pond
Milford
Bellingham
Sir Harry Frankland's Mansion

I

The River of Life

IT was Ralph Waldo Emerson, the wisest man to walk in the valley of the Charles, who likened man to a river whose source is hidden and who moved, like the river, to eventual freedom. It was Emerson, too, who feared that, if the race of man ever died off, it would die of civilization. And if the calm ghost of Emerson has gone far back in time or come forward in this same valley, the years have proved his wisdom. For he would have encountered, in one direction, the simple, idyllic life of the Algonquins. But in the other, he would have come across a web of ideas and convictions that led to intricate philosophies that flourished for a while and then passed away. He would have seen top-heavy industries rise throughout the valley and then topple in the dust of depression. Yet through it all he would have seen freedom as the goal of the valley's history, the quest of the poets and philosophers, and the fixed star of tradesmen along the riverbank, of printers, gristmillers, shipwrights, and those who plowed the fields and hewed the trees.

"Quineboquin," the Algonquins called the Charles, meaning "circular," and that is the way man's life in the river valley has been, moving from the wild freedom of the Indian through the tragicomic quest of the white man, who brought with him all his crippling institutions and then went systematically about inventing other institutions to break them down. The way of the red man came to its end early, for the Indian failed when the test came, probably because he knew too little of the trick of organization. But the way of the white man in the valley goes on. Some things he has tried which, far from setting him free as he dreamed, have brought him tumbling back to earth, so that he has had to begin again. And other things, rooted in three centuries of living here in the valley, have grown strong and are achieving their missions: the colleges have endured, and so have the songs of the poets and the words of the philosophers, the stubborn and ceaseless rumbling of the press. The young still walk upon the riverbanks and dream; and the old walk slower and remember. The moon still rises, in some places shining down on deserted mills and converting the hard daylight tragedy of blind ambitions into the soft emptiness of shattered dreams, and in other places shining down on the waters of the river as they leap over the rocks with the maple and ash and oak their only witnesses still. This last is the river the poets knew and loved, the river that Lowell and Longfellow stood meditating over and up which the wry little physician Holmes rowed away from his patrician patients.

But the Algonquins knew it long before that, for to them it was the River of Life. They, too, had their poets and their philosophers; and if they did not know as much of the letter of Plato as those who came after them in the river valley, they knew more of Plato's spirit. Through the years they evolved a host of legends which taught them the meaning of life, and they learned how to live. They sought the key of creation, too, in common with the prying curiosity of all mankind about things that do not concern them; and they came out of the whirlpool with a creed of passing wisdom.

In earliest times, the Algonquins believed, all the face of the earth was covered with water, and everything that lived floated about on a raft. Chief of all the animals was the Great Rabbit, who was the Great Spirit himself in mortal shape. After the raft had floated about aimlessly for a time, which might have been days or centuries, the animals were growing restless, so that the Great Rabbit saw clearly that there must be land to accommodate them and give point to their lives. So he called the beaver and sent him overboard into the depths, telling him to bring back with him a handful of earth. But the beaver went down and came up with nothing. Then the Great Rabbit called the otter and told him to go down and see what he could find. But the otter came up with nothing. Then the Great Rabbit considered the possible alternative measures he could employ to get hold of a little bit of earth and could light upon nothing of worth. As he sat in troubled silence there in the midst of the endless waters with the animals surrounding him and the raft floating impotently about, a little female muskrat came to him and offered to take a dive down into the deep. But the other animals, particularly the beaver and the otter, laughed at her and derided her. The Great Rabbit, however, gave her permission to try, and the little muskrat hopped off the edge of the raft and disappeared below the surface of the water. All that day and all that night and throughout the next day until evening, nothing was seen of the enterprising muskrat. Even the Great Rabbit had given her up as lost. But at the second twilight the body of the muskrat popped to the surface. They hauled her abroad the raft and found that the muskrat was unconscious; but in her paw she clutched a little ball of mud.

The Great Rabbit took the bit of mud and molded it in his hands. It grew larger and larger, first into an island, then a mountain and then the earth itself. The rabbit walks around and around it, looking to search out imperfections. He walks around it still, for it does not yet satisfy him. Thus, the Great Spirit envelops the earth forever.

The other animals meanwhile found homes for themselves, some in the hills, some in open fields, and some near the rivers in quiet nooks. Moreover, the Great Rabbit made trees by shooting his arrows into the earth and transfixing them with other arrows to form branches. Last of all, he rewarded the muskrat by taking her as his mate, and out of the union sprang the race of man. The Great Rabbit was the personification of the Great Spirit, and the muskrat the personification of earth. So the Algonquin saw his race as the creation of both spirit and matter; and if he recognized the earth as his mother, he recognized the spirit of eternity as his father. He conferred on the latter the name "Missabos," which came from the same route as his words for Light, Dawn, and the East.

All the mythology of the Algonquins, and all that they believed that man, in his little state on this planet, could ever know of eternity, was founded upon that simple legend. Thus, in all that followed and in the life and society of the Algonquins themselves, there was a certain clarity and directness. They probably put their lives in order and achieved a measure of satisfaction in living much more quickly than did any other ancient peoples. They may have been far behind in external signs of political and economic and even cultural development, but if so they saved themselves a good deal of bother. The ancient tribes of Israel wandered all over the Eastern world in search of a way of life; the Greeks and the Romans, embodying more nonsense in their mythologies than they could find even in their own annals, argued for years about the beginning and the end; the Egyptians reared great monuments and enslaved thousands of men to do it. The Algonquins did not concern themselves with such things. They saw that life, like the day, came from the east and ended with the setting of the sun in the west, on the very edge of night. And they had no complaint. The light made the earth worthy of life as it brought the endless succession of days, and it was the first thing that the Algonquin worshiped, for it was the first also that blessed him.

Never, therefore, did the Algonquin worship through fear or terror. His gods were the sun, the source of light; and the winds, the breath of life; the morning star and the rain; the lakes and the forest; the rivers and the moon. Deep within his silence, his soul was stirred by the world about him so that there was little in that world that he did not know intimately: the animals, the birds, and the fish; the rains, the winds, and the seasons; the trees, the plants, and the soil. He was a savage, perhaps, but he valued the gift of life while he had it.

This crude pantheism in the Algonquin, his mystical apprehension of eternity in the voice of the winds and the perpetual flow of the waters, led to an embracement of the natural world around him throughout both the years of his life and the days of his year. The Massachuset tribe, which inhabited the valley of the Charles, were a woodland people who found all that they needed to sustain life close at hand in the forests.

The Algonquin cut down saplings in the forest, stuck the larger ends of the poles into the ground in a

circle and bound the smaller ends together with tough bark at the top, and had the framework of his house. He then covered the whole framework with mats made of reeds and sewed together with the hemp that grew near by. Those mats were, in fact, the Algonquin's chief bit of furniture, for he used them as flooring, as walls, as beds, and as curtains and doors. He moved his house about at will in the spring and summer and autumn, but in the winter he and his fellows lived in primitive commons, community hotels in which as many as sixty people lived in peace together. These were relatively finished buildings, made of solid wood in much the manner of stockades. They were efficiently heated and had furnishings equal to those of the first settlers. Until the spring thaws came, the Indians lived a community life, whiling the winter away in making baskets and household utensils and clothing.

During the three other seasons, however, the Indian's life was freer and much more closely attuned to the natural world. The Algonquin's entire philosophy seemed to be that he had certain inescapable needs and that he had time enough to enjoy himself in the process of acquiring them. He was clothed adequately, he ate well, and his family life was of an order far beyond that of most other primitives and of many civilized peoples. But he made an ordeal of none of those things, and he knew nothing of economics, dietetics, or eugenics. Instead, he used the common sense with which he had been endowed. If it was cold, he dressed in a heavy cloak of beaver. If it was hot, he put on nothing but a loincloth. If he was planning to track through the underbrush, he put on tight breeches of deerskin to save himself scratches. He followed the same good sense with regard to his food; and without making an issue of it, he maintained a balanced diet. He hunted for flesh and fowl, he fished, he gathered berries, and he planted enough vegetables to last him through the winter and until the next harvest.

Early white men—those of reckless and adventurous nature who were always embarrassing the Puritans —found something relishing in the ways of the Indian, who apparently had every comfort and all the fullness of life that was supposed to be the reward of civilization. Thomas Morton wrote in 1637, a tone of envy creeping in occasionally: "The aire doeth beget good

stomacks, and they feede continually and are no nig-
gards of their vittels." Even in the dead of winter, the
Indian's larder was well stocked with dried corn and
beans, with smoked meats, and with preserved fish.
He had barns in the earth itself, huge holes which he
filled with great baskets of food. He ate as much as he
wanted, Morton said wistfully, and yet he had more
than enough to carry him through the year. What was
more, all this bounty was the fruit not of hard labor but
of leisurely sport. The Indian was swift, efficient in that
he wasted few movements, and silent; but work and
play were always one to him. Duty and discipline were
unheard of, for those imply a natural tendency in an
opposite direction that somehow has to be checked for
reasons of society. The Algonquins did not fit their
lives to institutions but to nature. Wrote Morton, whom
the Puritans despised.

"According to humane reason, guided onely by the
light of nature, these people leade the more happy and
freer life, being voyde of care, which torments the
mindes of so many Christians: They are not delighted
in baubles, but in usefull things."

Their lives were "voyde of care" perhaps, but not
of meaning. They respected age for its wisdom and they
could look upon the forest without seeing it as so many
cords of timber. They could use the deer and kill it for
their needs, but they knew it also as an ally in living.
They could snatch salmon from the river, but they
found companionship in the river too. Their lives were
probably a closer parallel to the life of the river than
those of any other men who have lived near it, if the
poets and philosophers be excepted; for, inarticulate as
they may have been to the rest of the world, nearly

every Indian was himself a poet and philosopher. He had a profound respect for human experience, for the odyssey of man's seventy years on the earth; he embraced life, and he never became panic-stricken at death.

It might well have been this self-respect that differentiated the Indian from those who displaced him on the banks of the Charles, for the Puritans had nothing but scorn for the mortal state of man. Yet it was pride that contributed to the undoing of the Indian as it was pride of a different kidney that eventually led the Puritan into the shadows. If one tribe was too proud to depend on another, it was destined that a strange race that knew full well the strength of unity would run all tribes into oblivion.

The legend of Papasiquineo, the oldest Indian legend to appear in English and the substance of a Whittier poem, was related to the world by Morton in his *New English Canaan*. He wrote the book "upon tenne yeares knowledge and experiment of the country" and entitled it as a gibe at the Puritans' preoccupation with the Old Testament. The Papasiquineo affair was brought up by Morton to show the English that stubbornness about maintaining one's reputation was no peculiarity of Anglo-Saxons; but it had deeper implications, for it was just the sort of stubborn independence that precluded any strong national organization among North American Indians.

Papasiquineo was the sachem of all the territory near the Merrimac River, some miles north of the Charles. The sachem of Saugus, of the Massachuset tribe, fell in love with Papasinquineo's daughter, and went up to the old sachem to interview him. Papasiquineo favored the match, and the marriage took place among the people of the bride's father, as was perfectly agreeable to the sachem of Saugus, who considered himself fortunate in getting the princess in the first place. After all the feastings and ceremonies at her father's seat in the north, the young bride went down to Massachusetts with her sachem of Saugus. Her father had given the couple an escort of warriors, whom the sachem of Saugus entertained royally and then sent back home to Papasiquineo.

The sachem of Saugus and his bride were happy, but after a few months the bride had a notion that she would like to go to visit with her father. Not only did her husband permit the visit, but he also appointed a company of his warriors to go with her. When the company arrived at Papasiquineo's headquarters, the warriors were feasted and then sent back to Saugus, whose bride stayed on for the visit with her father. In a few weeks, she thought it was time to go back again, and Papasiquineo sent word by courier down to the sachem of Saugus that his wife was ready to return and would he please send up an escort for her. The sachem of Saugus, although he loved his wife and had been lonely without her, sent word back to his father-in-law that he would do no such thing. He pointed out that he had sent the escorting party with his wife when she left his realm and that it was Papasiquineo's duty to furnish the convoy when the girl left his region. He said that neither he nor his warriors were going to make themselves servile.

Old Papasiquineo was enraged when he heard the answer from the sachem of Saugus, his son-in-law. He immediately dispatched another courier to the upstart and told him that if he did not have more respect than that for his father-in-law, and if he thought so little of his wife as to stand on the technicalities of ceremony in conducting her home, then he could do without her company. When this intelligence was delivered by the southbound courier, the sachem of Saugus refused to dignify it with an answer, for, said Morton, "hee was determined not to stoope so lowe."

For the ensuing years, the stubborn old sachem Papasiquineo would not send his daughter back to her husband. And the stubborn young sachem of Saugus would not send for her. The last Morton knew of the affair it was a stalemate, with the poor young wife stuck between two proud sagamores. The whole thing was an indication of what the Algonquin was not: he was no diplomat, no strategist, and no expert in either conversation or interrelationships. He could endure as long as it depended upon himself. If it depended upon his relationship with others, he was doomed.

The river valley knows now all that it will ever know of those first proud men who inhabited it; and that all is precious little, for they were silent men. The poets have caught their spirit, and the sculptors preserved their likeness. And all the men who have dreamed since those last days of the Algonquin have dreamed of a freedom akin to that which he knew, but none of them sought it in such a simple way. Some sought it through the fashioning of philosophies that would set their minds free, and some through material prosperity that would set their bodies free. But none has lived as the Algonquin, mind and body alike free, close by the River of Life and under the Moon, which brought the dews and ruled the tides and was goddess over all the rivers.

2

Admiral of New England

LEGENDS of the "Lost City" of America were already old when Sieur de Champlain of Saintonge, captain in ordinary to the King of France in the Marines, poked his way curiously along the eastern coast. As far back as 1530, Allefonsce had told tales of "a Town called Norumbega, and there is in it a Goodly Number of People, and they have manie Peltries of manie kinds of Animals." Nearly four centuries later, a Harvard professor (but not of history) went into the woods where a vivacious brook joins the Charles and erected a tower of field stone there in memory of the Norsemen. Moreover, he wrote numerous books, strangely documented, to prove that his tower was rightly placed; and for every book that he wrote, six more were written by other local historians all along the seaboard to prove that the lost city was on the Penobscot in Maine or the St. Johns in Florida or somewhere between.

Champlain himself, however, took Allefonsce with a grain of salt. As far as he was concerned, he himself was the first white man to see the river that flowed into Massachusetts Bay; and he exercised the prerogative of priority by christening the river, which he apparently never bothered to explore very far inland. "A very broad river," he called it. "It stretches, as it seemed to me, towards the Iroquois." The river, as a matter of fact, stretched nowhere. It wound and circled in every direction of the compass, but Champlain was not the last, even though he was probably the first, to be fooled. Coming up Boston harbor, one would judge, from the great size of the basin, that the river was a huge artery to the Pacific and the greatest river on the continent. But if one ventured three miles upstream, he would change his mind. The river bends where now the bones of Boston's great lie on the Cambridge shore, and it narrows so abruptly that only small craft can proceed farther.

But Champlain did not venture upstream. He took one look at the wide mouth of the river and dubbed it the River du Guast in honor of a great and adventurous friend. Champlain, furthermore, charted a map on which he represented his River du Guast as large and wide and straight. It was a worthy river named for a worthy man.

Pierre du Guast, Sieur de Monts, was once governor of Pons in Saintonge, which was not important. He was also a member of Henry IV's court, being no less a functionary than gentleman-in-ordinary to the king's bedchamber, which was hardly more important. What was important was that du Guast was a kindred spirit of Champlain's. In 1600, three years before Champlain made his first expedition, du Guast had crossed the Atlantic with de Chauvin and landed on this continent long enough to discover that there were valuable furs to be had from the Indians. He had gone back to France bubbling over with enthusiasm and planned to get all the merchants of La Rochelle to finance a colony in

America somewhere. Then, since he frequented the king's bedchamber on official business, he asked Henry IV for a grant. Henry was in an expansive mood and magnanimous, and he gave du Guast all the territory on the Atlantic seaboard (and as far inland as he wanted to go) from Philadelphia to Cape Breton. These formalities over, du Guast went out to collect a shipload of responsible settlers, while Henry IV's ministers gave his Majesty a serious rebuke for so foolishly tossing away the new continent, which might—for all he knew —be worth something.

Du Guast spent the autumn of 1603 trying to find pioneers. However, since he could line up no responsible parties, he turned to all the hovels and dives in the French coastal towns and by the end of the following winter had a motley crew of a hundred and twenty convicts, idlers, and wharf rats of varying degrees of degeneracy. By spring he had also a couple of ships and was ready to set sail for the New World. He didn't know where he was going to settle his portable asylum when he got there, but he did want Champlain to come along with him. Champlain had handled the Spanish navy satisfactorily some years earlier and had a reputation for being a hard man to best. And if ever anyone needed such a companion, it was Pierre du Guast with his six score derelicts. Henry IV, who was by now quite interested in the project, said that Champlain could have his royal permission to go along if he would make a chart of the American coast.

The two ships arrived off the New England coast toward the end of 1604. Du Guast, who probably was eager to get his convicts on land, grabbed the first opportunity, which happened to be at Passamaquoddy

Bay, to start his colony. Champlain, who had royal commands to attend to, continued to sail down the coast. He did not get as far as that "very broad river" he later christened before he had a hunch that all might not be going well with du Guast. So he turned around and went back up the coast. He found that only forty-four of the settlers were alive. Du Guast now decided that he'd better move down the coast and find a new location for what was left of his expedition. Together, he and Champlain probed the whole coast, as far down as Cape Cod, but du Guast could not decide on a place for his new colony. Champlain picked out the river as the most likely spot and named it in honor of the man who was responsible for the journey, but du Guast was not impressed. And he never did find a flourishing site for his colony, though he roamed the coast down as far as Maryland and back again. He went back to France and lost all his money in sending over supplies to keep a fragment of his colony going. Then he lost his reputation when Henry IV died, and no longer had access to the royal bedchamber.

The next man who charted the Charles was the Admiral of New England, Captain John Smith, a true explorer and the most persistent of colonizers. The region of the Charles was his kingdom come, for he lost all use for Virginia, as he had a perfect right to do, having three times been sentenced to death there—twice by his own people and once by Powhatan. There is probably a good deal of exaggeration in his amazing *Adventures and Discourses,* for the admiral was not above stretching a point for a zesty tale. Notwithstanding that tendency to toot his own horn which caused his listeners in the taverns back home to smile, he brought to his efforts more industry and more spirit than did his Gallic forerunners. He regarded the Virginia fiasco as an unfortunate miscarriage, but he became neither bitter nor discouraged because of it. He simply looked for a better land, perennial adventurer that he was.

That better land was the valley of the Charles, where, Smith said, probably meaning about half of it as usual, that he would rather live "of all the four parts of the world that I have yet seen not inhabited." He set out for New England in April, 1614, with two ships and elaborate plans "there to take Whales and make tryalls of a Myne of Gold and Copper." If he could not catch whales or find any mines, then he was going to limit himself to fish and furs. As the two ships drew near New England, they spotted a whale and wasted a lot of time chasing it, but it got away. As for the gold mine, Smith said that they had never seriously expected to find one anyhow: it was just a trick, he explained, to get backing for the expedition. Accordingly, when they arrived on the mainland, Smith turned his followers to catching fish and chasing beavers while he took notes for a book he was going to write on this paradise, at the same time making calculations for a map that he proposed to present young Prince Charles. Then he sailed back to England with forty thousand "dry fish," about a thousand beaverskins, his map, and a pocketful of notes.

Smith was a good publicist. He knew all the tricks of effective publicity, and he appointed himself advertising representative for his new land of hope. He went straight to the royal palace and gave his map to "the high and mighty Prince Charles," and gave him also the privilege of naming the settlements and the hills, the bays and the rivers and the capes. The prince was apparently delighted at the prospect of naming a maze of geographical landmarks that he had never seen, for he fell to the business with an enthusiasm surpassed only by Smith's own and, scratching out meaningless Indian

names, replaced them with good Stuart nomenclature. He changed Cape Cod to Cape James, Cape Trabigzanda to Cape Ann, Accominticus to Boston, and Massachusetts Bay, all-inclusively, to Stuart's Bay. A little cluster of islands which Smith had modestly named after himself the gracious prince endorsed as "Smith Iles." But he had no patience at all with the word "Massachusetts." The bay he had named for his whole family. The river of the same name, which Smith represented on his map as a couple of miles wide, Prince Charles named after himself. The admiral was greatly pleased with the map when it came back to him, and he published it with all sorts of decorations, the royal arms of Britain, the River Charles in discreetly large letters, and a huge picture of himself in armor, surrounded by four smaller pictures of rich symbolism: one of the globe, one of Smith on horseback, another of Smith sailing the high seas, and the last of Smith leading an army somewhere, with banners flying and lances fixed. Underneath the portrait was a highly laudatory poem, which concluded:

> So thou art Brasse without, but Golde within.

And brass without, the admiral certainly was. There was nothing he wanted more in this life than to go back across the Atlantic and start a colony near the Charles. Accordingly, he assembled all those notes that he had made on his 1614 journey and set to work writing a book designed to sell the idea to enterprising merchants. No riches, he implied, were beyond the grasp of men who had brains enough to send Captain John Smith, "Admirall of New England," over to start a colony. From a praise of New England, elaborate as it was, his book occasionally deviated to serve as a defense of New England, as though some cynic had looked over the captain's shoulder, as he sipped his ale and scraped away with his pen, and called him a liar. The admiral told of the opulent fields, the rich woodlands, and the satisfied natives. He was full of praise for the country; and if he did not happen to have sufficient information on any point to praise or blame, he praised anyhow. Like Champlain, he had not troubled to go up the Charles, but merely took it for granted that the river went far to the west. "The River doth pearce many daies iourneis the intralles of that Countrey," he said flatly, and that was all there was to it. Even if he had investigated farther and discovered that the stream tapered off to the southwest, it was not like the admiral to mention such a circumstance.

Under the skilled pen of Smith, every characteristic of the magic land became a glowing virtue. "The maine Staple," he said a little apologetically, was only fish, to be sure, but he asked his readers to look where the Dutch got from fishing. And by the time the admirable admiral was through with the fishing industry he would have the wisest man believe that all he needed was a net and an open boat to acquire a fortune. "Never could the Spaniard with all his Mynes of golde and Silver pay his debts, his friends and army halfe so truly as the Hollanders stil have done by this contemptible trade of fish!" The moral? Let someone finance Smith to the banks of the Charles and he would make that person as rich as the Dutch.

As he rambled on, Smith grew eloquent and lyrical. He was a man who dreamed, and he paraded his dreams before the whole world. He had ambitions too, but he was unselfish about them and willing to share them with all mankind—as long as they were Englishmen. Look, he begged his fellow loyal subjects, at that paradise in Massachusetts, "where there is victuall to feede us, wood of all sorts to build Boats, Ships or Barks; the fish at our doores, pitch, tarre, masts, yards and most of other necessaries onely for making"—look at all that, he exclaimed, and any man possessed of nothing more than a pair of hands could become as rich as Croesus.

Poor John Smith! He sat there in an Old World

tavern and achieved remarkable things on paper, for within his heart he was across the sea in his Valhalla. He was raising more corn than could ever be used; he was catching fish by the thousands and nabbing furs by the ten thousands; he was gathering precious berries which "hath been sould for thirty or forty shillings the pound"; he was building boats of native timber and tools of native iron. But never again did he get there in the flesh, however stubbornly he stayed there in spirit. He tried to get Bacon to finance a voyage, but Bacon was too busy with other matters. Then, when he heard that a group of Brownists were setting out from Holland, he tried to join their party as pilot, but they declined his services, "saying my bookes and maps were much better cheape to teach them than my selfe."

The Admiral of New England, Captain John Smith was the best friend that this valley has known. He loved it much and lied about it a little so great was his love. He praised it to the high heavens and was prepared to sell his soul to get back to it again. But Smith's soul belonged to eternity by then, not because he was dead, but because the day of the pure explorer was done. All that talk about the riches of the paradise of these parts was not for him but for a world which did not partake of his Elizabethan love of sheer adventure. Causes of religious complaint or of pecuniary ambitions were pretty meager in comparison with his own passion for pitting himself against the wilderness. "What so truely sutes with honour and honestie as the discovering things unknowne? erecting Townes, peopling Countries, informing the ignorant, reforming things unjust, teaching virtue; and gaine to our Native mother-countrie a kingdom to attend her; finde imployment for those that are idle, because they know not what to doe: so farre from wronging any, as to cause Posteritie to remember thee; and remembering thee, ever honour that remembrance with praise."

Hail and farewell, John Smith, godfather of the Charles, ever remembered and ever praised!

3

The Hermit of the Charles

I N its early days, the Charles liberated itself in the sea with a mighty thrust. All the restraint of its winding, narrow, sinewy course was brushed aside, the discipline of its years forgotten, as the river spent the full force of its strength in that final burst of freedom that flooded the marshes far inland on either side. Twice each day it converted the Shawmut peninsula into a virtual island when it mingled its waters with the flood tide.

It must have been a beautiful thing to see—a wild, impetuous beauty, belonging to the swooping flight of gulls against gray skies, to the virgin wilderness where great trees freed themselves by towering in the heavens, and to the music of the untamed, unharnessed stirring of all living things.

"That fairest reach . . . the Charles," Smith had called it. And his dream of a colony there, where men from a tired, overladen, and overpoliticized world could breathe once more the air of true freedom, never paled. He spent his last years wandering in and out of taverns, forcing his way into high places, penning broadsides in his rooms and circulating them in the streets—all to urge Englishmen to go forth and find a new life on the banks of the Charles. In 1631, the last year of his life,

he could pride himself only on his maps. Then, as a
hunter who failed to get his buffalo took some small
satisfaction in the deer he shot, so Smith observed that,
at least, "thirty, forty or fifty saile went yearly" to his
New England, although, he added ruefully, "only to
trade and fish; but nothing could be done for a planta-
tion, till some hundred of your Brownists . . . went to
New Plimouth." And of the Brownists Smith did not
think highly, for they had appropriated his maps after
refusing his personal services. Moreover, they missed the
river entirely.

Captain John Smith might have died a happier man
had he known that the banks of his favored Charles
had long since become the private Eden of one of his
countrymen. On the highest hill bordering the river,
and along its southern bank, William Blackstone, a
young man of bookish nature and solitary disposition,
who had come out of the night, set off nearly eight
hundred acres, built himself a house on the hill and established himself as master of that lovely wilderness.
He had left England to escape rule by the lord bishops,
which was bad; and he left the environs of Plymouth to
escape rule by the lord brethren, which was worse.

Four things Blackstone treasured above all else: his
books, the freedom of solitude, the growth of wild
things, and the sound of running waters. His books he
brought with him. The rest he found at the mouth of
the river.

Of orthodox education at the University of Cambridge and an ordained priest in the Church of England,
the young Blackstone was not so much a latter-day St.
Francis as an earlier day Thoreau, with somewhat more
demanding tastes. It was no hut or lowly cabin that

Blackstone fashioned there on his hill overlooking the Charles. It was a comfortable, rambling cottage, multi-gabled and with small-paned windows, woodbine creeping over the walls and up into the eaves. Living there in seclusion, the river flowing below him, the broad fields and unspoiled forest about him, and his two hundred books at his elbow, William Blackstone was one of the few men in the history of a gregarious people who knew complete liberty. Where Smith had but sipped of it and become intoxicated, Blackstone drank long and deeply and became mellow.

First among white men to know the river intimately and first to make his home on its banks, Blackstone was not, however, the spiritual father of those who came after. He was too far behind or too far before his time for that. Love of freedom and solitude are not enough to drive a man from his fellows into the wilderness or the desert. No hermit has yet been made who had not also some abiding hatred, even if it was only of himself. Otherwise he would stay at home, smiling perhaps at the frailty of man and keeping his love of unpopular things in reasonable check. But Blackstone was not of that kidney. Intolerance, bias, restriction from without or within, and persecution, intellectual or physical, he hated fiercely. Yet, for long and inglorious years, intolerance, the sine qua non of Puritanism, flourished on the very spot where Blackstone once sat in detached and sufficient peace with his Latin poetry and unpeopled acres. And all sorts of restrictions, cold and forbidding, flourished there too, damming the warm heart of man even as the river itself was dammed in later days. Little wonder, then, that decades after, Cotton Mather said of the hermit, "This man, indeed, was of a particular humor." For Mather could see no use in living if one did not dig a narrow path to walk in and force his fellows into the same rut.

Eight years Blackstone lived alone. On the slope of the hill he set out his apple trees; and in the fields to the south he planted crops sufficient to carry him through the year. He wore the clerical garb of the Established Church to the end of his days, but he lived among the Indians, trading with them and talking with them, without ever attempting to impose his faith on them. In the Indian, Blackstone seemed to recognize a fellow spirit, unfettered, happy and free. He saw nothing savage in the red man, for he had seen too much savagery among his own people. But he did see the proud, defiant freedom with which the Algonquins lived, disciplined only by the natural seasons. From the river, from the fields, and from the orchard he made a comfortable living. For the rest, he was content to read and meditate. He lived his life in simple solitude, and counted himself blest among men, confident that his river paradise would never be invaded.

As it happened, however, it was Blackstone himself who invited invasion. Directly across the river from him in the summer of 1630, he noted strange happenings and followed them from day to day with an interested eye. Gradually, from the things that he could see from his hilltop and piecing together reports from the Indians, he learned that white men had founded a community on the opposite bank. The presence of the river was a blessing to him, for it was no inconsiderable barrier. Besides, he believed himself to be sole proprietor of his eight hundred acres and beyond intrusion. Accordingly, he sat back, watched his apples change from buds to fruit and minded his business.

As the summer wore on, the serenity of the hermit of the Charles was severely jolted by reports from the other side of the river. There John Winthrop's colony was being riddled by the plague. Blackstone, who had come to Shawmut alone and who adapted the wilderness to his own needs rather than himself to the wilderness, probably wondered at the strange ineffectiveness of that whole shipload of people across the river. Experienced workmen they had among them, and the strength of numbers; and yet they allowed themselves to be defeated by the virgin country. For totally defeated Governor Winthrop's colony was in that summer of 1630, although he would not admit it. He wrote long optimistic letters home to his wife, and he was full of courage and faith. But inwardly he knew that the colony could not endure a winter. Many of the best men of his company were falling victims to the plague; many more were inadequately housed in tents; and the entire colony was existing from day to day with none of the pioneer's concern for the future but only fears for this day's safety.

From his private side of the river, the hermit Blackstone meditated on the relative importance of Christian duty and the ascetic's creed. Then he set out in his boat one morning, rowed across the river and sought out Governor Winthrop. In sad resignation at the loss of his wilderness paradise, he invited the colony to migrate across the river.

Much to Blackstone's surprise, they accepted to a man. They loaded flatboats and rafts, piled what worldly goods they had on them, and ferried the whole Massachusetts Bay Colony across the Charles. Then they forthright made themselves at home on Blackstone's peninsula. Governor Winthrop even brought the frame of his house over—"to the discontent of some," he added in his journal. The change was all that he needed to evoke all the talent for leadership that had lain dormant in the governor through the summer. At any rate, he lost no time in organizing his colony, doling out house lots and setting the people to constructing their homes. Most of the building went on at the very foot of Blackstone's hill. Sitting above the pounding of hammers and the ripping of saws where once he had read Vergil in peace, Blackstone marveled at his own stupidity and wondered why he hadn't let them all die on the other side of the river. But he had said nothing. Like every man who had ever found an Eden, he lost it through his own fault.

As soon as the Puritans asserted themselves, nevertheless, ironic resignation passed away from Blackstone. They had set up a General Court to guide the destinies of a region previously guided only by Blackstone and God. Invoking the help of God and passingly certain of His approval, they merely admitted Blackstone as a "freeman." The title was all wrong, and Blackstone, who understood freedom, knew it. The title, in fact, merely gave Blackstone the privilege of supporting a government he neither needed nor wanted and the responsibility of adapting himself to its laws. This infuriated him. For seven months he put off taking the freeman's oath. And when he did take it, he took it with his fingers crossed.

Gradually the hermit saw the population closing in on him. Nearer and nearer they came to his perch on the Shawmut hill, as the wilderness he loved faded away. He felt restless, ill at ease, and crowded in on all sides but the riverside. Cotton Mather, the arch-Puritan with the elastic vocabulary, sneered at Blackstone's point of view, which he could not understand. Mather said that "by happening to sleep first in a hovel" Blackstone thought he owned the whole town of Boston. As a matter of fact and as far as he was concerned, Blackstone did own it. Where would any hermit be if he was not an advocate of possession by prior occupation? Boston was his neck of the woods, the Charles his river, and the trees that the Puritans were cutting down were his companions. The problem of the Puritans' usurpation worried him greatly, but he could do nothing about it except sigh for the day when a man's home was his country. For three years he bore his agony in silence, turning his back on the new town and looking out over the river.

In 1633 his worst fears were confirmed. The General Court, in solemn session, had the brazen nerve to vote "that Mr. William Blackstone shall have fifty acres of ground sett out for him neere to his howse in Boston, to injoy for ever." The grant was all Boston Common and stretched to the river, but it was an insult to Blackstone. His guests were giving him one-sixteenth of his own preserves. Already his anger had been brewing for three years at their molesting his spiritual freedom by requiring him to take an oath as one of their alleged freemen. And now he was angered anew by their presumption in limiting his physical freedom to fifty acres. He rushed down to the court and relieved himself of a little speech. He did not propose to argue with them, for he knew that it would do no good. "Men are law-makers and tyrants by nature," he said, "even as tigers are carnivorous." He was further chided for his refusal to join the company's church—one of the pre-requisites of all freemen that he had steadily ignored. In a few words, as classical as any in the language, he repeated to the court: "I came from England because I did not like the Lord Bishops; but I will not join with you because I do not like the Lord Brethren." He then turned from the assembly to leave for what was left of his domain.

When he turned to leave the court that day, William Blackstone had every intention of staying on his reduced acres and abiding the Puritan invasion as best he could. But before he was out of the court his mind was changed. Legend has it that Blackstone tarried before the court a moment to see what the next case would be. That idle minute of curiosity, so unseemly in a hermit, cost him what little peace remained to him. For the case was of a woman, who apparently had as much desire for privacy as Blackstone himself had. She appeared shrouded in a thick veil and draped in a mantle of black that fell from her shoulders to the dusty floor. The clerk, in an automatic monotone, demanded her name. Blackstone, sensing a parallel in this woman's troubles and his own, bent nearer to hear her answer. But she spoke so softly that he could not hear a syllable. Blackstone decided, therefore, to indulge at least one of his rights as a freeman and stay there until he found out who she was and what she wanted.

He found out who she was soon enough, but he never learned what she wanted—nor did he much care. The Puritan court, which had little respect for privacy, lost no time in ordering the veiled lady to show her face.

Close enough to see her face even as she was lifting the veil, Blackstone's own face paled, and he gaped at her in wonder.

"Are you Magdalen Groves of Boirdly?" he asked, ignoring the court.

The woman answered that she was, simply and quietly. The clerk of the court said nothing, for it seemed inconceivable that this man who had lived for close to a decade on a lonely riverbank could be concerned about a veiled woman who was probably up to no good.

"I was told that you were dead," Blackstone said, and witnesses thought they smelled a rat.

"Then you have been deceived," Magdalen answered rather obviously.

"And you didn't join in the deceit?" Blackstone demanded.

The mystery woman looked away from him and did not answer. Blackstone, a man of few words, needed none. "I have my answer," he said, and went back to his hermitage, determined that the hour had come for what he should have done when first he espied the arrival of white men on the opposite shore of the Charles: push on upstream and fashion a paradise out of a new wilderness.

Rumors immediately circulated all about Boston that it was no love of Latin poetry and hatred of lord bishops and brethren alone that drove William Blackstone into solitude. And rumor, as often it is, was partly right. Blackstone had loved Magdalen back in Shropshire, had gone to the trouble of getting her father's approval and had elicited some sort of promise from her that she would wait for him. But a Knight of the Sepulcher had come to her Shropshire home, lured her away with his glamour and made her his wife at a fake ceremony. Thus, before the world she became Sir Christopher Gardner's wife. But Governor Bradford of Plymouth, for one, knew better. And he let everyone else know that they could expect little knightly conduct from this philanderer, who was no more fitted for New England than William Blackstone was for the society of Puritans.

"He came into these parts under pretence of forsaking ye world," Bradford wrote indignantly of Sir Christopher, "and to live a private life in a godly course, not unwilling to put himselfe upon any meane imployments, and take any paines for his living; and some time offered him selfe to joyne ye churches in sundry places. He brought over with him a servant or 2 and a comly yonge woman, whom he caled his cousin, but it was suspected, she (after ye Italian maner) was his concubine." And that was the man whom Magdalen chose in preference to William Blackstone! In later days he ran repeatedly afoul the colonial laws, and one thing at least he had in common with Blackstone. He frequently found it convenient to pass the time in solitude among the Indians. But even the Indians were suspicious of him, and they asked the governor once if it was all right to kill him. The governor, who was equally suspicious of the Indians and unwilling to set any precedent by allowing the liquidation of Sir Christopher at their hands, told them to bring him back alive. The Indians took him at his word, and Sir Christopher was returned in a living condition. But he was so badly beaten that no one, least of all the Indians, expected him to live.

Meanwhile, Blackstone had made up his mind that the world about the river mouth was becoming too crowded for his comfort and that anything could happen there. If his new world, once so vast and so quiet, was now so small and so turbulent that even his past caught up with him, then it was time for him to go his

way. But he would yield no further to Puritans. He was going away, but he was certainly not going to leave his fifty acres as a gift to them. So he sold to the town nearly all the fifty acres that they had so magnanimously awarded him of his original land, and he kept his house with six acres surrounding it. The town paid him thirty pounds for the area. To defray the cost, they taxed every householder six shillings, and the land became common property of the townsfolk, who pointedly referred to it through succeeding generations as The Common.

Of his thirty pounds, Blackstone spent twelve on some cattle; and he could count himself grateful that the settlers would sell him any. Then he packed his portable goods and his books and migrated upstream. After a few days, when he saw that the Charles was likely to wind around and end up in the miserable company of the lord brethren again, he forsook the river, hit across open country and located on another stream some miles to the southwest. It is improbable that he knew it, but his new river had its source only a few yards from that of the Charles. Here he set off his new domain and built himself a new house. The region was more grateful to him than the Charles had been, and they called the river and its valley, The Blackstone, in his memory.

There was something about the Charles, however, that always lured William Blackstone back. He had a trained bull in those days, and he used to mount the creature and storm through frontier outposts back to his old haunts. In fact, when he was over sixty and it was twenty-six years since he had left his home on the Charles, he rushed into town on his bull one July morning and surprised everyone along the banks by marrying the widow of John Stephenson of School Street. Governor Endecott, the dour old tyrant who hanged the Quakers, married the couple. With his bride and her sixteen-year-old daughter, Blackstone went back to his own river, paid his parting respects to a world of men which he did not love much by leaving it two children of his own, and followed his wife to the grave at the age of seventy-six.

This man was, indeed, "of a particular humor." He came to the Charles when its waters flowed to the accompaniment of Indian calls and the noises of the wilderness. And he left it as it flowed past strangely disturbed groups of men who mumbled incessantly of evil tidings.

Part Two

The Mouse and
The Snake

4

The Despot and the Sow

No two men in the history of this valley's settlement were more different than Blackstone and John Winthrop. The former loved a life of ease, a life of blissful, meditative solitude. He did not fight against the wilderness so much as he adapted himself to it, thereby finding a happiness that suited his contemplative nature perfectly. Winthrop, however, was no introvert. He was a man of dreams and a gifted leader of men. A Puritan by conviction, he was certainly not one by nature. There was a warmth in his heart, a sad yearning in his spirit for better things than this world offered, and a calm determination in his mind that helped him to succeed in a venture that might well have failed cruelly. He piloted his people across the Atlantic and settled them in a cluster of homes on the very edge of a trackless wilderness at the mouth of the Charles; and the realization that they might perish never vanquished his faith in himself and in his utopian dream.

For the early history of this valley is nothing more than a history of successive utopias. That is what Smith sought, what Blackstone found, and what Winthrop and his followers were determined to build. The latter nourished themselves through many a hard month on hope, and they never lost faith. A utopia did not mean to them, as it did to Blackstone, a life of ease. It meant a place where, unhampered by theological dissension, they could set grimly to the task of overcoming evil. Without faith in God, they could never have attempted such a mission. And without faith in themselves, they could never have persisted in it. But they knew well enough that faith was not enough, and that faith without not only discipline but iron hardness of character was an empty thing that would guarantee them nothing. So it was that they looked upon their leader, John Winthrop, to be more than a spiritual leader.

Nor did Winthrop let them down. He dreamed of a sinless world where men would live in sweet accord with the Hebraic Decalogue from a pure love of goodness. A benevolent despot, as he interpreted benevolence, he ruled with an iron hand and was jealous of his authority. But never in his life did he hold that groveling opinion of his people that was the stock in trade of the ministers who came after him. He was, in truth, a Moses of the New World, leading his chosen people out of the wilderness of evil into the promised land of the perfect man.

Like all Puritans who were not ogres, Winthrop's greatest sin was a denial of love, for he lapsed from his Calvinistic aloofness only when he wrote his wife long letters, which stand out in his prose in little quivering ripplets of light, like the incongruous luminescence of the waves lapping the dark New England coast. Thus, whether or not that tiny band of troubled people who huddled on the riverbanks loved their governor did not often enter his mind. He seemed to regard them as children and chronicled their doings and the growth of his colony in a taciturn, unfeeling way. Hence, even if joy and happiness were strangers to his diary and if pride for his fellows' achievements and inspiration from their courage did not animate its pages, useless sorrowing and empty repining also were alien to its tone of exalted reporting. Not even the tragic death of his son moved him to lay bare the grievous weight of the day that followed. "My son, Henry Winthrop, was drowned at Salem" was all that he wrote. The death of venturesome children likewise failed to stir his writings beyond the moral lesson implicit in such things, and he usually observed serenely that it was the will of God.

But Winthrop was a good reporter and a student of human nature. He had the reporter's instinct, and he knew a good story when he saw it, playing it up for all it was worth. "Two men servants to one Moodye of Roxbury," he wrote, "returning in a boat from a windmill, struck upon the oyster bank. They went out to gather oysters; and, not making fast their boat, when the flood came, it floated away; and they were both drowned, although they might have waded out on either side; but it was an evident judgment of God upon them, for they were wicked persons. One of them a little before, being reproved for his lewdness and put in mind of hell, answered that if hell were ten times hotter, he would rather be there than he would serve his master." Winthrop also exhibited a peculiar preoccupation with coincident and oddities, and he jotted them down in his journal along with the grave problems of church and state. "A company having made a fire at a tree, one of them said, 'Here this tree will fall, and here will I lie.' And accordingly it fell upon him and killed him."

In such happenings in that little autocracy where

the river met the sea, Winthrop seemed to take keen delight—almost as if he wished that he had the time to investigate them further. Sometimes his curiosity about the affairs of men and his interest in the small things of life nearly made him forget his business of overcoming Satan, and one supposes that he checked himself at such times. He could never, however, resist the temptation of making a story of human calamities, particularly when it involved some deductive sleuthing. The pressure of governmental matters could not distract his attention from the reconstruction of accidents, so that his diaries form the substance of scores of little dramas of the good intentions of men fighting the evil and of the small tragedies that invariably ensued.

Here is the case of one Jewell, a man full of good intentions and anxious to be of service but unfortunately fond of potent liquors. "He was bound to the Isle of Sable to relieve our men there," Winthrop wrote in his version of the affair. "His bark had lain near a week at Natascott, waiting for him, but he staid at Boston drinking and could not be gotten away. When he went, there was committed to his care a rundlet of strong water, sent to some there, he promising that upon his life it should not be touched; but as he went down in his bark's skiff, he went on shore at the castle, and then drank out about a gallon of it, and at night went away; but it being very cold and dark, they could not find his bark, and Jewell, his hat falling in the water, as they were rowing back to look for it he fell into the water near the shore, where it was not six feet deep, and could not be recovered." It did not matter to Winthrop that anyone who entrusted a keg of strong water to a notorious imbiber who was just rounding out a week of heavy drinking was no sage. Of sufficient interest to him was the fact that a man could lose his life by losing his hat.

Of interest, too, was the circumstance that too much of anything was not good for a man. Winthrop, with the best of designs and with purity of purpose, could see no sphere in which this was more apparent than government. He consequently kept the freedom-tainted charter discreetly out of sight, and he walked among his people clothed in authority of an order that the inhabitants of the province rose up in wrath against ever after. He created a variety of aristocracy made up of magistrates that worked well for a while, as long as the promised land was in a formative state. And since he was a benevolent despot, there was not much cause for complaint. He waited for the crime before he created the law to punish it, and on the whole the sentences of his courts were just in that they were uniformly severe. John Winthrop would yield no quarter to the devil. As time went on, however, and the rough cabins of the settlers became gabled houses, the stump-dotted fields rich farmlands, and the shaggy coastline a water front, there were undertones of liberty among the people. For twelve years, by a succession of devices, Winthrop kept them below the surface. But in 1642, Goody Sherman's sow ran away, and the issue between a "mixt aristocratie" and the "democratical spirit" took precedence over the classic duel between the mouse and the snake. And when the case of the sow was settled, not even the stratagem of church suffrage could thwart the democratic instincts of his people. The Great and General Court of freemen had begun to assert itself as a legislative body, and already the deputies were questioning the authority of Winthrop's little cluster of magisterial henchmen to overrule them. Nevertheless, they had often capitulated to the magistrates, for the rod of Winthrop still bore great weight.

Goody Sherman's sow changed all that. Goody Sherman was the wife of some obscure fellow who departed for London before the case of the celebrated sow reached the courts. Meanwhile, a man named Story was living at her house and whiling away the years with her against the return of her husband. George Story was a merchant, young in years and fresh from London. Having no stake in the colonies, he looked at Winthrop, the magistrates, and the churches with a nice objectivity that led him to treat them lightly. Had he not, he would never have lived with Goody Sherman, in the first place, nor would he have taken such considerable interest in her sow, in the second place.

The Sherman sow ran away in 1636. It ran through all the streets of Boston, and finally it wound up in the yard of that same Captain Robert Keayne who had fleeced the carpenter of thirty-eight shillings and who had pressed a claim against poor Sarah Kinge to the extent of taking the clothes from her back. Keayne had a sow of his own in the yard, and he let the two stay together. Six years later he swore by all that was holy that he sent the town crier yelling all over the town that there was a stray sow in his yard, and he claimed that half the population accepted his invitation to come and see it. But that is, at best a doubtful story: Keayne was too much the type of man who holds that finders are legally keepers. He may have given up the sow, after some persuasion, if the owner had chanced to come across it in his yard; but he certainly was not the man to put himself out to find an owner.

Since he now had two sows and wanted to support only one, Keayne executed one of them—which, he said, was his own. Goody Sherman heard about it and

promptly went around to Keayne to see about it. She looked at the surviving sow, inspected its markings closely, discovered that it was not her own and, with deadly logic, accused Keayne of willfully butchering the stray sow. Keayne, of course, denied it. Everybody knew about the captain's parsimonious nature and was in a highly receptive mood for Goody Sherman's story that he had stolen and killed her sow. The sow was a common topic of discussion in Boston, its fame spread far and wide, and soon the elders, who did not want particularly to concern themselves with the critter, were forced to take action. The elders called in Goody Sherman and Captain Keayne, and picked out a few witnesses who promised to clear up the case with due dispatch. Then they announced that Captain Keayne undoubtedly had butchered his own sow, that the sow currently inhabiting his yard was the stray one, and that it was too bad that it did not happen to be Goody Sherman's. The matter was then dropped, and bicameral legislative bodies might never have been a political institution in America if Captain Robert Keayne had not gone out of his way to mind someone else's business.

But Captain Keayne, who could not afford to stretch his court record out indefinitely, harbored a grudge against Goody Sherman and kept his weather eye peeled on her private affairs. The arrival of young George Story and his continued stay at the Sherman house, when everyone knew that Goodman Sherman was in London, gave him just the opportunity he had been waiting for since the stray sow was suggested as possibly the one he butchered. Accordingly, he stalked into the governor's presence one day and informed him that Goody Sherman was living after ye Italian manner with the visiting merchant, young George Story.

Story, whom Goody Sherman had told all about the sow and who considered his position in the Sherman household none of Keayne's business, was properly indignant. He urged upon Goody Sherman to repay the captain in kind, pointing out that her sow was never really accounted for and suggesting that the elders' witnesses were perhaps prejudiced. Anyhow, he said, he didn't see what authority elders of the church had over stray sows. Goody Sherman considered the matter; and her ponderings, plus the emotional effects of the source of the advice and her explainable anger at Captain Keayne, resulted in a visit to the "inferior" court, where she entered a complaint against Captain Keayne, not for slander, but for stealing that sow which had long since been strung and quartered.

Goody Sherman fared no better with the court than she had with the elders, for it derived its authority from the same source. In fact, she fared rather worse. Before the elders, both she and Captain Keayne had got away scot free. The inferior court, undoubtedly taking into account the problematical relationship between Goody Sherman and George Story, not only sent Captain Keayne away vindicated but also awarded him three pounds for his trouble in coming to court, when he might have been jumping the prices on his merchandise, and twenty pounds for the grave damage done his character by the Sherman-Story alliance's reports that he had stolen the sow.

Six years had now passed since the stray sow had first precipitated a great crisis by leaving the Sherman preserves. In that time Captain Keayne had had some fun at the expense of Goody Sherman, and was twenty-three pounds richer. Goody Sherman, on the other hand, was still short one pig, had had her name dragged in the mire, and stood now in disgrace before her neighbors. She may have been resigned, by this time, to the loss of the sow, and she probably did not think the game of pursuing the matter worth any more candles. But

Story was ready for anything to turn the tables on Keayne.

With a vengeance, Story immediately set out and combed the town of Boston, the villages across the Charles, and the settlements upstream, all to find people who had been around six years ago when Goody Sherman's sow wandered through the town. At last he found one who had previously testified in Keayne's behalf but who had apparently since been bitten by the latter's sharp commercial teeth. He told Story that he was ready and anxious, for his conscience' sake, to go before the court and confess his perjury. Story, fully aware of Captain Keayne's potentialities, wasted no time in accommodating the man. Once the perjury confession was duly filed, he made another visit on official business. This time he went to the Great and General Court, where magistrates were periodically riding over the acts and resolves of duly elected deputies.

The General Court admitted Story to a hearing, and he said that a conscience-stricken church member had confessed false testimony in the Sherman sow case. Would the honorable Court hear the case anew? Since Captain Keayne was a man of limited popularity among the deputies, the court said it would. For seven days, therefore, during the hot summer of 1642, nine magistrates and thirty deputies sat in solemn judgment on the Sherman sow case. Every detail of the sow's anatomy was discussed, and every possibility of a sow's meanderings was investigated. Every witness who could be mustered was examined carefully, and every aspect of the case was debated thoroughly. At last, a vote was arrived at, and a most unsatisfactory one it proved to be. Half of the deputies wanted to return a finding in favor of

Goody Sherman; eight of the deputies wanted to have done with the matter and let the lower court's verdict stand; and seven of the deputies, in spite of the seven days' testimony, evidence and arguments, could not make up their minds whether Goody Sherman had really lost a sow and, if she had, whether it was the one that Captain Keayne had slaughtered. On the part of the magistrates, two of liberal tendency thought Goody Sherman had been accorded rather shabby treatment; but their seven associates rose as a man in defense of Captain Keayne.

Here was a situation that the people of the Colony, far beyond their concern over Goody Sherman's sow, were anxious to settle. The vote of the deputies, the only popular voice in the state, was clearly for indictment of Captain Keayne. And the vote of the magistrates, who derived their authority from Winthrop and from God, was as clearly for acquittal. Winthrop, who was seeing his authority slowly slipping away and genuinely feared that the voice of the people would undo much that was good for them, whether they knew it or not, held that the vote of the magistrates automatically negated the vote of the deputies. Such a sound and fury was raised to the rooftops that everyone, including Winthrop himself, immediately forgot all about the sow. What the people of Massachusetts wanted to know was whether this was a land of freemen or a petty aristocracy.

Winthrop was honest enough. He said it was a petty aristocracy. Moreover, he added, even if the people did not appreciate it, it was the best thing for them. As for the relative merits of Story and Goody Sherman and Captain Keayne, he pointed out—without the

slightest trace of injustice, that Keayne happened to
be justifiably unpopular ("being of ill report in the
country for a hard dealer . . . as divers others in the
country were also in those times, though they were not
detected") ; that the testimony of Story's witnesses was
remarkably resilient; and that the whole case was tried
by rumor three or four times before it ever reached the
General Court anyhow.

What is more commendable, John Winthrop did
not then, nor did he ever, evade the question of democracy as opposed to his tightly bound rule of theocracy,
which he loved to call a "mixt aristocratie." For the
present, nevertheless, he did not talk too much about it.
Instead, he issued "a declaration in the nature of a
pacification." He proclaimed that, although the magistrates and the deputies had come to diverse conclusions
in regard to the sow, yet they continued to hold ex-
ceedingly high opinions of one another. Since, at that
particular moment, each division of the court was ready
to exterminate the other, it was fortunate that Goody
Sherman's friends in the court tabled the declaration
before it was posted on the meetinghouse. From that
hour, the inspired despotism of John Winthrop was
doomed.

But it was not vanquished, any more than was
Puritanism itself eventually, without putting up a fierce
death struggle. As a last defense, Winthrop said in a
hundred words instead of seven that democracy was an
instrument of the devil, for, as far as he could see (and
he was right), to give the deputies chosen by the people
any powers was to create a democracy. He could think
of no more tragic thing to befall his people. "We should
have no warrant in scripture for it: there was no such

Governm't in Israell." And he feared deep in his heart that democracy would spell the end of this utopian commonwealth that he had journeyed across the seas to found. Democracy "hath been allwayes of least continuance & fullest of trouble," he said sadly.

Goody Sherman and democracy, despite Winthrop's feelings, triumphed. The Great and General Court split into two houses. The deputies said that, if the magistrates wanted to nullify their votes, they would reciprocate by nullifying the magistrates'. Thus, the powers of the two houses approached equality; and the seeds of a government by the people on this continent were sowed by no founding fathers but by an indignant little company of inconsequential folk, who happened to be as jealous of their rights as Goody Sherman providentially was of her lover and her sow.

5

The Apostle and the Wind

JOHN WINTHROP and his Puritans at the river mouth, in their rigid determination to endure against the wilderness, had no time to concern themselves with what would happen to the Indians who had lived there before them. Looking back now, their posterity find it easy to imagine that the red man just gracefully withdrew to the west, fading out of the picture as the town of Boston grew and the valley expanded. But one wonders what the Indian thought at the very start, when the white men came out of the east and established themselves in a community of rude houses by the sea.

If the Indian was not too awed at the spectacle of shiploads of dark-clothed figures disembarking on the strand that had been the edge of his own realm, he may well have doubted the strength of those people to endure the New England winter. But they clung to life and their purpose with fierce tenacity, and they huddled close together in their strange wooden homes. Then, later, when the white men's confidence in their own strength brought new courage, the Indian watched them begin their first exploratory journeys upstream during the first year of their settling here. Seeing the little parties of explorers stamp their way through the forests or flap their way up the river in awkward, graceless boats, well might the Indian have wondered whether to turn his own face to the west and the setting sun. For the test that had come to the river with the glaciers had come to the red man—and he never achieved that fresher independence that follows a victory over the ravages of unforeseen adversity.

Many things the white man brought with him in his vessels that transplanted a population from one side of the ocean to the other. He brought firewater with him, giving it to the Indians and condemning them when they drank it. He brought firearms; and when the Indians yielded the clean flight of the arrow to the smelly fire of gunpowder, he accused them of murder. He brought his trickery in trade and called the Indians' resentment of his ways savagery. He brought, too, his singular religion and his more fantastic schemes for the ordering of men's lives. The Indians were surprised, alternatingly bitter and impressed, and always confused. . . .

Unmindful that it was autumn in his people's history but aware of October along the Charles, Waban, the Algonquin prince named after the wind, went downstream to meet the white apostle of the new religion before the colony's first year was over. The yellow sun of the October afternoon slanted down through the trees, flecking the winding ribbon of the river with pale gold as it flowed softly and quietly until it broadened its way into the marshes. In frequent places, where the boughs of the maple and the ash tree leaned out over the river's edge, the rippling waters seized upon a fragment of color—of scarlet or orange or purple—and

reflected it briefly before the tiny ripplet itself passed
on to meet the tide.

Waban, who had left his father's land to the northwest and had fashioned his own wigwam for his young
squaw here on the gently sloping north bank of the
Charles, did not speak as he led the file of his companions, a half dozen braves, down the narrow path to
where the apostle would meet them. He did not speak,
for he sensed something oddly holy about that afternoon and knew the sad parable of October, that what
was beautiful was also transitory. Autumn was the season of change all along the river. The colors of the
woods, the habits of the animals, the appearance of the

moon, even the surface of the eternal river—all changed in the autumn. On one day everything was green and alive and free. On the next the breath of the north wind had touched the earth's surface; the world crouched for a moment and then burst forth in a proud, defiant flame of final glory. And on the next day all the world was brown and ready for sleep, imprisoned by winter.

As Waban, with his six braves, was pacing in long, silent strides downstream, four white men made their laborious way upstream. Never were two peoples in one river valley more opposite than were these. The Indian lived not only in but with the natural world surrounding him, and he left it unchanged. The Puritan

huddled as close to the sea as he could get, the wilderness at his back; he lived not only without it but despite it. In the lore of the Indian, in his traditions, his daily life, his religion, and his thought, there is nothing unrelated to nature. And the Puritan, in his literature and his customs, in his philosophy and his religion, left not one sign that he cared about nature in the least; for what was natural was necessarily evil. No wonder that Waban approached the white men in silence.

As for them, three of their number were Puritans, and one was a Christian. John Wilson was there—he who interpreted the affair of the mouse and the snake. Not at all sure of the reception that awaited them, he proceeded prudently, with less faith than fear in his heart. One could not tell about savages, though God knew that they needed some preaching. He was condescending in his attitude, a little contemptuous, and very much one of the elect going forth into the wilderness to pray for a flock of dirty, unspeakable heathen, who probably would not appreciate it and might even hatchet him for his pains. "Perishing, forlorne outcasts," he called them—these tall, lithe men who had loved the spirit of the earth and the waters and the winds and who had understood the mysteries of the seasons. "That dark and gloomy habitation of filthinesse and uncleane spirits," he called their unspoilt world which even now he was penetrating without seeing, blind to the blaze of color, deaf to the rippling of the river and the distant drone of the wind through the tops of the cedars. But he was not and would never be the bearer of any message to them. Like two of his companions, he was not much interested in the expedition and probably came only in deference to that brassy voice of Duty that he valued so highly.

One of the four, however, had troubled himself to learn something of the Indian's heart and to understand the soul of the red race. He was a slight and slender man, who walked more quickly and with less reluctance than the others; and he bore in his mind the words of the sachem: "When you came over the morning waters, we took you into our arms; we fed you with our best meat. Never went white man cold and hungry from Indian wigwam." Thus, when John Eliot, the apostle, saw the sinewy form of Waban loom up so suddenly and so silently before him that the Algonquin seemed to have sprung full-grown from the earth at his feet, he went forward with an impetuous step to meet him. The others, startled by the surprising noiselessness of his appearance and with suspicious glances at the six braves behind him, stopped dead in their tracks, leaving it discreetly to Eliot to handle the formalities.

Eliot the Apostle and Waban the Wind greeted each other there on a tree-lined trail beside the river, not verbosely or with forced familiarity but with the restrained sincerity of two men who trusted each other. Then Waban, his sharp, piercing eyes having penetrated to the backs of the skulls of the three standing in the background, pointed his arm upstream to the west, where his people waited to hear the words of the apostle.

The wigwam of Waban stood in a grassy clearance high above the river. Before it his family and his friends sat, and around them was a circle of his people, silent, expectant, trusting. Sachems were there, full of the wisdom of their own lives and the poetry of the wilderness. Old squaws squatted on the ground, their faces lined but their black eyes sparkling at this strange happening in their old age. Little children looked on in wonder, bronze-skinned and with nervous, fleeting smiles. Old men, their skins hardened and browned deeply by a thousand rains, stood on the outer edge, patient and like those who stand waiting at the threshold of death.

In his superior tongue, the Reverend John Wilson offered an entirely advisory prayer to his superior God. The prayer was long and hard in tone, as befitted the communication of a Puritan with his Deity. His voice rumbled on, heavily, coldly; and the autumn wind hummed an antiphon in the treetops. The Indians, aware that this was solemn business, were still and motionless, but they peered from their bowed heads at the man in black who talked the alien tongue so inexhaustibly. And when it was over, they stirred in restless thanksgiving.

After that prayer and when the apostle to the Indians rose to speak of the faith of the white man, half the sins of those cold, overbearing, and unfeeling Puritans were atoned. He spoke earnestly to them in their own language—the language of their lips and the language of their heritage. Two years he had spent learning that tongue, and he knew not only how the Indian spoke but how he felt, what things were precious symbols to him and what things raised him far above the naked wild man for whom other races mistook him.

Throwing off the Puritan's mantle completely, John Eliot went straight to the core of Indian philosophy with the words of Ezekiel the prophet: "Then said he unto me, Prophesy unto the wind, prophesy, son

of man, and say to the wind, Thus saith the Lord God;
Come from the four winds, O breath, and breathe upon
these slain, that they may live. So I prophesied as he
commanded me, and the breath came into them, and
they lived, and stood up upon their feet, an exceeding
great army." Waban, himself called after the wind,
standing straight and still before his wigwam, listened
and knew that this white man would be loved by his
people.

For Eliot realized what no man had discovered
before, and few afterward, that the heart of the simple
savage is often closer to the truths of eternity than that
of the inventors of evil. As the rigid circle of red men
listened, the penetrating darts softened in their eyes,
their immobile faces relaxed, and their hopes rose anew
that the white men would not bring to their future the
gloom of that forbidding new village of theirs down
at the river's mouth. The apostle brought with him no
word of damnation and eternal writhings in fire that
was endless, but told in quiet, unruffled tones of the
religion of love.

Waban looked down at the river, which deepened
in color as the sun went down in the west, and knew
that changes would come. He thought of silent nights
on that river, when he had glided downstream under
the starlight, the world on either side peaceful and
noiseless; of how, casting his spear into the water, he
had loaded his canoe with salmon; and of how, on so
many October nights before, he had paddled close by
the shore, snatching pike from the shallows. He thought
of his days on the riverbank, when he had gathered
berries and precious herbs that the white man trampled
underfoot, and of the snows that had blanketed these

forests, when he had tracked the moose with fast furious running until one of them was exhausted. And he knew that changes would come.

But with this apostle, Eliot, it would not be so bad. Waban called together his people, after the white men had gone; and they decided to build themselves a village, where Waban's wigwam stood on the riverbank, after the pattern of the white man's village downstream and there practice the white man's religion. They called their village Nonantum, which meant "rejoicing." John Eliot dreamed beautiful dreams about it, and he was passingly certain that he could make a utopia of it—just as Winthrop had dreamed of his colony.

The Reverend John Wilson had gone back downstream highly pleased with himself, although the Indians had not understood a word of his prayer nor he a word of Eliot's sermon, and quite sure that he was a step closer to heaven. The other two Puritans were so apathetic about the whole thing that even their names have not come down to posterity. But Eliot went back full of his dreams, the happiest man on these shores. He made plans for his new people and lived his long life for them:

"And this Vow I did solemnly make unto the Lord concerning them; that they being a people without any forme of Government and now to chuse; I would endeavour with all my might, to bring them to embrace such Government, both civil and Ecclesiastical, as the Lord hath commanded in the holy Scriptures; and to deduce all their Lawes from the holy Scriptures, that so they may be the Lord's people, ruled by him alone in all things."

Faithful Eliot, whose simple, pure life shone like a

beacon in the Stygian severity of the Puritan night! His sterling dream was never realized completely; and when kings were popular again in England and the Bay colony modified its political philosophy, it caused him trouble. But for many days during the four years of Waban's village of Nonantum, he talked and walked among the Indians. Then his Indian commonwealth had to move up the river.

That is what is always happening to utopias. Blackstone had to move his habitation far beyond the river's source before he could find peace again. And in later years the Puritans' own posterity moved all the way across a continent. But the Indians did not go so far. They merely went upstream and founded a new village on the banks of the same river.

Eighteen miles they went, around falls and turning the countless bends. Some paddled the aged canoes, and the young walked with Eliot along the bank. When at last Waban at the head of the procession to utopia came to a cluster of hills, he stopped; and all the company agreed that this was the place for the new commonwealth. They called it Natick, the Place of Hills. Then they threw a footbridge across the river, using stones for piles, and built their village on both sides among the slopes of the hills.

But the day of the Indian was drawing toward its end. The onpressing white men pressed farther and farther upstream, and far beyond the western limits of the Algonquins. Waban the Wind, who had once been free, died with a Puritan prayer on his lips and was buried not in the land of his fathers but among a new people, whom one man had made strangely attractive to him.

Yet Waban never really understood their ways and was a little impatient with their institutions. It is doubtful whether, even if his land at Natick had never been encroached upon, his ideal state that Eliot conceived for him would ever have flourished. The swift freedom of the Indian could never become reconciled to the intricate workings of a white man's mind and social organization. This was blatantly evident in Waban's efforts as justice of the court at Nonantum. In one of his warrants, wherein he tried hard to emulate the precision of the white man in his legal dealings, he said: "You, you big constable, quick you catch um Jeremiah Offscow; strong you hold um; safe you bring um before me, Waban, Justice Peace." But in one of his decisions, it can be seen that he despaired of the processes of law necessary to an ideal commonwealth and confessed defeat: "Tie um all up, and whip um plaintiff and whip um 'fendant and whip um witness."

6

The Duel

As the star of the Indian descended, that of the Puritans rose ever higher. Far from meaning only that they had endured the first winter in the wilderness, had earned for themselves some slight physical security, and had achieved even a small degree of material prosperity, this meant also that there was no relaxing of their common effort to vanquish evil, to which any material expansion was secondary. In no place is this more noticeable than in the journals of John Winthrop himself and in those also of the men who carried his mission forward long after he was gone.

"At Watertown," he wrote in his journals, "there was (in the view of divers witnesses) a great combat between a mouse and a snake; and, after a long fight, the mouse prevailed and killed the snake."

This was grave news in the theocratic little state along the lower Charles, and a courier was quickly dispatched with the tidings of the mouse and snake to the seat of all authority, civil and ecclesiastic, in Boston three miles downstream. Winthrop, who considered even his own wisdom in such matters limited, immediately turned the matter over to the learned ministers, who went into a long conference. At length, after a good deal of solemn speculation, the responsibility of interpreting the affair was entrusted to the Reverend John Wilson, who promptly returned an engaging verdict: "The snake was the devil; the mouse was a poor contemptible people, which God had brought hither, which should overcome Satan here and dispossess him of his kingdom."

Satan was thus the third party to be dislodged, following the hermit Blackstone and the Indians. But Satan lacked the hermit's bitter resignation and the Indians' confused acceptance of the new order, and he lingered a spell. Consequently, the puritanic mice had but one avowed business for a century, and that was the eradication of the satanic serpent. Everything else —and this is important—was incidental to it.

It took a hundred years to fight the serpent, and the Puritans did not win, as Cotton Mather well knew when he cried, as that century drew toward its close, "I would bewayl the sins of my people." For Satan found the region of the Charles to his liking, probably because he received so much attention and was credited with so many and such varied achievements. Accordingly, he outstayed the Puritans themselves.

The duel, however, bred in the mice of John Wilsons' grim verdict a few qualities of passing merit. They grew into hard, practical, resolute men, not given to compromise. In their long court records and vigorous church papers, you can see that some of the mice fell victims to the snake but not one of them compromised with him. And the battle went on, at times quietly and steadfastly, like a Puritan propagating his species, and again vehemently and furiously, like a Puritan composing a sermon. It was the first war fought on the banks of the Charles—this hundred-year war against the powers of Satan, and those characteristics with which it left the aggressors have penetrated to the core of the New England character.

Since idle hands were the consort of the devil, industry was the first weapon that occurred to the Puritans as jointly effective both against sin and against the wilderness. It is not insignificant that they first built homes, and not a meetinghouse, next to William Blackstone's orchard. Or that they never doubted that it was perfectly possible to serve two masters. Community life in that wild country presented practical problems that the hermit never encountered, and the Puritans, whatever their righteous attitude in their dealings with one another, did not for a moment forget that it was every man for himself.

This necessity, inflicted by their surroundings, to work hard and to deal sharp was the parent of Yankee shrewdness—a euphemism full of virtue, which also covered a multitude of sins. There were frequent court cases against the colonists for overcharging or driving too sharp a bargain, but no one seemed to mind them much. Edward Palmer's was the prize case. He was haled before the court for taking too much money (about five dollars) "for the plank and wood-work of Boston stocks." The court, with an active sense of humor and letting the punishment fit the crime, fined him five times the exorbitant price he had demanded and sentenced him to sit in the stocks for an hour. No one, however, thought less of Palmer.

A more chronic offender was Captain Robert Keayne, who met his Waterloo at the hands of Goody Sherman. Keayne was a merchant, and one of the most highly respected in Massachusetts Bay. Yet he was always before the court for his questionable business ethics. Thomas Wiltshire, a carpenter, had done some work on Keayne's house, but the merchant never paid the thirty-eight shillings that Wiltshire demanded. He said, however, that, since Wiltshire was such a good carpenter and had done the job so well, he, Keayne, would let him in on a fine bargain. Then Keayne produced a bolt of what he called "Spanish broadcloth," which he offered to sell Wiltshire, as a favor, for seventeen shillings a yard. Wiltshire, proud of his bargain and convinced that Keayne was not such a hard man after all, brought the cloth home to his wife and exhibited it with some small commentary on the high privilege it was to enjoy the friendship of a man like Keayne. His wife, however, changed his tune and informed him that he paid just twice what the cloth was worth. At her instigation, the case was brought into court, the cloth was officially pronounced as worth no more than nine shillings per yard, and Keayne was fined and told to mend his ways.

Keayne paid the fine and did not alter his ways one iota. He was back in court repeatedly. In one instance, he was fined as much as a thousand dollars, a tremendous sum in colonial Boston, for charging outrageous prices for merchandise. Nor was there anything too far below him, as the following court order testifies: "Captain Keayne was willed to returne Sarah Kinge her necessary cloathes againe." The captain, nevertheless, had a front pew in the meetinghouse, and was accepted as a shrewd man, whose only sin was being unnecessarily careless.

Through the years, that Puritan attention to the

technicalities of business has persisted. But it has been modified somewhat, and profiteering finally passed away, probably because men like Robert Keayne discovered that it was bad business to pay constant fines. And Yankee shrewdness now is a complimentary term: it means a sort of technical honesty. Practically, what it amounts to is a certain ingrained ability in the Yankee to get the better of a bargain.

The Puritan's second great weapon against the devil and the wilderness was his firm conviction that he was the chosen of God. Being of the elect, he had definite obligations. He had, for example, to make himself worthy of the honor bestowed upon him; he had to see to it that the forces of evil were kept underfoot, and he had to keep an eye on his neighbor's business to make sure that the neighbor was having no traffic with sin. And these things have not passed away. Those who are born and grow old along the Charles today still regard the rest of the world with slight misgivings. There may be other cities in the world, but there is none equal to Boston. There may be other colleges, but there is none equal to Harvard. There may be other regions—a West, a South and a Midwest, but none is equal to New England. Even Emerson, whose clear and great intellect rose far above those others that have frequented our riverside, said that he did not know that "Charles River . . . water is more clarifying to the brain than the Savannah or Alabama rivers; yet the men that drink it get up earlier, and some of the morning light lasts through the day."

Much of the light may have been filtered through a Calvinistic haze in those early days, but it was at least a beginning. No religion in the world ever approached

that in the delta of the Charles for its weightiness and
wordiness. Constant self-examination and the perpetual
search after new evidence to damn the devil require a
certain amount of intellectual exercise, just as keeping
track of your neighbor involves much mental curiosity
that amounts to a primitive variety of psychological
study. All this, also, developed among the New Eng-
landers a certain facility in the handling of words, so
that a preacher could, and not infrequently did, de-
scribe the fires of hell for three hours at a stretch without once repeating himself. Gloomy as it may have been,
it was just such essays in redundant verbiage that par-
ented that literary aspect that lingered about the
Charles for over two centuries.

These, then, are the things that endured from the
days of the first Puritans at the river's mouth: that
early cupidity, which has survived as Yankee shrewdness; that Calvinistic conviction of being the chosen of
God, which has survived as a marked indifference to the
rest of the world; and that deep interest in words as
darts to be thrust at Satan and in books as a weapon of
God, which has survived in old men walking along the
riverbanks with their green-felt bags full of books, in
the Boston Athenaeum where other old men run ele-
vators from book-lined floor to book-lined floor, and
indeed, all along the valley when you can see the sad
ghosts of yesterday's glorious golden age in village historical societies.

At some time, as we shall see, the Puritan, whose
heart was damned up with a fierce doctrine as cold and
as craggy as the glacial rocks that damned the river,
freed himself, even as the river itself eventually found
the sea again. But, like the river that wound its way

through a tortuous, craggy course, Puritanism did not emerge in the clear breadth of reason until it left itself scarred, nearly broken, and as narrow as the river flowing through the granite gorge.

It took many years, that twisted course, to reach final liberation; and it is not a pleasant story in some ways, for there were dark days when little children were frightened into panic, when innocent women fell victims to superstition, and when the "lecturers" raved hour after hour in a hailstorm of words that debased everything that was noble in the unfettered heart and mind of man. Many of the stones struck deeply and left bitter wounds.

Samuel Sewall saw his daughter of fourteen plunged into a mania of fear, with not the slightest trace of compunction on his part. "It seems Betty Sewall," he wrote calmly in his diary, "had given some signs of dejection and sorrow; but a little after dinner she burst out into an amazing cry, which caused all the family to cry too. Her mother ask'd the reason; she gave none; at last she said she was afraid she should goe to Hell, her Sins were not pardon'd. She was first wounded by my reading a Sermon of Mr. Norton's . . . Text Jn 7. 34. Ye shall seek me and shall not find me. And those words in the Sermon, Jn 8. 21. Ye shall seek me and shall die in your sins, ran in her mind and terrified her greatly." If anything, the judge recorded the incident with a full sense of satisfaction at having put the fear of the devil into the child.

Cotton Mather, the last champion of the Puritans, gloried in a similar experience that he thrust upon his daughter of eight. "I took my little daughter, Katy, into my study," he wrote; "there I told my Child, that

I am to *dy* shortly [as a matter of fact, Mather lived thirty-one years after that] and shee must, when I am Dead, Remember every thing that I said unto her. I set before her the sinful and woful Condition of her *Nature,* and I charg'd her, *to pray in secret Places,* every Day, without ceasing, that God for the Sake of Jesus Christ would give her a *New Heart* and *pardon* Her Sins." The tragedy of such episodes was not willful cruelty to little children but that the souls of their fathers were really tormented, their hearts withered in their breasts.

Strange and dark, indeed, were those grumblings that drowned out the soft sounds of the free waters of the river. "Are we at our boards? There will be devils to tempt us unto sensuality. Are we in our beds? There will be devils to tempt us into carnality . . . I am verily persuaded that there are very few human affairs whereinto some devils are not insinuated." At no period and in no place in the history of the race did man's opinion of man reach a lower ebb than it did during the first century the white man lived near the Charles. "Every man and woman is born full of all sin; as a toad is of poison, as full as ever his skin can hold; mind, will, eyes, mouth, every limb of his body, and every piece of his soul, is full of sin; their hearts are bundles of sin . . . Thy mind is a nest of all the foul opinions, heresies, that ever were vented by any man; thy heart is a foul sink of all atheism, sodomy, blasphemy, murder, whoredom, adultery, witchcraft, buggery; so that if thou hast any good thing in thee, it is but a drop of rose-water in a bowl of poison."

Thus the duel went on, the Puritans tongue-lashing Satan all through that little patch of civilization at

the river mouth, and Satan merely sitting back and biding his time. The fight was virtually over in 1700, but not until Cotton Mather, the last participant, had had his round with the devil. He came to the battle equipped with diverse strong instruments, not the least of which was his nose for evil, his tongue for invective, and his taste for the ink of the printing press. More-over, he claimed God for his father, his servant, his friend, his employer, and his literary agent.

Cotton Mather was a self-confessed genius of the first water. A freshman at Harvard when he was eleven, he had already read Homer and Isocrates, Vergil and Ovid. Even as a child, he had wandered among the children of Boston, pointing out to them the error of their ways. At fifteen, when he was graduated from the college, the president told the assembly that the youth was destined to great things, and nothing thereafter could convince Mather that he was not supernatural. At twenty-two, he was the associate minister of the North Church and was beginning to walk with God in the fields along the river at the back of the town, during which times he was assured, he said, not only of being blessed but of himself being a blessing to the rest of the world.

From the age of fourteen, he made it a practice to fast periodically, hoping that his face would turn black. Every fortnight he prostrated himself "in the Dust on my Study-floor." Altogether, he reckoned, he fasted four hundred and fifty days during his life, and he prayed privately one hundred and five thousand times. In every ramification of life and in the pettiest daily occupations, he searched for some relationship with the stern voice that was bellowing in his ear and echoing through his mouth or flowing through his finger tips. The most ordinary business of life he made a terrible ritual. If he looked at the clock, he mumbled, "Teach me to number my days." When he saw laborers, he thanked God for his nobler occupation and higher station. On seeing people who were busy, he muttered,

"Let not that person so mind the affairs of this world as to neglect the one thing needful." If he met children in the street, he babbled, "Let not those children forget the great works they are sent into the world to do." On seeing a tall man, "Let him fear God above many"; on seeing a Negro, "Lord, wash that poor soul." If he had a toothache (and he had many), he accused his teeth of sinning. When he had a cold, he suffered "exquisite Miseryes."

No employment of life was beneath his notice if it presented an occasion for railing at his own race. "I was emptying the Cistern of Nature," he wrote, in his characteristic soberness, "and making Water at the Wall. At the same Time, there came a Dog, who did so too before me. Thought I: 'What mean and vile Things are the Children of Men in this mortal State! How much do our natural Necessities abase us and place us, in some regards, on the same Level with the very Dogs!' My Thought proceeded, 'Yett I will be a more noble Creature; and at the very Time, when my natural Necessities debase me into the Condition of the Beast, my Spirit shall (I say, *at that very Time!*) rise and soar and fly up, towards the Employment of the Angel! Accordingly, I resolved that it should be my ordinary Practice, whenever I stop to answer the one or other Necessity of Nature, to make it an Opportunity of shaping in my Mind some holy, noble, divine Thought."

His lowly opinion of his fellows can best be judged from his opinion of himself, whom he considered "a Monument whereon *Mercy* shall be glorifed forever" and "Surely, if the Lord intended not to glorify mee in Heaven, Hee would never have putt it into my Heart that I should seek to glorify him on Earth."

Nevertheless, he referred to himself, the choicest of the chosen, in extremely uncomplimentary terms. Reading his voluminous diaries at random, one encounters any number of disparaging pseudonyms he adopted. He is successively "a vile Worme," "one of the most inconsiderate Wretches in the Land," "a Sluggard," "a silly and shallow Person," "a poor, broken, sorry, despicable Vessel," "a barren Tree," "a foolish and filthy Creature," "the most Lothsome Wretch in the World," "the vilest of Men," and "an horribly guilty and filthy Sinner." And he was also, according to his own testimony, any variation or combination of those things.

The only virtue that touched him was his industry, as a matter of fact, and even that was based on his egoism. But industrious he certainly was. He wrote six hundred books in his lifetime, and he saw four hundred of them published. Mather would write a book at the drop of a hat, tearing his works off at a merry clip that has never been equaled. He wrote books on crime, on medicine, on pirates, on witches, on politics, on religion, on history, and on vague subjects that defy classification. He wrote the lengthy history of the New England churches, which amounted to a history of New England, labeling it *Magnalia Christi Americana*. He wrote the equally lengthy and much less coherent *Wonders of the Invisible World*, which purported to be an explanation of the witchcraft phenomena. The book was far from an explanation and might more truly be described as a manifestation of it. All it did in effect, between page after page of totally delirious ramblings, was to pile more and more abuse on that poor snake that was the devil.

As for himself, except for those purely rhetorical

references, Mather found only two things worthy of serious criticism. One was his stammering—a difficulty that he brought to the attention of the Almighty in a three-page, astonishingly argumentative prayer. After filing a long bill of particulars, he said, "My Lord, I have one Argument more," and he proceeded to point out that, since many men who ill knew how to use it had the gift of perfect speech, he who knew far better the best employment of it certainly deserved that gift above all men.

And one January morning, when the cold penetrated to the core of Mather's being, he bemoaned his "hard Heart" and resolved to read books to "cure" it. But that was no flaw in Cotton Mather's character; mention of it was merely an inconsistency. On the same page of his diary he referred to the "happy Death of that Greater Monster King Charles II." And the hard heart turned to stone in the face of his enemies. "A wondrous Lump of Ignorance and Arrogance," he called a preacher whom he did not like. He later warned the "wicked Incendiary" that he might be shown up in a bad light if he did not stop inciting public rage against Cotton Mather. Mather even went to the trouble of getting "several sober, modest and virtuous Women" to swear before a magistrate that the man "had often affronted them with lewd, vile, uncivil and lascivious Actions, and watching Opportunities to gett them alone would offer them rude Things." No one could brook such opposition as that. "Thus," Mather wrote triumphantly, "the Wretch went off with a Stink."

Satan wagged his tail and waited. And Cotton Mather had his bad years. One of his daughters was always falling in the fire, with a relevancy that was unaccountably vague to Mather; he was twice widowed, and his third wife went mad; and his younger children were given to fits on the kitchen floor. Above all, his "bowels were troubled for Increase," his son. "My miserable, miserable, miserable son Increase," he wrote. "The Wretch has brought himself under public Trouble and Infamy by bearing a part in a Night Riot with some detestable Rakes in the Town." Not only that, but "an Harlot big with Bastard accuses my poor son Cresy and layes her Belly to him."

It was more than the toughest of men could stand. Cotton Mather, tormented, furious, squealing in impotent rage, was the last mouse to attempt to vanquish the snake in Massachusetts. He may not have lost the fight until he was lowered into his grave. Or he may have already lost it years earlier, when he wrote significantly in his diary: "On Tuesday I was married. . . . The next sabbath after that I preached at Boston on *Divine Delights.*"

Part Three

The Near Frontier

7

Upstream Migrations

A RIVER is an invitation to adventure. Pioneering souls at the mouths of countless rivers have always cast longing eyes upstream, just as those at their sources have invariably been drawn to follow the river downstream. Blackstone had eventually gone up the Charles, and the Indians of Waban's praying tribe soon followed him. Moreover, the eyes of certain adventurous leaders among the Puritan settlers were turned westward almost as soon as the river mouth was crossed by Winthrop's desperate company. As the Charles had lured John Smith, it captivated the fancy also of Sir Richard Saltonstall, an enlightened man, who was haled into court as defendant and went there as plaintiff more often than any other man in Massachusetts Bay. Sir Richard went up through the marshlands and around a few bends, and founded a town of his own where the river narrowed suddenly to refute John Smith's guesses about its greatness. Throughout the remainder of that century, little settlements, which gradually acquired the dignity of towns, appeared all along the riverbanks. At every turn of the Charles there was a new town; and a peculiarity of each was that it was founded by pioneering spirits who became restless in the town immediately preceding it. Thus, there is a sort of lineal descent from Boston in the towns extending upstream, and each is parent to the next.

The Great and General Court, sitting in solemn conclave, viewed the westward, upriver movement with mixed feelings. They feared, first, that distance would lessen their authority over the footloose pioneers and, second, that the Indians might close in someday and make mincemeat of all of them. Steps were taken, therefore, to exercise control over all the moving that was going on along the river. The General Court decided that no one could move thereafter without getting official permission and that every town furnish itself with a militia, with "knapsacks and other neces" to ward off Indians. With this paternal interest, the General Court also doled out little stretches of farmland to deserving settlers. Thus, the upriver movement had the court's tacit blessing, if not its enthusiastic support. The court caused garrisons to be built and manned in each town and even contemplated seriously the wisdom of erecting an eight-foot fence from the Charles river to the Concord and thence to the Merrimac, enclosing all the inland towns in a huge area and saving them "from the rage and fury of the enemy."

The fence, however, cost far too much to build, and would take too long. Besides, the migrators were made of stern stuff and dealt satisfactorily with hostile Indians. There is not a town along the river where the local historians will not first tell you of their forebears' incredible exploits against Indians. You will hear of old ladies, since rewarded by suitable bronze tablets, who snuffed out half a dozen red men singlehanded and, when they got through, turned their hands to putting out the fire on the roof. And oldest inhabitants always have great-great-grandsires who went through some such terrifying ordeal as staying all night in a swamp, with only their heads sticking abovewater, while a hundred Indians took pot shots at them. "But the old cuss got home safe and sound, and lived to be ninety." Then the old fellows will spit reverently on the hallowed ground and allow that the old graveyard is full of men of over ninety who never sat down to breakfast until they had chased a dozen Indians out of town.

In truth, those relatively unsung heroes, whose names are sacred now only in local historical societies, did develop an extraordinary resourcefulness, born of the necessity to adapt themselves to their wilderness homes. No man went upstream from Boston and brought even that primitive outpost of civilization with him. The vision of the devil in his eternal struggle with God paled in his mind, and was replaced by the reality of himself, alone, fighting against the wilderness. And he fought on the latter's unrelenting terms and not on his own. The Bible often lay undisturbed on the crude pine table in the kitchen, while the musket was repeatedly snatched from its perch over the fireplace and the knife snapped up from its place near the door. The pastures of Boston were forgotten, and the empty Sabbath of the Puritans forgone. The ways of the Algonquins became the ways of the white men, for the latter had no time for the missionary spirit. The upstream settler hunted as the Indian hunted; he planted as the Indian planted; and he lived with some of the hearty freedom that the Indian lived. He came to terms, at last, with the wilderness, and the struggle ended in a compromise. At the price of his heritage from centuries of civilization, he made his peace with his new home; and he adopted new ways. He had tested the strength of the wilderness and found it to be all that he had bargained for. Wisely, therefore, he molded himself to fit it.

All that is, perhaps, what rural resourcefulness is today. You do not find a master carpenter or a master ironsmith or a master cobbler on Yankee farms. But you can find a master farmer who is also a journeyman carpenter and ironsmith and cobbler, with a hundred other crafts thrown in for good measure. For the upstream settler, who was his ancestor, had the unqualified choice of work or perish. He did not perish.

The up-river towns also gave full way to that spirit of independence which first startled Winthrop when his people at Boston became curious about the charter and which came to a head when Goody Sherman made up her mind to press the affair of the stray sow. Owing to the difficulties of transportation over a maze of Indian trails or up a capricious river, the towns upstream were physically and materially independent. There was no sending down to Boston for a hunting shirt or for advice on planting corn. The hunting shirt was fashioned after the method of the Indians from deerskin; and the corn, if it did not grow, was planted thereafter with a herring at its roots, as the Indians used to plant it. No one town could expect much help from another town, so they took care of the situation by not needing anything. What they could not provide for themselves, they went without.

Because a man could be materially independent upriver, in contrast to the commercial interrelation that was already apparent in the port town of Boston, many men deserted the seacoast for the inland towns. Many more, aware that where a man is economically independent he can also live his private life with less intrusion, went because they sought a fuller life than the Puritan autocracy permitted in the closeness of the Boston settlement. Later still there was a continuous stream of migrants going up the river for eminently worthy reasons of their own, and it became characteristic for ambitious young people to liberate themselves from that tight world at the river's mouth by choosing the harder and freer life in the "frontier towns." They might perish upstream, but at least they could live without the piercing eyes of the elders constantly searching their ways.

This capacity for living as one wanted to live and in freedom, as opposed to living as the Puritans thought seemly downstream, was never more clearly illustrated than in the career of Sir Charles Henry Frankland, who found even the Georgian Boston of the eighteenth century too puritanic for his liking. Sir Harry, as he was called, went from one end of the Charles clear to the other just to live without interference. A baronet who was always out of place in Massachusetts, he had a mixed ancestry; on his father's side, he was of aristocratic blood, but on his mother's side he was a descendant of the arch-Puritan, Cromwell, whom he did not admire and in whose honor he named his bastard son Henry Cromwell. Sir Harry came to Boston, full of a zest for living, in 1741. While he was officially collector of the port, he had a large private income and a whole list on nonpuritanic hobbies: expensive wines, women, Restoration literature, art, horticulture, and high living in general. Handsome and with a deceptively melancholy expression, he was twenty-four on his arrival and ready for the adventure of life.

Sir Harry was not here long before he had urgent business in Marblehead, and it being summer, he stepped into a tavern there to bend his elbow and quench his thirst. He saw a girl of sixteen, barefooted and bare-legged, scrubbing the floor. She was meanly dressed but as beautiful a creature as Sir Harry had ever seen, with her black hair and vivacious eyes. He engaged her in small talk and learned that she was the maid of all work at the tavern and that her name was Agnes Surriage. She was, further, sufficiently quick-witted to parry his light remarks, and he was so pleased that he gave her a crown, to spend on a pair of shoes. Then he went back to Boston, daydreaming about her all the way and after he got there.

Not long after, Sir Harry had some more urgent business in Marblehead. Back to the tavern he went for his first stop, and there was Agnes still scrubbing the floors and still barefoot. Recalling the crown he had given her, he asked her where the shoes were. When she said that she kept them for meeting, Sir Harry, allegedly, was startled by her brilliance. An early biographer, who was constantly embarrassed by his subject's playful nature, summed up the results of this interview. "The elegance of her lithe and slender form . . . quite entranced the heart of Frankland," he said; "and he sought and gained the permission of her parents, who were then poor but pious people, to remove her to Boston to be educated." The relevance in Harry's mind between her lithe form and her adaptability to education does not appear, but he brought her to Boston anyhow. He then proceeded to set up a bizarre arrangement.

First he saw Peter Pelham, a most respectable schoolmaster, and arranged for his Agnes to attend the school. Then he went to see the Reverend Dr. Edward Holyoke, who was the president of Harvard College, and arranged with him to take care of Agnes's religious welfare. After that he bought a tract of useless land up in Maine from Agnes's mother at an exorbitant price, just to obligate that poor but pious woman. And when all this business was attended to, and since he had become increasingly fond of Agnes, he installed her in his house and adopted her as his mistress. He explained that he could not marry her, because he was a baronet and baronets simply did not marry barefoot girls who scrubbed tavern floors.

In a matter of days, every tongue in Boston was wagging violently. Here was a religious charge of the president of Harvard living in open sin with the collector of the port. The situation was intolerable: wherever Sir Harry went, heads shook in solemn judgment after him; Dr. Holyoke immediately lost all interest in Agnes's eternal salvation; Peter Pelham lost all interest in her education. She was cut dead in the street, and Sir Harry himself was treated no better. It was all right to found a paradise at the mouth of Charles. In fact, that was a feature of the region. But Blackstone's had been properly ascetic and with books—not a woman. And Winthrop's was pledged to God. Sir Harry was acquainted with both those Edens and was hardly transported at the thought of them. Blackstone may have lived with his books, but look at what happened to him. When he was over sixty and should have known better, he came racing into town astride a bull in hot pursuit of a widow! But Sir Harry took a leaf from the journal of the hermit, and decided that it was time for him to move upstream.

He went to the very source of the Charles, high in the hills of Middlesex. There he bought nearly five hundred acres of land on a chestnut-covered hill full of springs and brooks and commanding a view of the country for miles around. He reared a great mansion, multicolumned and with chimneys of Italian marble. He built a huge barn, elaborate houses for his servants, and numerous summerhouses. Then he landscaped the grounds with imported plants and rare trees. The following summer, the tongues of Boston still wagging and the heads of Boston still shaking, he set out with twelve slaves, his bastard son Henry Cromwell, and Agnes his beloved. There, where the Charles bubbled out of the ground, he proposed to enjoy life as he could not where it emptied into the sea.

Neither the tolerant little village of Hopkinton nor the entire Massachusetts Bay colony had ever seen an establishment or a modus vivendi of the order that Sir Harry created on his hill. In the morning he entertained his guests with fox-hunting, an oddly colorful rite in the heart of a country not yet out of homespuns. In the evening he served banquets that were the equal of Continental feastings. In the afternoons he had chamber concerts, and the thin sounds of a violin mingled with the distant scrape of a plow. Late in the night, when the rest of the countryside was asleep, he had drinking bouts that developed every earmark of a marathon. Sir Harry himself had a trick glass with a false bottom, which made it appear to hold somewhat more than the glasses of his guests when in reality it held but half as much. The convivial host counted no pleasure higher in this world than to use his private glass to drink his cronies under the table; and when the last one slipped under in blissful unconsciousness, Harry marched upstairs, cold sober but mellow, to his waiting Agnes.

The startling feature of all this rhapsodic living was that it should be taken with a grain of salt by a tiny village in the hills when the growingly important port of Boston rose up in horror at the thought of it. For three merry years, Sir Harry and Agnes and Henry Cromwell lived exactly as they wanted to in Hopkinton. Then Harry and Agnes went to Europe on a holiday, during which Agnes was scorned by Harry's family and Harry himself was badly shaken up by an earthquake. By way of apology and contrition, for the earthquake scared the daylights out of him, he married Agnes. To make up for his past, he married her twice in rapid succession: once by a Roman priest in Portugal and again on board ship. Thus the Marblehead waiting-girl came back as Lady Frankland; and to celebrate, Harry bought another house, this time on the edge of the river at Boston. Sir Charles Henry Frankland now controlled both ends of the Charles, and he used to shuttle his parties from one end of the river to the other. But he did not live long, and Agnes, who still had no love for Boston, moved permanently up the river to the Hopkinton elysium. Henry Cromwell, Sir Harry's bastard, went with her, and then half of her own family moved in on her. Agnes, however, bore the weight of her riches graciously. She ended up her days happily enough, surrounded by friends and half the Episcopal clergy of the Eastern Diocese, to whom she was particularly partial for their representation of everything that the Puritan elders had not been, notably their love of music and good living.

Sir Harry and his effervescent Agnes were very much living people, but they were also very much symbols. They were symbols of the slipping of the Puritan yoke with the geographic expansion of the colony up the river and then to the west. They were symbols, too, of a tiny town's insistence on being independent of every other place on the face of the earth. Its acceptance of Sir Harry and his joyous retinue was an expression of that independence and nothing more, for no one sought to emulate him. Perhaps if Sir Harry had started his merry life within hailing distance of the village green, the townspeople would have made life miserable for him. But that would have been their own business. Boston, however, was a different matter. There was no law requiring its code to be Hopkinton's. To prove its moral independence, the village took in Harry's flock with open arms; and more than one bellyful of Harry's port was the joy of a Hopkinton freeman. The whole business was not so much a question of the town's being less godly than the citadel of Puritanism down the river as it was a matter of the several towns' asserting themselves as communities distinct from the capital on other grounds than geographic.

The most important manifestation of that independence, and the fount and life of American democracy, was the town meeting—the purest form of democracy that this world will ever see, notwithstanding that it was never the community of saints that the Puritans dreamed of founding. It originated as an informal, extralegal body made up of proprietors of the town, that is, of everyone who owned land within the limits of the township. It worked so well, however, that it was early organized as an authoritative and recognized legislative body, omnipotent about domestic affairs of the town. Foreign affairs did not matter, because no town cared what the next town did anyway. The first town meetings were held weekly; and not only was everyone invited but in many of the towns along the river was required to pay a fine if he did not attend. It was not until the town selected commissioned agents from among themselves (whom they called, with nice directness, "selectmen") to conduct the week-to-week business that the town meeting became an annual event of great importance. And from those days on to the present, the town meeting remains unchanged. It would be as easy to dry up the river at its source as to alter the procedure at a town meeting. Even the immigrant Irish, who came to the river valley with a veritable genius for local politics, knew that, and they never tried it.

One of the first signs of spring in the towns was the posting of the warrant, a document of prodigious length which specified every item of business that the townsfolk must act upon. It ended with an article that further provided for the bringing up of new business, which was always taken advantage of, and with the exclamation: God Save the Commonwealth of Massachusetts! Town Meeting Day was the only real holiday on the outlying farms of the township. It was the only day when, in the heat of the democratic process at work, the barber could call the bank president a fool in public. He might not get his note renewed the next time he went around to see the banker but he would have had his little hour. It was the only day when fond relatives who weren't "on speaking terms" would yield their tradition of leaving the room if "that cousin" entered. There was nothing sufficiently serious to keep the townsfolk away on Town Meeting Day.

On every farm the chores were hustled on that one day, and some sins of omission were overlooked. The heads of the households were too busy with greater things to be concerned with particulars at home. Equipped with statistics on the town's operation during the past year and usually with an ax of his own to grind in addition to his notations of his personal feelings toward various articles on the warrant, the townsman packed his family and the hired man into the carry-all and deposited them at the Town Hall steps promptly at ten o'clock. Then he went into the hall with his fellows and became an articulate element of the body politic. Often he was a changed man, once he was a part of the meeting. A man might be meek as a mouse at home and let his wife rule him and his hired man scare him; but let him arise in town meeting to speak his mind and threats of death could not sway him.

The first thing the meeting did after order was created out of the preliminary arguments was to choose a moderator. There was no contest usually. The moderator of the past forty years had always been as efficient as any man could be and certainly knew his business and the limitations of his office well. So it was simply understood that he would continue moderator, duly elected each year, until he permitted mayhem during the course of a debate or died. Once elected, the moderator cleared his throat, banged his gavel, and announced that balloting was open. The rest of the morning was spent in the long business of casting ballots. Every official from selectman to dogcatcher was voted upon, and judiciously. There was no formality about voting, however, and it was not regarded as an especially clandestine business, where one had to sneak up to an enclosure, mark his ballot with due dispatch, and then sneak out again, as though there were a time limit on the privilege of voting. A man, if he was of firm convictions and had his mind made up thoroughly, hunched forward in his chair, drew another up before him to use as a desk and, beginning at the top of the list and going systematically down through to the bottom, checked his preference for every office with his silent, unhurried determination. If he was of a more deliberative character, on the other hand, he strolled all over the auditorium, ballot in hand, consulting and conferring and checking names here and there all over the slip, filling in the unchecked gaps whenever he got around to it. He could take an hour or more to cast his ballot if he wanted to, and frequently he did. Then he sauntered up and dropped his ballot in the town clerk's box, probably telling the clerk that he didn't vote for him this year and wandering away to argue about an appropriation while the town clerk laughed at a joke of a few decades' standing.

The rest of the morning was taken up with the counting of the ballots, which was done in plain sight of everyone. But no one bothered to watch. The female population of the town had already adjourned to the vestry across the Common to prepare dinner. And the men were busy going over their financial statements and that long warrant of articles headed "to see if the Town will" do this, that, or the other thing. They discussed budgets, plotted strategy to break the opposition, arranged to second motions for one another, and went over last year's expenditures with a fine-tooth comb. Then the moderator, who might have been anywhere during the ballot counting, hopped up on the platform, reeled off the results, and entertained motions for a recess. Briskly he put the motion, yelled in a rapid monotone, "All-those-in-favor-say-Aye—those-opposed-No — the-ayes-have-it — it-is-a-vote," before anyone had time to say Aye or No, banged his gavel and told everyone to go across to the vestry, ordinarily making some little jest about the women's proficiency in cooking.

The reassembly after dinner, when the body politic was reinforced by too many pies, constituted the meeting proper. The moderator banged his gavel again and read out the first article of the warrant, and democracy started to function. Immediately half a dozen citizens in scattered places bounded to their feet and clamored for recognition. The moderator recognized one, according to some mysterious principle which no one questioned. A flood of oratory was then let loose as the speaker urged the article's immediate adoption. Someone else opposed violently. More speakers rose in its favor. The opposition, embittered by loneliness, shouted that he had made a particular study of the issue and could say, well advised, that his opponents knew little whereof they spoke. Finally the moderator put the question to a vote, which was affirmative and almost unanimous. But the opposition wasn't through yet, and had saved his trump trick. He bellowed that the meeting wasn't legal because the warrant was posted thirteen days ahead of the meeting day instead of the fourteen required by law and that the meeting, in fact, therefore, did not exist as a legal body. He moved, in view of that circumstance and for no reason at all concerning the nature of the vote, that it forthwith adjourn. The town logician then jumped to his feet to offer that you could not adjourn a meeting that did not exist.

The moderator took it all in his stride. After the tumult, he banged his gavel once more and rendered his decision, and a wondrous one it was: You could not adjourn a town meeting sine die until all the articles of the warrant had been acted upon. Therefore, he could not entertain the motion, and he said so. Everyone accepted his decision, because the moderator knew everything about legal procedure. As a matter of fact, the "sine die" did the trick: the opposition had never bothered to investigate the term and did not appreciate that if he had specified a later date in his adjournment motion, he could have had the satisfaction of seeing it put to a vote, even though it was dead certain to go down in defeat.

Anyone could talk about anything at the town meeting, and no holds were barred. If a motion was made for an action that would benefit a certain landowner, that gentleman was named and, what is more, he got up and defended the measure himself. He might first expatiate on generalities and talk loudly and at great length on the welfare and progress of the town; but eventually he got down to business and said that he had been waiting for ten years for that road from his wood lot to the highway and it was about time that he got it—he noticed that Sam Bacon had had two roads connecting his properties in those ten years. Sam Bacon was up in a flash to grieve and regret that a fellow townsman should stoop so low as to imply that he had ever urged a public project for private gain. Nevertheless, if the meeting felt that the landowner did have the road coming to him, they voted to build it. If they didn't, they might decide to let him wait another year. And in five minutes he and Sam Bacon would be rising in sweet accord to object to something else.

At every town meeting some old inhabitant had a favorite motion which he had been making for the past half century. When a certain lull came in the proceedings, he would totter to his feet, make his motion, wait for it to be defeated, and sit down again to fall asleep. It was only respect that led the moderator to entertain the motion, for he habitually exercised discrimination.

People expected him to. A man of patriotic demonstrativeness might rise in sober sincerity to move, after a long speech molded on the Public Addresses of George Washington, to hang bunting on the town hall on February twenty-second. As soon as he sat down, a humorist would take the floor to make the motion that the town hang the speechifier on April first. Situations like that were up to the moderator; it took a nice sense of differentiation to know what motions to put before the body and what ones to avoid hearing, for humor lost its point on repetition.

But the moderator never tried to control a man's freedom of speech. At the town meeting a citizen said what he wanted to say, and "to speak up in meeting" became a New England virtue, a criterion of a man's independence. His motion might fail ignominiously, but he exercised the right to make it. His speech might fall far short of due appreciation, but he delivered it. His wife might curtly inform him on the way home that he made a perfect idiot of himself and never was she so embarrassed, but he was not embarrassed himself and knew that deep in her heart she was pretty proud of that speech that made them all sit up and take notice.

As independent as its several members was the town itself as a unit. No motions failed more consistently than those which were favored because another town had adopted them, and the best way to cut an appropriation was to point out that some city had increased one in a similar department and prospered greatly. The town's business may have been transacted in a flood of words that flowed from hard concern over dollars and cents to poetry and Scripture and that sank to low comedy only to rise to metaphysics. But independence was there throughout. It is significant that the town of Dedham, at the sharpest bend in the river, in town meeting assembled, anticipated the Continental Congress by two months in 1775 by declaring themselves independent of Great Britain whenever Congress got around to declaring it for the rest of the colonies.

8

Farmers and Almanackers

THE countryside of the river valley was full of wonders to the settlers who migrated upstream, and visitors from England never ceased to marvel at the remarkable things in those parts. Most of the latter wrote books, when they went back home, to acquaint their astounded friends with the wondrous Massachusetts country. John Josselyn, Gent. topped them all with his volume entitled *New England Rarities*. The most ordinary thing was a great discovery to Josselyn, and he had numerous adventures with the rarities he found.

"In the afternoon I walked into the woods," he wrote, "and I wandered till I chanc't to spye a fruit as I thought like a pine Apple plated with scales; it was as big as the crown of a Womans hat; I made bold to step on it, with an intent to have gathered it; no sooner had I toucht it, but hundreds of Wasps were about me; at last I cleared my self from them, being stung only by one upon the upper lip, glad I was that I scaped so well; But by that time I was come into the house my lip was swelled so extreamly, that they hardly knew me but by my garments."

Other English travelers lacked the enthusiasm of the born naturalist that led Josselyn to take the attack of his animated pineapple in such good spirits. Some of them were openly skeptical about the region's adaptability to agriculture. "There is much cold, frost and snow," one Englishman wrote home, "and this land so barren that unless a herring be put into the hole that you set the corne or maize in, it will not come up." Another felt rather defeated about the quality of the hay downstream, where it was extremely bad: "Hay we have here of the lowlands," he wrote peevishly, "such as it is . . . for it is so devoid of nutritive virtue that our beasts grow lousy with feeding upon it and are much out of heart and liking; besides it breeds among them sundry diseases which we know not how to cure." The man should have gone up the river, beyond the salt marshes, and he would have found as opulent hayfields as he could wish. Moreover, cattle were new to the Charles River valley. Josselyn knew that, and he noted it carefully. Of the Indians, he said: "Tame cattle they have none, excepting Lice."

Josselyn was, in fact, kindly disposed toward everything in the virgin country of Massachusetts except the weather; and he was not very optimistic about the future of a people who made up their minds to endure it. It was much too warm in summer, tending to corrupt the settlers. "So much more heat any man receives outwardly from the Sun, so much wants he the same inwardly, which is one reason why they are able to receive more and larger draughts of Brandy and the like strong spirits than in England without offense." Of the cold weather of winter Josselyn was even more apprehensive. "Cold is less tolerable than heat," he said flatly. "Too much cold diminisheth the flesh, withers the face, hollows the eyes, quencheth natural heat, peeleth the hair and procureth baldnesse."

But the Massachusetts farmers became neither drunker nor balder than other men, although they were probably the most gregarious farmers in the world. The Valley of the Charles is not a segment of a great plain, but is a rolling, hilly area. Consequently, the

farms were small and close together. Each home lot was a narrow strip of land running back from the main street, and each had a house, a barn, a garden patch, and a tiny pasture. The bulk of the farming was done on outlying fields, so that the farmer's land about his house was invariably the smallest part of his holdings. Each day he commuted six or seven miles to the edge of the township to till his holdings. Often he owned a piece of tillable land "in common" with his neighbors. Each of them built a section of the fence that enclosed it, and a majority of the owners decided what to plant. The cows were kept in a distant community pasture. A town official of considerable importance, the cowherd blew his horn at sunrise to warn all the villagers to milk their cows before he came around to collect them. Then he tramped along the street, collecting a few cows at every door until he had a great herd, which he drove out to the pasture. The cowherd stayed with them all day, driving them home again toward sunset. Often, when the danger from wolves was great, he simply stopped before every door for the housewife to come out and milk her cows and then continued to the town common, where the animals were penned for the night. The common was securely fenced—a matter of such importance that the town elected fence viewers at every town meeting, and the towns along the Charles still do.

It was the middle of the seventeenth century before the river valley was extensively taken over by the farmers. And life was hard and living rugged. The houses had thatched roofs of reeds, oiled-paper windows, and rough-boarded walls. But they were practically built around a huge chimney, and they endured like the farmers that built them. The people downstream were condescending about them, looking down on the "frontier" farmers as a pack of rude, poverty-stricken rustics. As a matter of truth, however, wealth became the rule. Men, who—had they stayed at the river mouth— would have become underlings, achieved independence, and the upriver towns took on an aspect of prosperity that the passing of a few years made surprisingly general among them.

The English travelers changed their tunes: "Gentlemen's houses appear everywhere and have an air of wealthy and contented people. Poor, strolling and ragged beggars are scarcely ever to be seen; all the inhabitants of the country appear to be well fed, clothed and lodged, nor is anywhere a greater degree of independency and liberty to be met with . . ." In a few full years, the upriver farmer had come into his own economically and politically.

Culturally, too, he came into his own—for the first book published in America was not a sermon but a farmer's almanac, printed by Stephen Daye at the press at Harvard College. That was in 1639, and thereafter the farmer's almanac was an institution. It had all the authority of the Old Testament and all the glamour of the Sears, Roebuck catalogue. Every year its arrival was awaited with interest, and every year its circulation was increased. The almanacs were what some disturbed contemporary critics might have called functional to begin with, their purpose being to help the farmer plan his year. From their tables of computations of moons and tides and sunrises, however, the almanac makers were naturally led to an absorbing interest in astronomy and thence to astrology and every variety of natural phenomena. Moreover, there was usually some space left at the bottom of each page, underneath the tables, and the fillers used to fill it up gradually gave the almanacs distinct characters, like the editorial pages of the later newspapers but far less serious. Poems, fragments of religious thought or of philosophy, and scraps of scientific information were scattered through the almanac, some of them gracing the bottom of the pages, some of them inserted at the beginning or end of the little books, and some just put in arbitrarily where the compiler thought they would receive the most attention. Eventually the character of the compiler himself could be quite fairly judged from the nature of his filler, as well from the selections he made from other authors (and any one was likely to turn up in a farmer's almanac) as from his own effusions.

As was more or less appropriate, the almanac poetry was largely of the time-is-fleeting-and-human-life-short school, like that of the village graveyards. Although it was usually bad verse, there was a certain sad sincerity about such poetry. The treatment of death, too, had that same fatalistic tone that New England headstones sounded, even though the compilers tried to approach it with light resignation. Sentiment was still something fearfully repugnant to the soul of New England, but it cropped up on most pages of those almanacs in the guise of flippancy or curtness:

> Death *is a Fisherman,* the World *we see*
> *His* Fish-Pond *is, and* we *the Fishes be:*
> He sometimes, Angler-like, doth with us play,
> *And slyly takes us One by One away;*
> *At other times he brings his Net, and then*
> *At once sweeps up whole* Cities *full of them."*

And always the preoccupation with the passage of time left the compiler and his readers deeply moved. References such as "Swift-winged Time, feather'd with flying hours" and "Time devouring all that she brings forth" were consistently present. Words like that, flowery as they may have been, were not insignificant, coming as they did from the "practical" men of New England who wrote the almanacs. They were evidence of some slight liberation from the yoke of cold Puritanism, for you cannot bemoan the passage of time as too rapid unless you value life on this earth.

Most of the almanac makers were educated men, widely read and full of rhymes. They had their private theories, enthusiasms and antipathies, which they indulged from year to year and which became features of their publications. Josiah Flint, for example, did not like the names of the several months—he thought they were irrelevant and meaningless—and he accordingly omitted them from his almanac and did not bother with them at all. A man compiled an almanac as he pleased.

In 1676 John Sherman appended to the table of contents of his almanac a lengthy prophecy that morally New England was on the road to hell. For a while after, the Puritan elders wondered if the almanac vogue was not another opportunity for putting the fear of God in the people; but, although Cotton Mather once wrote an exhaustive and grave homily, the strategy failed, and the almanacs went their own way.

The almanacs were expected, of course, to offer some prophecies about the weather, and most of them did. But no one, least of all the compilers, took such technical features seriously. The almanac maker merely decided whether to couch his prognostication in such general terms that he was bound to be right, to invent a good deal of scientific hocus-pocus and offer it as sober truth, or to treat the whole question of the weather humorously.

In its long-range forecast for the year 1676, Foster's almanac reached the height of being very general and very correct: "The Wind blowing Much from the South without rain: wormes in oak-apples: Plenty of Frogs, flyes and poysonous creatures: Great and Early heates in Spring; Year with little Wind and thunder; Flesh or fish soon putrefing in the open air." Foster could have been wrong on no count. There were always worms in oak apples in New England, always plenty of frogs and flies, usually early warm spells in spring, and flesh or fish would putrefy in the open air as quickly and as consistently as anywhere else. As for the wind from the south, it seldom brought rain; and it was pretty safe to say there would not be much thunder.

Russell, in 1684, to appease his readers' curiosity about the weather, offered a detailed study of the nature of lightning, which was always a popular subject. Besides, it made them forget his limited prophecies. "Of Lightning," he said, with comfortable self-assurance, "there are three sorts, viz. piercing, dashing into pieces, burning." The first sort was a "subtile and thin exhalation," which would go right through a small hole but would pierce its way through an obstacle. The second sort of lightning, he said, was thicker and "burnes not to ashes but blasts and scorcheth. With this Lightning there happens to be (yet seldome) a Stone, that is called a Thunder-bolt, which . . . breaks into pieces whatever it meets." The third sort (and here the almanac maker's imagination failed him) was "more fiery than flamy; of a more grosse and earthy substance." The Sunday supplements were born in those early almanacs, for they abounded in such meaningless sensationalism. "If Lightning kills one in his sleep, he dyes with his eyes opened, the Reason is because it just wakes him and kills him before he can shut his eyes again: If it kills one waking, his eyes will be found to be shut, because it so amaseth him that he winketh and dyes before he can open his eyes again."

The important thing about all this talk about the weather is that not once was it blamed on the devil. Toward the end of the seventeenth century, in fact, the humorous treatment of the almanac's role in prophesying the weather had become the rule rather than the exception. Tully, who published his almanac in Boston under the noses of the Mathers, could begin with the following observation for January:

> The best defence against the cold
> Which our Fore-fathers good did hold
> Was early a full Pot of Ale,
> Neither too mild nor yet too stale,
> Well drenched for the more behoof
> With Toast cut round about the Loaf,
> The Weather is very cold; but when *Jeal-Lousie* is hot, that house is Hell, and the
> Woman is the Master Devil thereof.

That is about the lowest ebb that almanac poetry reached: the continuity is bad, the rhyming is atrocious, and the division of jealousy is unfortunate. But nothing could point more emphatically to the waning of the chill Puritan moon. Tully himself, in no way deceived about the quality of his verse, specialized in that sort of thing. For February he ignored the weather completely and wrote a terrible poem touching upon St. Valentine. To amend, he made the observation, in much more palatable prose: "The Nights are still cold and long, which may cause great conjunction betwixt the Male and Female Planets of our sublunary Orb, the effects whereof may be seen about nine months after and portend great charges of Midwife, Nurse and Naming the Bantling."

Tully was one of the rare geniuses of New England, a man born out of time and therefore forgotten. He was the lightest, the most independent of all almanac makers, and he did not care a shilling what his public thought of him. He cared less about his confreres. He persistently made fun of his own business and lampooned the senses out of those almanac compilers who looked upon themselves as inexhaustible founts of knowledge and their creations as compendia of universal understanding. The private antipathy which he indulged in his own almanac happened to be toward compilers of almanacs. "If some great Person do not die this month," he said of his own gift of prophecy in March, 1688, "let them light Tobacco or make Bum-Fodder with our Observations." And his prophecies were all of a piece: he wrote with pointed ambiguity of September:

> Perhaps a Sudden Frost,
> By which the Tender Plants are lost.

and of March, simply "Dirty Weather." He may have been bawdy, as he was uniformly when the winter months occupied his attention. He could not resist writing of January:

> Now Virgins will own
> 'Tis hard lying alone
> Such Weather as this.

or of December:

> This cold, uncomfortable weather
> Makes Jack and Jill lie close together.

But he brought freshness and humor and warmth and the ability to laugh at himself to a cold, bleak world that had been imprisoned by the thought of that diabolic snake too long. Doing this, he did much to set his fellows free.

The serious almanackers, however, carried on, and their annual productions flowed from the presses with a consistency worthy of the river. The explanations of natural phenomena went on, the free medical advice was dispensed, and that eternal anatomical figure with the bared entrails and the signs of the zodiac continued to greet the reader at the beginning of each new year. The compilers themselves got sick and tired of the last feature and tried to give it up, but their readers would not hear of it. One of the compilers summed up the situation sadly:

> The Anatomy must still be in
> Else the Almanack's not worth a pin.

The valley of the Charles formed the very core of the almanac makers' fraternity. In some families it became a tradition to produce an annual edition, and the greatest dynasty of almanackers lived in the town of Dedham at the river's bend. For half a century, one of the Ameses of Dedham published an almanac. Nathaniel Ames, the father, was born in 1708, at the height of the almanac's popularity, and published his own first edition at the age of sixteen. He was gifted with considerable wit and, except where lawyers were concerned, was cheerful and friendly. He was given to the making of astrological prophecies until it proved a boomerang, for he later complained that more knowledge of the future was demanded of the almanac compiler than was possessed by the devil. Although he was a physician by profession and practiced medicine widely in Dedham, he also turned his hand to tavernkeeping, because he married a girl who happened to own a tavern. After a couple of busy years, during which Ames was at once husband, physician, almanac maker, and tavernkeeper, his wife died. From that time on, Nathaniel Ames had no use for the legal profession and let it be known in his annual report to the world.

The trouble was that Ames, being a man of amiable disposition, had grown rather fond of his tavern. It backed right up to the Charles, and opposite it was a lane that led up to the graveyard, called "The Beere Waye." This captivated Dr. Ames's fancy, for the lane clearly led from his beer to the biers of the cemetery and the name of the lane was almost a philosophy of life. Accordingly, when Dr. Ames's wife died in 1737 and her mother thought the tavern ought to revert to her, Dr. Ames thought quite differently. There was a good deal of legal dispute over the matter, which apparently tried the physician's naturally pleasant disposition sorely. But he won the case. The Supreme Court decided that he was entitled to the tavern, although two of the judges dissented and said his mother-in-law ought to have it. The doctor, by way of expressing his opinion of those two, had his tavern sign taken down and a painting of the Supreme Court hung up in its place. All the judges were clearly recognizable, and each of them had a copy of the Province Laws before him, the volumes open and ready for their study. And every judge was studying the laws except the two who had decided against Dr. Ames. Those two had their backs turned to the laws. Since one of the dissenting judges happened to be the chief justice, he immediately sent the sheriff out to confiscate Ames's painting. Ames was in Boston at the time and, having heard of the order, raced the sheriff up the river to Dedham and saw to it that his tavern signpost had nothing on it but a perfectly legitimate legend. When the breathless sheriff ar-

rived, he found only the words: "A wicked and adulterous generation seeketh after a sign, and there shall be no sign given unto it."

Dr. Nathaniel Ames was a good physician, kept a good tavern, and published a good almanac. His poetry, of which he wrote reams, was rather wretched and much too long; but his scientific observations were interesting and his astrology diverting. He kept his weather forecasts brief and safely general, like "Hot and looks like Thunder." But he never forgot the lawyers. They were like quack doctors, he said, "Scabbed Sheep among the Flock, one Devours and t'other breeds the Rot." Through thirty-nine editions he jibed at the lawyers, matching their tongues with his own pen:

> The lawyers' tongues—they never freeze,
> If warmed with honest client's fees.

Then he died from exhaustion, having been in three trades all his mature life, and turned his medical practice, his tavern, his almanac, and his very name over to his son.

The second Dr. Nathaniel Ames was known far and wide as a veritable hellion. Even as a college freshman, his diary reveals, he was blessed with an astonishingly disagreeable nature. "Fit with the Sophomores about Cust," he wrote in 1758; and two days later, he added, "Had another fight with the Sophomores." In 1762, two years before he inherited the almanac, he wrote, "Mr. Haven preached a pretty affecting funeral Sermon for the Old Meeting House. Snivelling Women." While his father hated lawyers, the second Nathaniel hated everybody. He called merchants "lobster princes." His political foes, the Federalists, were "fudderalists." The lawyers were "pettifoggers." Farmers he hated least of all, calling them "lords of the soil" and defending their causes at the expense of the others.

Since he liked printers no more than anyone else, the second Dr. Ames had difficulty carrying on the almanacs. If his almanac compiling was not interrupted by family affairs, he was being bothered by the printers, "for they are all Knaves, Liars, Villains . . . and when they appear most Friendly have most of the Devil in their Hearts." The trouble with Nathaniel, Jr., was that he was not a born almanacker, who had to be a man well disposed toward humanity. Disagreeable, rude, churlish, and ferocious, he apparently kept the almanac going only to help himself forget all the fools in the world. But he approached the compiler's task with no joy. He kept strict records of all the other almanacs then published, and he made a close examination of their production and editorial methods. His own he compiled while he was in bed in the mornings, usually finishing it early in the year. The almanac for 1775, for example, was entirely finished in January, 1774; and the cantankerous young doctor spent the rest of the year fighting with the printers over it. After 1775, he became tired of the almanac and exasperated with the printers, and the Revolution seemed an opportune time to discontinue the publication. He spent the rest of his days in a long grouch, and the mothers of Dedham used to frighten their children with threats of Dr. Ames.

The work of the almanacs had been done by then anyway. The first books to be printed in America, they were also the first to print the English poets for the great body of the people and the first to shake off in clear print the heavy weight of Puritan oppression. The almanackers are forgotten now, and literary histories pass them by; but with their understanding of time, that would be just what they would have expected:

The Year is past away, our Glass doth run,
And while we speak, the Present Minute's gone.

9

Spillways

Having experienced the glaciers and conquered their thrusts, the Charles was not much disturbed by what the race of man did with its waters. Dams were built, canals dug, spillways made and fishing weirs constructed, but the river still flowed on, its course unaltered. In later days, there were gigantic works afoot at the river's mouth, where half the river basin at flood tide was filled in with old oyster shells and dirt so that the best people of Boston could build long, sedate rows of brownstone houses to live in, huge stone churches to contemplate eternal things in and a great Renaissance library—oddly enough, after ye Italian manner—which they dedicated to the "Advancement of Learning." They built, too, a great hall in which they could listen to Beethoven on winter afternoons and a greater one still in which they could look at Copleys and Sargents. They reared a little theater with a terrace, which was always too polite to make a living, and scores of schools, and several hotels whose ballrooms were occupied more by lectures in the morning than dances at night. That was their "Back Bay" and their whole world; and they sat back and enjoyed it, growing ripe like apples in late September, while the rest of the human race poked gentle fun at them. It was all built right on top of the Charles River, but the river itself was complacent and merely made a quieter entry into the sea as its living waters lapped the hem of Boston's skirt on the south bank and licked the boots of Cambridge on the other.

Upstream, and in earlier days, the river bore no such colossal weight. Men tampered with its ancient waters for their own little purposes, but they were practical men in those times and had little leisure for growing ripe. Consequently, whenever they looked upon the waters of the Charles it was with a naked utilitarian eye. The river had fish, and they could use fish. It had power too, and they could use power. But first they were concerned with the fish, for power was needed to grind corn into meal and without fish, which the Indians taught them to use as fertilizer, there would be no corn.

Shad and alewives abounded in the Charles, where they used to come upstream in great swarms past Sir Richard Saltonstall's village of Watertown. Catching them by hand took a good deal of time—more than the settlers at the outpost could spare. Moreover, the first year's corn crop was far below expectations, and fish was seriously needed for fertilizer. A committee was appointed, therefore, to investigate the feasibility of building some sort of trap in the river whereby they could catch thousands of fish in one day. The committee went down to the river bank and wistfully watched millions of the potbellied herring surge upstream. It was simply a question of constructing a wooden weir, which would take very little time, and snaring the fish in it as they swam along. The committee were justifiably enthusiastic over it and went downstream to get the permission of Governor Winthrop.

The governor told them that he had no power to grant such permission and that the river was under the official guardianship of the General Court. This did not help at all, because, by the time the court sat again, the season for planting corn and putting herring in the holes would be over. On his own responsibility, Winthrop told them to go ahead and build the weir anyhow and to get the approval of the court later, for he saw no sufficient grounds upon which the court could withhold approval. He said that in any case he would use his own influence with the body and that he was perfectly willing to "sink under it if it were not allowed." And sink under it Winthrop nearly did, for Thomas Dudley, his irascible deputy, raised a fearful rumpus over the affair when he found out about it and was all for impeaching Winthrop without delay. But the court had already approved by voting that "the towne of Waterton shall have that previledge and interest in the wayre they have built upon Charles River," and there was little that Dudley or anyone else could do about it.

Watertown had its fish weir for years, catching as many as a hundred thousand alewives in two tides. The towns beyond the weir, when they came into being, did a good deal of formal protesting, however, because no herring ever got beyond the weir to fertilize upstream corn. But the dispute was evidently settled amicably, for there was no civil war in the Charles River valley.

Conditions approached a civil war, on the other hand, when the river started to turn the wheels of grist-

mills. It all started when Abraham Shaw, one of the
first to venture up the river, decided that the settlement
at Dedham would be much better off if meal could be
ground more efficiently than it was by hand. In the
winter of 1636 he rose in town meeting and told his
townsmen that he would be willing to undertake the
erection of a gristmill if somebody would help him. He
didn't have the remotest idea as to where he would build
the mill, but he would welcome advice on that question
too. With a predilection for committees common along
the river, the town appointed five men then and there
to "accompany him and his workmen to find out a
convenient place: and viewe what fitting [timber] is
about yt place soe found for yt purpose; as also to order
every thing concerning ye perfection of ye same."

The six men went out to look over likely places for
the mill. They stamped up and down the riverbank,
searching for a place where the current could be har-
nessed and for trees of sufficient sturdiness to furnish the
heavy timbers needed. They finally decided upon a
spot and reported back to another town meeting a
month later. By now the town was so deeply interested
in Abraham Shaw's project that they dropped all formality and took him to their bosom, thereafter referring to him pleasantly as simply "Abraham" in their
records. They voted to give him sixty acres of land for
his corn mill, which was an offer very generous for the
purpose, "to belong unto ye sayd Mill soe erected provided allwayes yt the same be a Water Mill, els not."
There had been too much trouble with windmills.
Watertown had erected one and had to move the whole
mill down to Boston to get enough wind to operate it.

Abraham died before he ever got around to building the mill, but it was no fault of the town. The latter ordered every man within its confines to go down to Watertown "by land" and get some millstones at the boating place near Haynes's farm and tote them back to Dedham. Moreover, to make Abraham feel perfectly confident that the town was not merely offering all this aid to snatch up the mill as soon as he had finished it, he was given legal title to the mill itself and to all those sixty acres with all rights to sell at his pleasure, as long as he let the town match the price of any prospective purchaser. But Abraham Shaw's days were numbered; and without his inspiration the matter hung over the fire.

Three years later someone spoke up in town meeting again and wanted to know whatever became of that gristmill that Abe Shaw was going to build. After a good deal of recollecting, alternately damning and praising the memory of Abraham Shaw, and orations to the effect that a gristmill was now twice as necessary as it had been three years ago, the town took action once more. This time it reckoned directly with the river, for the upshot of the debate was that the Charles wasn't very amenable to pushing a water wheel in Dedham. The town resolved, therefore, to go out and dig a ditch through a meadow bordering the river in such a way that the waters of the Charles should be diverted to form a brook running into the neighboring Neponsit. The mill would be built on this artificial brook.

The scheme was greeted with great enthusiasm and hailed as an engineering project of inestimable courage, until it was asked who should build the mill. No one came forward. It was spring then, and there was not much time left if the town was not to go without a mill through another winter. An order was accordingly posted offering anyone who built a mill all the sixty acres that had already been given to the late Abraham Shaw together with all the rights and privileges awarded to Abraham in his hypothetical mill. The only catch was that the mill had to be erected and grinding corn by the first of the following December.

A man named John Elderkin, who thought the proposition a sound one, talked it over for a few days and then volunteered to erect the mill. For some unknown reason, the town gave him only thirty-eight acres, ten of them being the river meadow where the brook was dug. But Elderkin preferred going ahead and building the mill to squabbling over a few acres of land, and he finished it in due season. Pretty soon he was grinding out a respectable living by making corn meal for every house in Dedham. He enjoyed building the mill, in the first place, and he was rather surprised at its success, in the second. Moreover, he got his original investment in labor and material back by selling a half-interest to Nathaniel Whiting. Then he sold the other half to the minister and a couple of his friends, having found the day-to-day operation of the mill much less exciting than going out in a wild spot and actually erecting the mill. He left Dedham, with all the money he had made, and went all around New England building water mills for any who wanted one.

Owning a mill was something of a novelty, and the minister and his two friends probably just bought their shares because they thought the experience of owning a mill might be valuable. But the experience did not last long, for Nathaniel Whiting bought them out of the business and owned the mill by himself. The town, however, took a paternal interest in the place and frequently called Nathaniel Whiting on the carpet to have him explain away complaints of "the insufficient p'formance of the worke of ye Mille." But Nathaniel was as clever as any of them, and told them to appoint two men, as he himself would choose two, and send them down to see whether the mill was running efficiently. The issue could result in a deadlock at worst.

The mill stayed in the Whiting family and supported them through five generations, a period of nearly two centuries. The town continued to look after its welfare. They built roads leading to it, placated disgruntled landholders around the artificial brook with new awards, and when one of the Whiting heirs complained about a new mill built by Ezra Morse a few miles upstream in 1699, the town decided, with quaint reasoning, that "it may be benefishal to our medows and the other mill to have Ezra Morse's mill let fall & to let the water run in its anchant naterall corse." To make Ezra happy, they gave him forty acres of land at the other end of town as an outright gift.

While Ezra Morse was quite easily pacified, the town of Newton, a few miles downstream, was not. Diversion of the waters of the Charles into a millrace for Dedham's corn mill irritated the inhabitants with mounting effect until in 1767, one hundred and twenty-seven years after the Dedham ditch was dug, the townsfolk took action. Whether the people of Newton, which happened to possess the most beautiful stretch of the river, were actually incensed at what they regarded as a sacrilege in diverting the waters or were jealous of Dedham's corn mill or merely wanted more water power for their own industrial plans is not clear. But

vociferation came in handy enough. Smallpox epidemics were regular in the valley of the Charles; and once when Newton was having its bout, Judge Fuller's powerful voice was its only communication with the outside world. Judge Fuller used to get up on a hill on his farm every night and yell to Dr. Spring at Watertown, three miles away, a communiqué on the situation. The people of Cambridge, some miles farther, said that they could hear his thundering ALL'S WELL! passing right over their heads on its way to Maine. His voice was no petty consideration, therefore, when it came to appointing a delegation to deal with Dedham.

There were other reasons for the selection of Judge Fuller. One was that he happened to be a man of solid convictions. He had no use for people who incurred debts, and he lived without owing any man a penny overnight. Ludy Harris used to repair the judge's shoes and would willingly have extended the magistrate credit. But when some member of the family went around to get the judicial boots while the judge was ill on his deathbed, Judge Fuller raised a fearful clamor and shouted until the house shook. When he calmed down, he dispatched his wife to the cobbler's with the exact sum due. He died a little while after, his stentorian voice stilled forever. But when the physician unfolded the judge's hand to place it in a properly imposing position on his great belly, the fee tumbled out into the physician's own palm.

All this is far ahead of the judge's connection with the Dedham gristmill, but it is necessary information to the appreciation of the rise in importance of industry in New England. It is necessary to know that Judge Fuller was persistent in his convictions, and not very retiring physically; and to know that, one has to go beyond his death. For some years, in fact, there were grave fears in the Newtons that Judge Fuller was physically immortal and that an echoing roar might even emanate from his tomb. At any rate, his body was embalmed in the not overcareful method of the day, deposited in an ordinary coffin, and placed in an ordinary tomb. Nine years afterward both the tomb and the casket were opened, and there was the judge lying in as perfect condition outwardly as he was when last seen on Newton streets. Somebody tapped the corpse in various places and confirmed the rumors of its indestructibility, for it was as hard as rock. Immediately there was a grand rush to Judge Fuller's tomb to see his remarkable body. Nor did the public interest soon die down, for it was necessary to close the tomb before the townsfolk would go about their business. Twenty-five years after that, a new generation arose, and most of Judge Fuller's contemporaries were dust. Not so Judge Fuller. His tomb was opened again so that it might be seen how he was getting along. He was still in perfect condition, his body as impressive as ever and his features as recognizable. The coffin itself had molded away, and a new one had to be provided. When the judge was thus made comfortable again, his tomb was closed and he was left to the years. Seventy-two years after, the new coffin, which was made advisedly of better wood than the first, was opened, for the judge's body had now passed the century mark after its original entombment. On this opening, however, Judge Fuller was just a pile of bones.

It may be assumed from all this moral perseverance and physical persistence that Judge Abraham Fuller

was not the man to take a commission lightly. He went
down to the State House with two other delegates, who
were entirely superfluous, and roared to the governor
and his Council his demand, in the name of Newton,
that something be done about Dedham's purloining of
Charles River waters. But nothing was done. Again
and again Judge Fuller and his confreres went to the
State House, and over and over Judge Fuller bellowed
damnation on Mother Brook. Eventually his fellow
delegates dropped out of the mission, but it may be
counted upon that Judge Fuller did not. Yet he whose
voice was heard over three towns and a river elicited
nothing more than vague promises from successive officials at the State House.

To his fellow citizens of Newton the failure of
the admirable magistrate was representative of subtle
changes in the river valley. A boon to industry, even if
it involved a serious moral offense such as altering the
course of a river's waters, was not to be nullified by the
government of Massachusetts. And industry even then
was taking over the river valley, as Newton well knew,
for they themselves were joining in the theory that it
might be quicker to grow rich by chaining the river
for manufacture than tapping it for agriculture. For
the final settlement of Judge Fuller's futile howl in the
case of Newton versus Dedham came in 1840, and an
odd bargain it was: it provided that "one-third" of the
Charles River should flow forever into Dedham's sluice
and the other two-thirds flow on in its natural course
to Newton.

What can be made of that? No one could measure
the flow of water in the Charles so that one-third might
be sent one way and two-thirds another way, and no

one could control the flowing even if the measuring had been possible. It was a strange compromise, indeed, reflecting a singular state of mind. Many people were leaving the Charles valley to go west, fired with an ambition which those who remained home turned into as diverse channels as the river itself had known. And one way—the way of the poets and the philosophers at the river's mouth—led to freedom and a kind of peace, as one way of the river led to the sea. And the other way —the way of those who piled brick on brick in a mad building of factories—led to disillusionment and a feeling of being lost, as surely as the way of the river through the Dedham sluice led it to a lesser stream where *it* was lost.

But during those first years of the water mills, when the turning of the water wheels were attuned to the needs of the men along the riverbanks, the Charles played a useful and noble part. It was only centuries after, when the wheels were caked with moss and the mills covered with dust, that the practice of being industrious at the price of other things ended, like a current of fresh water in a stagnant pool, in torpor and tragedy.

Part Four

Truth's Current
Glides By

IO

Calm Rising Through Storm

A COLLEGE across the river at Newtown was voted into existence out of thin air by the Great and General Court in the autumn of 1636. It was a bold step for a little cluster of men in the lower Charles valley to take, for there was still much physical work to be done and Newtown was not much more than a frontier settlement. But the way to freedom was the way to truth, and the General Court counted it a solemn duty to perpetuate learning. Then, having founded the college by merely voting that there should be one, they forgot all about it and turned to more pressing matters.

No one bothered about the hypothetical college across the river until the following autumn. Then it was decided that if the college was to start the business of polishing the colony's youth, it ought at least to have one teacher. The overseers were in no position to offer any very attractive proposition and they had to take whomever they could get as "professor." They could get Mr. Nathaniel Eaton, and—though they later cursed the day—they took him.

Nathaniel Eaton was a relatively new arrival in Massachusetts, having come in the summer of 1637 with his brother Theophilus and his wife and, in all probability also, John Harvard, an ailing young cleric. Theophilus Eaton was a man of great importance and no end of influence, for he contributed greatly to the Puritan migration across the Atlantic. When he got here himself, however, he ventured farther afield than Nathaniel, who preferred the comparative comfort of Boston. Nathaniel was a good Puritan and was educated, though he had no degree, at Cambridge in England and at the University of Franeker in the Netherlands. At Cambridge, the English fountain of Calvinism, Nathaniel Eaton acquired a reputation for hellraising, loose living, and Sabbathbreaking. He probably did it, not because he liked to enjoy life, but because he wanted to be contrary. For when he got over to Holland, where the good-natured Dutch made Sunday a feast of revelry, he turned right around and became a strict Sabbatarian. He came to America, he said, because he was constantly beset with sinful temptations in England. Although he was appointed to head the college in November, he stayed in Charlestown, where John Harvard was, until the following June. Then he went upstream to a forceful career at the college.

When Nathaniel Eaton was running it, the whole college was located in the professor's house. It was a small, two-and-a-half-story frame building, probably built of green wood, with a steep roof, a large central chimney and a lean-to ell. The building was first used in the summer of 1638, when a few students, Nathaniel Eaton, and Mrs. Eaton all moved in. Eaton had gone to the further trouble of planting thirty apple trees and setting up the frame and digging the cellar of a new building. He also fenced in the yard with a six-foot fence, because the college was situated on what was nothing but another pasture in Cowyard Row, where all the residents of Newtown kept their cattle at night under a guard of the watch. Here in this unimposing cottagelike building in the midst of a community cowyards a great university was born.

But Nathaniel Eaton was at best a clumsy midwife, and it is no credit to him that the institution lived. William Hubbard, the only one of his students who thought the professor worth commenting upon, said that he was "fitter to have been an officer in the inquisition or master of an house of correction than an instructor of Christian youth." Cotton Mather, who took occasion to review the history of the college in his *Magnalia*, said, "Though his *Avarice* was notorious . . . yet his *Cruelty* was more scandalous than his *Avarice*. He was a *Rare Scholar* himself, and he made many more such; but their Education truly was *In the School of Tyrannus*." That isn't very heavy condemnation, coming from Cotton Mather; it is almost veiled approval. Certain it is that Cotton Mather had a great infatuation with italics and felt not nearly so strongly against the methods of Nathaniel Eaton as his underscoring would indicate.

For Nathaniel Eaton was a bad man, a worse teacher, and a chronic sadist. His wife, who was butler, steward, and matron of the college, was a simple woman who was just as bad. Eaton used to browbeat his students and drive them to the point of distraction both with his constant prodding of their minds and with frequent applications of his walnut cudgel. He was aided and abetted by his spouse, who used to starve them. This state of things went along for some time in the cowyards along the riverbank, and the students used to look longingly at the gentle-eyed cattle whose lives were passed in such serene beauty. The man whose job it was to watch over the cattle looked sadly at the rough college building and sniffed contentedly at his more lowly estate. Matters concerning the college at last came to a head when the watch heard a fearful racket one day with much slamming of doors. Moreover, it was the Sabbath, when even the cattle were quieter than usual.

Mr. Eaton had apparently engaged on his own initiative an assistant named Nathaniel Briscoe to help him teach and perform other duties consistent with the assistant's scholarly attainments. Briscoe had been in the establishment for just three days when Eaton had a terrible argument with him about some triviality. It was after sunset on a Sunday, so that technically the Sabbath, about which Eaton was particular, was over; and he let loose a barrage of expletives in Briscoe's direction that aroused the entire college. Briscoe replied in kind, and Eaton fired him on the spot, opened the door and pushed him out into the night. Briscoe lingered on the doorstep a minute, wondering what to do next; while Eaton, on the other side of the door, relented a bit, opened the door and told Briscoe that he could stay for the night. This evidently annoyed the assistant considerably, and he told Eaton many of the things that the students had been saving until after commencement.

Eaton's anger mounted until he could control it no longer. He grabbed the assistant by the collar, pulled him into the house and slammed the door shut. Once inside the house, he commenced a fist fight. The two were quite evenly matched and equally enraged, so that the fight ended in a draw with both the professor and the usher of the college in a clinch, from which Briscoe eventually broke loose and went upstairs to his chamber. Eaton then sent up a howl for the constable.

The constable, with no understanding of academic niceties and no eagerness to mix himself in the complicated situation that Eaton outlined in an incoherent tantrum, made some polite suggestions. He said that if he were a master with an undutiful assistant, he would first "admonish" the man and then, if that did not change the fellow's ways, he would go to the magistrate. Then he said good evening to Eaton and went out through the cowyards to the peaceful night.

Eaton, of course, had no intention of following the advice of that angel of peace, the constable. As soon as the oaf was out of the college yard, Eaton sent his man for his walnut cudgel (which John Winthrop described as "big enough to have killed a horse and a yard in length"). Then he got another man, and the three went up to Briscoe's room. That was about eight-thirty. At ten-thirty, Eaton's two men were still sitting on Briscoe, pinning his body down, and Eaton was still walloping him with the walnut cudgel. Blood streamed down Briscoe's back, which was pocked with wounds; and as the blows from the professor's cudgel came nearer and nearer to his head, Briscoe started to yell loudly, screaming bloody murder.

The constable had put a considerable distance between himself and the college, for he had not liked the look on Nathaniel Eaton's face during the interview he had had with him. But the Reverend John Shepherd, who lived among the cowyards too, heard the screams of Briscoe, rushed out of his house and aroused a couple of neighbors and hurried into the college prepared for the worst. The minister and his reinforcements grabbed

Eaton's arm as it was raised for another blow and over-
powered him. Briscoe, with understandable anger, took
a small knife from his pocket and made a harmless poke
at one of the men who had been sitting on him. Eaton
was, of course, the first to get the ear of Mr. Shepherd,
whom he told that he was beating Briscoe because Briscoe was taking the name of the Lord in vain. Briscoe,

as a matter of fact, was praying to the Lord to spare
him from murder, and it was only due to Shepherd's
timely arrival that it was not in vain.

But Mr. Shepherd, in deference to his seniority,
listened to Eaton and even went with him to Winthrop
to enter a complaint against Briscoe for his "insolent
speeches and for crying out murder and drawing his
knife." Eaton and Shepherd wanted the usher brought
to public acknowledgment, but Winthrop's magistrates
would do nothing until they had first heard Briscoe's
version of the affair. Eaton, a brave man when he had

the upper hand, stormed out of the gubernatorial presence in another tantrum.

Briscoe had his day before the governor, and the first thing Eaton knew he was the one brought to public acknowledgment. Moreover, he was requested to bring his wife along with him. There were complaints from some quarters that all this publicity might be bad for the college and that the professor might fall short of the respect of the students as a result. But Winthrop had heard too much of the happenings across the river, and he was determined to examine Eaton. The latter, Winthrop said, offered a lot of answers that "were full of pride and disdain." Anticipating the drift of events, he remarked further that the magistrates need not bother to fire him, because he was quitting anyway. Winthrop asked him why he beat Briscoe and habitually beat the students. "He said that his rule was that he would not give over correcting till he had subdued the party to his will." He was then asked about the food served at the college, which Winthrop termed an "ill and scant diet . . . it was ordinarily nothing but porridge and pudding and that very homely." Eaton said that he had nothing to do with that and they'd better ask his wife.

Simple-minded, shrewish Mrs. Eaton rattled off a "confession" of great length, in which she denied, admitted, and disowned any knowledge whatever of every charge put to her. The students had gone into minute detail about her mismanagement of the buttery and her complete indifference as to whether they had enough to eat or not. They accused her of hoarding the food and of careless preparation of what little she dished out in commons. Mrs. Eaton was alternately afraid that the charges were all too true, indignant that she should be accused of such things, and "much ashamed" and "very sorry." There is nowhere in Americana a more radiant gem of inconsistency.

Breakfast, she admitted, had been pretty bad, "the flower not so fine as it might, nor so well boiled or stirred." She confessed freely that that was a sin of neglect and that, since feeding the students was in the nature of a sacred trust, she was guilty of a sad sin. As to their complaint that she took their beef away, that she denied for the simple reason that she never remembered giving them any, although she said that she should have. The students had also noticed that when Nathaniel Eaton was present there was more food than when he was absent. This coincidence she could easily explain. She was by nature more judicious than her husband and, on looking over the table, invariably decided that nothing more was needed. Her husband was more extravagant; when he was at table, "he would call sometimes for butter or cheese." As a result, the table was somewhat less barren when he was present. Hard on this explanation came Mrs. Eaton's admittance that her own parsimony had more to do with it than anything else and that she always refused the students any more butter and cheese even if they asked for it.

Besides being scarce, she said also that the food was probably poorly cooked; and she "took shame to herself for that" also, although she didn't know anything about it. "And for their mackerel brought to them with their guts in them, and goat's dung in their hasty pudding, it's utterly unknown to me; but I am much ashamed . . . and I humbly acknowledge my negligence in it." She was also sorry that the students were frequently required to make their own beds, in which her Negro servant often slept in their absence. The latter, she said, was "just cause for offence" and she personally took the shame and sorrow for it. But she said she knew nothing about the students' being fed the Negro's crusts and that "the swine and they had share and share alike." Nor did she know anything about the Negro's having a tankard of beer when the students were denied it. And she was greatly indignant because John Wilson claimed that they had twice had bread "made of heated, sour meal." She said that they had had it only once, as far as she knew. Then she went on to admit that beer was often completely off the board between brewings and that she had tried to force dry pudding, that is without butter or suet, down their throats under the pretext that such a dish was "miln of Manchester in Old England." She concluded by saying positively that if she had everything to do again, she would do none of those shameful things.

But Mrs. Eaton never had that sole academic year in Cambridge to live through again. Nathaniel had expressed no such sorrowful shame and refused to admit that he was guilty of the slightest sin. The elders spent a whole day talking the matter over with him between court sessions, but Eaton was stubborn, stuck to his theory of his right to inflict his will on his charges with the walnut cudgel and held out against the elders until nightfall. Then he changed his tactics dramatically and confessed his sins with a flood of tears such as his wife had never been able to shower. The elders were deeply moved and recommended strongly to the court that the poor fellow be forgiven. Since it worked so well on the elders, Eaton tried his confession again in court—"a very solid, wise, eloquent and serious (seeming) confession, condemning himself." But the court was not so deeply moved as the elders had been, and Eaton was fined, ordered to pay Briscoe thirty pounds damages, and debarred from teaching at any future time in the colony.

As soon as the court had finished with Nathaniel Eaton, the church in Cambridge was after him. He had made a fool of the Reverend John Shepherd, and nothing was bad enough for him except excommunication. But Eaton was then on his way to Pascataquack. The governor, however, said that he would send three couriers after the miscreant and bring him back for the ecclesiastical trial. They caught up with Eaton, who said that he would just as soon go back to Cambridge for a church trial as not. But first he wanted to go out to a bark offshore to collect some goods. The couriers guessed that that was all right, if he would let them go along with him. The four of them, three messengers and Nathaniel Eaton, got into an open boat, and rowed out to the bark. Eaton collected his goods, and then the four of them rowed back toward land in the open boat. When they reached land, he told the two couriers near the bow to hop off first—which they did. Then Nathaniel helped the third off with a healthy kick in the ribs, turned the boat around and headed back to the bark alone. Nobody knows where he went after that, but he was excommunicated in absentia and up to his ears in debt. Cotton Mather, although he called Eaton "a blade who marvellously deceived the expectations of good men concerning him," betrayed his real admiration for the fellow's cleverness even in discussing the serious business of excommunication. Mather said that, in returning the compliment, Eaton "did himself excommunicate all our churches" before he departed.

If you ask most Harvard men today who Nathaniel Eaton was, the chances are that they will never have heard of the man who was the college's first head. But if you asked them who John Harvard was, they would reply promptly enough that he was the man who sat in amused tolerance in front of University Hall, who was periodically smeared with Yale's blue paint and who once had the toe of his boot decorated with hamburg so that Dan, the Yale bulldog, could be photographed abjectly licking it. Yet, compared to Eaton's tempestuous relationship with the college, John Harvard's association with it was quite remote.

That summer of 1638, when Nathaniel Eaton had first moved into the cowyards in Newton (which, from the college's presence and in due respect to the citadel of the Puritan faith in England, the General Court dignified with the name "Cambridge"), was an unpleasant one. There were earthquakes in New England and hurricanes and heavy rains. John Harvard, who had inherited none of the robustness of his butcher ancestors, lingered in a mounting consumption all summer and died quietly in September. His few hundred books he gave to the new college struggling for life under the tyranny of his fellow Cantabrigian. He gave it also one-half of his remaining estate. It is possible that he had seen the college, for he lived not far away in Charlestown; but it is extremely doubtful, for the college building had been opened for but a few weeks before he died, and four miles in the wilderness was a long journey for an invalid. But the General Court, in fitting gratitude to the young cleric who had come across the sea to die on the edge of an unknown wilderness, named the college after him.

Harvard has grown now until it has spread to the very river's brim and across it to the other side. It has had its bad years: there have been grave questions raised in the interest of the college's search for truth which often resulted in great crises over orthodoxy, but the college survived them all and fought upward to intellectual freedom; there have been serious times finan-

cially, before the days of rich men's gifts, when rich men stole from the college, as John Hancock did when he was treasurer, but from the college has sprung a great university of physical immenseness; there have even been architectural miscarriages, so that Harvard has brought to the Charles, besides its native Georgian order, neo-Romanesque, Italian Renaissance, Greek classicism, Illinois Victorian, and that huge Memorial Hall which Harvard calls its architectural hiccough. Despite all that, it is the magnificent work of the Puritans that endured through three centuries and more; and the moss has been washed from its errors by a river of truth.

11

Type of Our Ancestors' Worth

Sitting serenely on the banks of the Charles, like an aged dean in his study, Harvard has always been a wise uncle to Massachusetts and the nation. Although its innards might occasionally have been disturbed with academic dyspepsia, to the outer world it has remained calm, sagacious, imposing. Harvard has ever known what was best for the people, and it will let matters go only just so far before saying something or doing something. It was responsible for many things, from which nothing but grief accrued to the college, but which were fostered for the public weal. One such was the printing press.

Ambition, love, and sudden death on the high seas all had a hand in associating Harvard College with the first printing press in America. It happened that the Reverend Joseph Glover, an English clergyman full of ambition, embarked for America in 1638, with great plans to enter the iron industry and to start a printing press. He had made thorough preparations, for this was no wild-goose chase. Already he had a house in Cambridge waiting for him; he had a font of type with him; and he had also, besides his wife, four assistants. The four assistants were all members of the Daye family, who came because they thought the Reverend Mr. Glover's enterprise was as good a means as any other of getting free passage across the Atlantic. Stephen Daye was head of the family, which included in the migration his sons, Stephen and Matthew, and a stepson named William Boardman. Stephen Daye himself was a locksmith by trade and knew nothing at all about printing, so that it was possible Mr. Glover had intended to use him in the iron industry. Matthew Daye, however, was a printer's devil and could, in an emergency, operate the press—although he was no master of typesetting. The other two men weren't of much use.

Unfortunately, the Reverend Mr. Glover, who would undoubtedly have made things hum on his arrival here, died when he was only halfway across the ocean. That left poor Mrs. Glover with a lot of printer's type, a locksmith, a printer's devil, and two other men in mid-Atlantic. But she gathered her wits about her quickly and determined, though she did not think she would bother about the iron industry, to carry out her late husband's plans for a printing press. She went directly to the house at Cambridge, close by the college, had the press set up on the ground floor and put the Dayes to work running it. Stephen Daye, the man who is currently awarded all the wide fame that belongs to the first printer in America, did not in fact have much to do with the actual printing. He was a locksmith anyhow, and all he did at Mrs. Glover's press was act as manager—and not a very good one at that. The man who did the printing, who wore the black apron and etched his fingers with honest ink, was his son Matthew. The first production of the press was a copy of the Freeman's Oath, and its first book was the almanac of

1639. After them came a psalter called the *Bay Psalm Book* and a succession of pamphlets on religious or political questions.

Meanwhile President Dunster of Harvard College, in the kindness of his heart, dropped around to pay a neighborly call on the Widow Glover. Cambridge was still on the edge of the wilderness then, and life was quite lonely. The Dunster-Glover friendship grew and waxed warm. In the second June after her arrival, Mrs. Glover was Mrs. Dunster, and the president moved into her house; for it was easier for the president of Harvard to move than it was for a printing press, to which the new Mrs. Dunster had become very attached and which she was unwilling to desert. Harvard College, however, now controlled the American press.

Stephen Daye, a restless man in the wrong business, came to an inglorious end. He made so little money at the press that he was always running into trouble, and he was always going to the General Court for help in extricating himself. Although the work his press did was consistently bad, it was the best that Matthew could do and much better than no printing at all; so the General Court gave Stephen three hundred acres of land, because he was "the first that sett upon printing." If the court thought it was thereby ridding itself of Stephen Daye, however, it was in grave error.

In little over a year Stephen Daye had mortgaged nearly two-thirds of his land grant. Part of the money thus raised he invested in one cow, one calf, and one heifer. The rest he used to pay his grocery bills. Running short of cash again, he tried some legerdemain and was promptly taken across the river and deposited in jail "for defrauding severall men." The summer of 1643

was then spent in the greatest security Stephen Daye
ever enjoyed in New England. In September, just as
the cold weather was coming on, they turned him loose.
For five years, Daye struggled along, trying to make
money out of a press he neither owned nor operated.
Then he gave up the fight, he renounced the press and
went up the river with the idea of starting a new settlement somewhere.

The star of Stephen Daye seems to have set the
moment he landed in Boston, and his exploratory efforts
were as unsuccessful as his previous ones. In April, 1656,
seventeen years after his arrival, he was still in embarrassing circumstances. He deserved most of his troubles,
however, for he was totally lacking in principles and
entirely shiftless in his ways. Eight years after he had
given up the press, he had the effrontery to sue President Dunster, who was up to his neck in his own troubles, for a hundred pounds for labor and expenses.
The labors of Stephen Daye were pretty well limited to
wasting time, and whatever expenses he incurred in that
pursuit were certainly not the responsibility of Dunster.
Even the suit itself was a waste of time, for Daye lost it.

Having failed with Dunster, he tried the General
Court again. He told the court that he had suffered
considerable damage from having started the press at
Cambridge in the first place, that he had never got a
living from it, and that the colony had not even given
him any satisfaction for his troubles. As a matter of
fact, the court had given him those three hundred
acres; but the mortgagees had long since foreclosed on
them and Daye was penniless. The General Court, which
fully appreciated the value of printing, remote as
Daye's association with the trade was, gave him three

hundred acres more. But Daye lived to be again a poor man, his acres dwindled away, his debts mounted, and he was no sooner dead than his creditors pounced upon his pitiable estate. Stephen Daye's life was empty, lonely, and tragic, for he was one of those misguided persons who find themselves in the wrong environment. Daye belonged in his English locksmithy, making his locks and keys and rounding out his prosaic days in peace where he began them. The pioneer's life was not for him, nor was the printer's. And of all the lost souls who must have bemoaned the day they forsook their humdrum spheres for the wilderness, none was more defeated than Stephen Daye.

His son Matthew, though neither a very bright man nor a very good printer, stuck to his type without complaint. For eleven years he worked on President Dunster's printing press, turning out a succession of works for Harvard College and an occasional sermon or governmental sheet. He died in harness at the age of twenty-nine, probably of malnutrition, for his faithful life was truly a sacrifice to the cause of the printed page.

Dunster was now the sole owner of the press, barring the implied ownership of Harvard, for his wife, the Glover widow, died two years after her marriage to him. Practically everyone associated with the first press was destined to sadness: the original sponsor was deep in the Atlantic, his widow was now dead, Stephen Daye was penniless, Matthew Daye was dead, and his brother and stepbrother had wandered off to obscurity. It was not strange, then, that both Dunster and Matthew Daye's successor at the press should be headed toward hard times.

Having already prevailed upon Harvard College to get some new type for the press, Dunster had no intention of letting it go to waste by lying idle after Matthew Daye's premature death. He accordingly employed Samuel Greene, who had spent some time around the press when Daye was running it, as printer. Sam Greene inherited all the monetary troubles of Stephen Daye and all the ineptitude for printing of Matthew. It is probable indeed that he had gleaned all his slender training from the latter, for there was no improvement in the poor workmanship after he took charge of the establishment. But he inherited Matthew's tenacity too, and that was no mean heritage.

While Samuel Greene was plugging away at his printing, the honest, open, sincere President Dunster was fired from the presidency of the college. Henry Dunster made the mistake of disagreeing aloud with an element of Puritan orthodoxy. He rose to his feet in meeting one day and nearly sent the ministers into a convulsion by saying that he disapproved infant baptism. He was forthwith accused of heresy and summarily asked to resign his post. The fact that he had sacrificed fourteen years of his life to drag the college up from the wreckage of Nathaniel Eaton to a position of dignity and genuine worth to the colony did not matter. Nor that he had lived on a pittance all during that time and had never spared himself. Nor that he had built with personally solicited funds and given the college the very house out of which he was being turned. It was November when he was ousted, and Dunster was forced to beg for the privilege of staying in the house until spring, in a humiliating petition wherein he pleaded that he was totally without funds, had no place to go, had a sick child, and could make no immediate preparation for housing his family during the winter. So they let him stay in the house until March.

With the unseating of President Dunster for his great heresy, the printing press passed into the direct ownership of the college. Samuel Greene still operated it and seemed also to assume charge of its affairs. Like Stephen Daye, therefore, Sam Greene had frequent recourse to the General Court. But while Daye had approached that body with a self-assurance bordering on brazenness, Sam Greene nearly fell prostrate at its feet. He constantly referred to himself in meek, servile terms and beat all around the bush before coming to the point. Stephen Daye could rush in and fairly demand three hundred acres of land from the court with a good deal more confidence than lowly Sam Greene could creep in and beg for a few pounds' worth of new type. Since Sam had little control over his press and less over his modesty, his petitions are classics of misery. Here is one composed in 1658, after the original type brought over by Glover had been used for nineteen years:

"Whereas yor poare Servant hath (although with many wants & difficultyes) spent some yeares in attending ye service of ye country in that worke of printing, the Presse & the appurtenances thereof, without a speedy supply & yt especially of letters & those principally for ye printing of English, is now almost wholly uncapeable of farther improvement, either for the answering of ye Countryes expectation, or for the benefitt of such as are employed therein, & ye Colledge (to whome ye presse doth properly belong) have not ability in theyr hands to helpe, so that unless some care be taken by the wisdom . . . of this Hon'rd Court . . . yor poore servant must bee forced to change either his habitation or employment or both."

Although it sounds like a veiled request for Boston Common, this petition was merely for twenty pounds' worth of new type to print a Bible that John Eliot had translated for his Indians up at Natick. The court told Sam Greene that it would send his petition to the commissioners of the colony in England, which was the nearest place to get type. Evidently disturbed at the desperate tone of Sam's plea, the commissioners went around to the Society for the Propagation of the Gospel amongst the Heathen Natives of New England and Parts Adjacent in America, and told them that Sam Greene over in Cambridge needed some new type rather badly in order to print a Bible for the Indians. That was all the spur the society needed, and they immediately went the whole hog and overwhelmed Sam Greene, who never expected much of life, with a deal more help than he had prayed for. The society agreed to pay the expenses of the printing, to send Sam not only the new type that he had begged for so humbly but also a new press and to send over a printer to assist him in the work. In fulfillment of this last promise, Marmaduke Johnson arrived, a full-fledged printer.

Unlike anyone else hitherto associated with America's first press, Marmaduke Johnson was a man of action, a good businessman, and a first-rate printer. He was also systematic. He started off right by not bringing any dependents over with him and by equipping himself with a written contract. According to the terms of the latter, he was to have his name mentioned as printer of Eliot's Bible in the imprint and was to receive "diet, lodging and washing" in addition to his pay of forty pounds per year—which were handsome terms. Johnson figured that a page set in type and printed per day was a reasonably fast rate, as it was with his press, and that it would allow him sufficient time for the life more abundant outside the printing shop.

Marmaduke's difficulty, however, was that, though he was sure of food, shelter, and clean linen, he would get no cash until, the Bible finished, he got back to England. So he kept borrowing money against his salary and diverted himself by making love to one of Sam Greene's many daughters.

Required to work in a measure of harmony, Marmaduke Johnson and Sam Greene were exact opposites in temperament. While Marmaduke was carefree, Sam was bowed under the weight of heavy responsibilities. While Marmaduke's private life was unknown, Sam had a family of eight children. And while Marmaduke could get along very well in a godly way of life without money, Sam had to have funds. Moreover, Marmaduke took his pleasures lightly, while conscientious Sam spent all his spare time drilling with the militia on Cambridge Common. It was impossible that the two should not eventually come to a quarrel.

Soon enough it developed that all the time Sam was doing his duty with the militia, Marmaduke was lurking around his house courting his daughter. This had been going on a full year before Sam discovered it; and, being a sober man of good standing in the community, he flared up as soon as he did. For the first and only time in his life, Sam hustled to a court without first humbling himself, for he certainly did not want any such lighthearted fellow, and a better printer than himself, for a son-in-law. Besides, Marmaduke had made enviable progress and apparently had the girl

deeply in love with him before Sam knew about it; and there was no time to lose over formalities.

Sam outrightly accused Marmaduke of "obtaining" the affection of his daughter without his knowledge or consent. He further accused Marmaduke of threatening to kill anyone else who came near the girl, which annoyed Sam because, although he was unwilling that his associate assume the responsibility, he did not want to support all his daughters forever, especially in view of the fact that he was just marrying a second wife. So in Marmaduke's second April in America, he found himself facing serious charges in the Middlesex court. The Indian Bible, the pride of John Eliot's career, lay deserted in the print shop while the two printers fought for justice.

Marmaduke was direct and unafraid of the Puritan magistrates who glared down at him. He admitted that he had courted Sam's daughter and that the daughter had capitulated and that Sam did not know anything about it until the day he ran to court. He said that he did not, however, threaten to kill anyone else who came near his love. Since he denied one of the charges, there had to be a trial, but it was found that Marmaduke was right on the second charge and Sam Greene was wrong, for no one appeared to swear that Marmaduke had threatened to kill him. During the course of the trial, Marmaduke raised havoc by announcing that he had a wife in England anyway. Therein he made an almost fatal error and was saved only by John Eliot, who thought more of his Indian Bible than he did of the marital affairs of printers.

The court dealt severely with Marmaduke Johnson. Although it did not specify how he was to get the money, he was to pay a fine of five pounds immediately for making love to Sam Greene's daughter; he was to go on probation for making the threatening speeches, even though he was found innocent of making the actual threats; and for having a wife in England all the time, he was to take the first boat back to her. He was also to pay all the costs that this threat involved in the Middlesex court. Samuel Greene was happy for one of the few times in his life at the sentence. John Eliot, who thought less of Sam's printing abilities than he did of Marmaduke's morals, was greatly upset.

Marmaduke Johnson himself was not bothered in the least. He simply stayed in Cambridge, practically next door to the court building, and went about printing the Bible for the Indians, although he did give up his pleasantries with Sam's daughter. In October, 1663, a year and seven months after its banishment order, the court awoke to the fact that Marmaduke was still around. He was promptly haled into court again and told to leave within six weeks. John Eliot immediately went to the General Court and pointed out that Marmaduke, being a good printer, was one of the rarest and most necessary men in the colony and that the question of his morals was a distinctly minor matter. This was the acme of human bravery in Puritan Massachusetts, and it served Eliot in good stead. At his insistence, Marmaduke was given another year of grace; and it proved his salvation.

That additional year saw much progress in the history of American printing. John Eliot's Bible was completed—a work of excellent quality that pleased the translator highly and vindicated his consistent faith in Marmaduke Johnson. Two more works, *Psalms in Metre* and *Call to the Unconverted,* appeared over Johnson's imprint. Moreover, his personal affairs took an abrupt turn for the better. When it was time for him to answer another court complaint about not going back to England, he introduced a letter to show that his wife was no longer there to go back to and would not be worth the journey even if she was. The letter stated that Marmaduke's wife had taken up with a man named Tracy and that the latter, having grown tired of her, had shipped her to Barbados, where she never arrived, having died on the way. In view of this evidence, Marmaduke was allowed to stay until he could get a death certificate as proof of his claims. The following year, although his accomplished relation with American printing was not yet ended, he went to England on his own account to collect the hundred and twenty pounds owed him by the Society for the Propagation of the Gospel.

There were now two presses in America, both of them in Cambridge: one, the Daye relic, in the president's house; and the other, the one sent by the society, in the "Indian College" in the Harvard Yard. The Indian Bible being finished, Sam Greene was faced with the questionable pleasure of going back to the old Daye press. He was so disturbed at the idea that he made overtures to certain officials to keep Marmaduke Johnson in England so that he himself could run the society's press. Reports were then dispatched across the Atlantic in Marmaduke's wake, saying that he was "very idle and nought and absented himselfe from the worke more than halfe a yeare att one time." Moreover, the society's agents in America confirmed the reports. But John Eliot and President Chauncy of Harvard wrote strong commendations of Marmaduke, and the society chose to retain him as their printer.

Marmaduke Johnson came triumphantly back to Boston in 1665, bringing with him a certificate of his wife's demise on the high seas and a printing press of his own together with some new type for the society's press, which he was to continue to run. He had apparently intended to set up his own press in Boston had the society failed to give him the management of their press in Cambridge.

Sam Greene meanwhile had gone back to his ancient press in the president's house. The thought of either Johnson or the society moving their presses terrified him, for he would then have no one from whom to borrow type to work the college press. He brought the attention of the college to the type shortage, and a measure was quickly pushed through the General Court making it illegal for anyone to have a printing press anywhere except in Cambridge. And as long as the court was on the subject of printing, it passed a law requiring that everything printed first have the approval of a board of four censors.

For the next three years, printing went along calmly. Greene, with his bad press and scanty type, was doing indifferent work on the college press, raising a new family of eleven children in addition to his other eight and constantly begging the court to help him out financially. As recreation he was marching around the Common at Cambridge with the militia, of which, from sheer constancy, he had been made captain. Marmaduke Johnson wisely stayed single and ran two presses, his own and the society's. He was reasonably busy, having printed and bound an Indian grammar for his good friend and defender Eliot and a host of sermons. After some experimenting, he and Sam Greene decided that a spirit of deadly competition might be fatal to both of them as printers; so they decided to co-operate to a limited extent, and they published nineteen books together in the next nine years while Marmaduke published twenty of his own. Greene was by then in the awkward position of using the society's press, of which Johnson was manager, for the college press was totally useless.

In 1688 the entire printing trade was summoned before the General Court—which meant that both Marmaduke Johnson and Sam Greene were in danger of the judgment. Someone had published a book too playful for the court's approval, and both printers were asked to bring in a list of their publications the next day. Sam was there bright and early with his list of perfectly innocuous books. All of them were as dry as the dust on the old college press and as harmless. Marmaduke sauntered in with his list, on which was one book called *The Isle of Pines,* which was what the court was after. It was a volume of tall stories about the beautiful, utopian life one could lead on an imaginary South Sea island—a book that was the vogue in Restoration England. Although it was comparatively racy reading for Massachusetts, it was neither too exciting nor too interesting. But it was the vogue in Restoration England. The court sternly demanded of Marmaduke why he had published the volume without the censors' approval. Marmaduke, who was always refreshingly frank in his dealings with courts, said that what the censors did approve simply did not bring him much money and implied that if he was permitted to come across the river and practice his craft in Boston he might not have to print things of that sort to make a decent living. The court fined him five pounds, which he could not afford, and sent him back across the Charles to Cambridge.

Johnson repeatedly tried to get permission to bring

his press to Boston and was repeatedly stopped. In a few years, he resigned himself to printing in Cambridge, which he thought too small to support two presses, and to being Sam Greene's neighbor. He even married, and accepted a post as constable, in Cambridge. But his dream of setting up his press in Boston never failed, and at last he prevailed upon the court to lift the ban on printing outside Cambridge. That was in the fall of 1674. Jubilant, Marmaduke bought a piece of land in Boston, put up a building and moved his wife and daughter and press across the river. But he never realized his ambition to put Boston on his imprint, for on Christmas Day, 1674, he died.

Sam Greene carried on in Cambridge amid many woes. After Johnson's death, he wrote influential people, begging them to get Johnson's management of the Society's press for him. But John Eliot, still mindful of Greene's poor rating at a printer, would not hear of it, and the job went to a young Harvard graduate. So Greene wrote more letters, running on at great length about his troubles and unhappy life and nineteen children and the equally sad prospects for his sons if they were ever fools enough to follow in his footsteps. Nevertheless, Sam Greene stuck to his type, and printed in Cambridge for fifty years. He stuck to the militia too; and as an old man he used to direct the marching while carried around the Common in a chair. Despite his troubles, he did not die until he was eighty-seven.

These were the men who saw the American press through its growing pains and on the way to freedom: miscast Stephen Daye, humble Samuel Greene, and obstreperous Marmaduke Johnson. Their greatness lies in their ability to have kept the infant printing industry alive at all, and their monument in the great presses that are today built along that same river over which they shuttled back and forth to court.

12

Heralds of Light

LIKE a strong whiff of the east wind, Benjamin Harris blew into the valley of the Charles from sea in 1686. A robust, hearty, independent man, he was preceded by his reputation, which had the tang of jails and countless troubles, for Benjamin Harris was possessed of a genius for getting into trouble, for tactlessness, and for honest opinionating.

Sick of the inside of British prisons and discouraged at the prospects of his favored Whigs at home, Benjamin Harris brought to Massachusetts all his enthusiasms and aimed to give them free rein. He plunged himself into the midst of things by opening up a "Coffee, Tea and Chucaletto House, by the Town-Pump near the Change," which was the very heart of Boston, which was in turn the heart of New England. Half his troubles in England were the result of his dabblings in journalism, and he was evidently full of good resolutions on coming to America to mind his coffeehouse and subjugate his taste for the printed word. Experience had taught him that it was far healthier to air one's opinions verbally in a coffee house and that his audience was likely to be just as large. But Benjamin Harris had ink in his blood. Soon he was neglecting his coffeehouse and hiring a printer to issue an almanac that he had compiled and which he offered for sale at his London Coffee House. He now regarded himself as a publisher, which was what he always wanted to be, and he gave the printer almost regular employment. He published several works, the most important of which was the famous *New England Primer*. Since his editorial and bookselling activities occupied much of his time, his coffeehouse suffered, and he was forced to keep moving it up and down Cornhill in search of a more prosperous location. In addition to being "by the Town-Pump," Benjamin's coffeehouse was also, at various times, "over against the Old Meeting House in Cornhill" and "over against the Blew Anchor" still in Cornhill, and finally "at the Sign of the Bible" in Cornhill.

On Thursday, September 25, 1690, Benjamin Harris sprang a surprise on the colony of Massachusetts Bay. Without telling anyone about it and without asking the censors' permission, he published a newspaper, an unheard-of thing in these parts. Bolstered with good intentions, he announced that the paper would appear once a month; or "if any Glut of Occurrences happen," he said proudly, he would issue an extra. He was doing all this, he said further, for three altruistic reasons: first, he thought it was a good thing to remember "Occurrents of Divine Providence" (this was evidently to please the clergy, for shrewd Benjamin Harris had lost no time in sizing up the political situation in New England); second, people's thinking would be straighter and their businesses better conducted if they knew what was going on; and third, it was desirable to correct the too-fallible habit of gossiping by "Charming that Spirit of Lying" by the bright truth in his pages.

Harris's paper was a courageous little journal, encumbered heavily with the title, *Publick Occurrences, bothe Foreign anl Domestick,* and he had tried hard to make it pleasing to the Puritan mind. Of four pages of two columns each with the last page left bare, the paper was a well-disciplined publication, when one considers Benjamin Harris's energetic mind. As a lead item, he had chosen the Indians' action in appointing a day of Thanksgiving for themselves—which was something he did not care at all about personally but which he thought the clergy would like. And the rest of the paper was given over to innocent and historically inconsequential news which must have been on everyone's tongue when it happened. A couple of children were missing and believed kidnaped. A "very tragical" accident took place at Watertown, where an old man, grieved by the death of his wife, hanged himself in the Cowhouse, for "the Devil took advantage of his Melancholy"—an observation which might make it safe to publicize a sin. Various epidemics and fevers were rampant, "though many dye not." The smallpox, which had been bad, was abating. A fire destroyed six houses. It destroyed also a young man, for whom Harris expressed little sympathy, for "he some way lost those Wits that should have taught him to help himself." But the fire destroyed, too, a PRINTING PRESS, with the passing of which Harris sympathized deeply, for it was a loss "not presently to be repaired." An army of a couple of thousand was sent off to make a "Descent upon Mount Real [Montreal]." Some lengthy news about the war was also given, but Harris said frankly that it may not have been exact. King William had landed in Ireland and was heading an effective army; and the King of France was having trouble with his son, because "he used to lie with the Sons Wife," which was as tasty an item as any columnist two and a half centuries later ever hit upon. Harris injected an editorial note into his newspaper by bewailing the rough treatment of French prisoners by the Indians and implying that if his own people could not do without an alliance with the incensed red men, they might with better grace lose the war.

It took Boston four days to get over the shock of seeing a newspaper in its midst, and there was the rumble of distant thunder in high places. Samuel Sewall, the relatively enlightened judge who kept an exhaustive diary, noted the paper's appearance and said that it gave great offense because Harris had not bothered with the formality of getting the censors' approval and because of its reference to the love life of the House of Bourbon. As soon as he saw the paper, Cotton Mather, bristling with indignation, sat down and wrote a letter about the great evil of newspapers and about the unholiness of a people who would read them. The governor and his Council read the paper with grave fears for the people's welfare, thought the matter over for four days, and then issued an edict forbidding the publication of a second edition. They found the paper contained "Reflections of a very high Nature and sundry doubtful and uncertain Reports," and they expressed their personal "high Resentment"—although why the Governor of Massachusetts Bay and his Council should resent personally allusions to the capers of Louis XIV is not clear.

Having learned the error of his ways, Benjamin Harris gave up the notion of publishing a newspaper and mended his manners. He did not storm at the governor as he had stormed in England. He did not make tactless remarks that might have landed him in jail. Instead, he worked his way back into the good graces of the authorities and devoted himself to the good works of printing governmental documents, until two years after his noble experiment he was styled "Printer to His Excellency the Governour and Council." But his abortive and quite readable little paper, far as it was before its time, had paved the way for the rise of American journalism, though nothing more was heard of it in the seventeenth century.

In the third year of the following century, 1703, a humble and timid little Scotsman named John Campbell was eking out a meager living by serving as postmaster at Boston. Since his duties were not sufficient to occupy all his time, he passed away the hours by listening to all the news that came his way as postmaster and sending it in long letters up the river valley to the frontier and down to Connecticut. He was doing this for a year when it occurred to his Scotch imagination that he might turn his tendency to relay news in, if not a profitable, at least a self-supporting channel. Accordingly, he went around to the print shop of Bartholomew Greene, the son of that woe-stricken Samuel of Cambridge and the man whose burnt press aroused Harris's sympathy. Greene told Campbell that he thought, since the Scotsman was postmaster and could get the paper in circulation quickly and cheaply, that the newspaper into which Campbell planned to turn his letters could be made to pay its way. Campbell was a cautious man, however, and did not know as he wanted to be the publisher, although he would edit and furnish copy. Greene thought he could take care of that too. So Greene dropped in on Nicholas Boone, who ran a bookshop at the "Sign of the Bible" where Benjamin Harris once had his coffeeshop. Boone was ready for anything and agreed to act as publisher.

Campbell did two things which Harris in his enthusiasm had forgotten to do: first, he secured permission of the licensors to publish a paper; second, he kept all editorializing and racy news items out of his journal. But his Scotch canniness and his natural timidity were not a happy combination for journalism. His *News-Letter* was a masterpiece of dull circumspection, full of such appetizing items as week-old ship arrivals and civil appointments which everyone but John Campbell knew about some days before they were made. The most space was given to the editor's willingness to take paid advertisements and new subscriptions. As time went on and even his old subscribers did not bother to pay their subscriptions, Campbell devoted much space to the complaints of the struggling editor, pointing out at great length that he was a poor man and needed money badly if the paper was to continue. Repeatedly he begged his subscribers to pay up. To add to his troubles, which were all due to his own lack of imagination in editing the paper, Bartholomew Greene walked out on him as printer and Nicholas Boone, the nominal publisher, dropped out of the picture completely. However, John Campbell was another mediocrity redeemed by perseverance. He was determined that his *News-Letter* should carry on in all its dryness.

To get a new printer and a new seller of his journal, he merely had to go next door to the post office, where John Allen, of Pudding Lane, ran a printing press—for printing had become a favored trade in Boston, once Marmaduke Johnson had broken through the pro-Cantabrigian ban. Allen and Campbell bungled along for four years, when a fire burned down Campbell's post office and spread next door to burn down Allen's printing office with many unsold copies of the *News-Letter*. Campbell, greatly discouraged but prodded by his Scotch obstinacy, went back to Bartholomew Greene and asked him, for old time's sake, to help him out in the emergency. Greene helped out for eleven years, though the *News-Letter's* emergency became chronic and lasted much longer than that. The paper was made up largely of scissor items clipped from stale London papers as world news, routine public announcements which could be read free at the Town Hall as local news and only Campbell's bewailing about his pecuniary difficulties as feature matter.

In January, 1719, something snapped in John Campbell's chary mind; and he made the discovery that maybe a change in the paper would cure its ailing condition. Accordingly, he doubled its size, because, he said, he did not have room enough for all his European news and was always thirteen months behind on it. In other words, instead of throwing away all the accumulated clippings of the past thirteen months, he was going to print them all, but catch up by printing twice as many in each issue. After seven months of this, he proudly proclaimed that he was now only five months behind, having caught up eight. In view of this amazing gain, he wondered in print why people did not give him **more** financial support.

Before catching up any further on his foreign news, John Campbell was visited with more troubles. First, he lost his job as postmaster to one William Brooker. Second, no sooner had Brooker taken office than he started publishing his own paper, which he called the *Gazette*. The prospects were bad for Campbell. If the *News-Letter* could not prosper as the only paper, how could it even survive as one of two? And Campbell's stubbornness caused him still further unhappiness. To get even with Brooker, he refused to patronize the post office, an extremely poor way of retaliation for a newspaper publisher. Campbell simply would not have Brooker put his foul hands on his paper, and consequently he lost his entire outside circulation. As for Brooker's *Gazette*, Campbell said in one of the rare items of interest in his own journal: "I pity the reader of the new paper: its sheets smell stronger of beer than of midnight oil."

Neither the *News-Letter* of Campbell nor the *Gazette* of Brooker prospered under the new competitive spirit. During the next couple of years Bartholomew Greene, for old time's sake, was still helping out Campbell in the emergency; and Brooker's paper was being printed by James Franklin, whose young Brother Benjamin was helping him out. Both papers continued to exist as merely enervated calendars, and the feud ended with Campbell's unceasing appeals for more money and with Brooker's being fired from the postmastership. Brooker thereupon gave up his paper, for he could not afford to keep it going without the use of the post office. His successor promptly took it up, and from then on the *Gazette* seems to have been regarded as part of the job. Every new postmaster inherited the paper from his predecessor.

When Brooker was fired, James Franklin decided that he might as well get deeper into the journalistic fray. So he started a paper of his own.

It is a peculiarity of the Charles River valley that, while people were always moderate in things of the flesh, they were always extremists in things of the mind. When it was popular to publish sermons, there was not a clergyman in the whole valley up to Hopkinton at the river's source who did not have "books" to his credit. When it was popular to run a printing press, even if one starved doing it, printing presses sprang up at every street corner. When it was popular, years later, to write poetry, there was a poet in every other house, and two in most of those in Cambridge. When it became popular to write letters to the papers, old men all along the valley regarded it as a weekly duty to sound grave warnings or observe with misgivings or note with new heart. So it was, in 1721, that Boston was threatened with a flood of newspapers. But James Franklin's, if we except the courageous but stillborn attempt of Benjamin Harris, was the first to bring intelligence and vigor to American journalism.

In his first issue, Franklin stated flatly that John Campbell's now venerable *News-Letter* was just a "dull vehicle of intelligence, very dull," and not a newspaper in the aggressive, assertive sense at all. Poor old Campbell, pretty near the end of his rope, was furious. And his fury gave his staid old journal a little twinge of life. He likened the upstart James Franklin to "soure Ale in Summer," called him a "Jack of all Trades, and it would seem Good at none," and accused him of doing his writing "after you had been Raking in the Dung-hill" when "the corrupt Steams got into your Brains and your Dullcold Skul precipitate them into Rib-aldry." Those were fighting words for John Campbell, the meek and cautious little Scotsman who had put up such a good fight, defeated as he was from the start by his own prudence. The following year he gave up for good, and sold his paper to Bartholomew Greene, who was faithful to him to the end.

James Franklin's *New England Courant* was the first paper to have a personality of its own (though Cotton Mather said it stank to high heaven of the Hell Fire Club), and it was strong, aggressive, and solid. Passing by trite news to comment editorially on questions of public importance, it stuck fiercely to its convictions. No quarter was safe from its attack: government officials, clergy, or Puritan survivors. It was the work of no one man armed with a pair of scissors and a pile of British journals, but of an entire staff, the vigorous Hell Fire Club, and of the captious office boy, Benjamin.

The *Courant's* gibes at Campbell were only an incident. The first real storm of its career began with a paradox, for it was a feud between Franklin and Mather. James Franklin was an unlettered man with great intelligence, while Cotton Mather was a much-lettered man with a minimum of intelligence. Strangely enough, Franklin opposed Mather on the only occasion that the Puritan priest ever exhibited the slightest trace of common sense. There was another smallpox epidemic, and both Increase Mather and the old man, and Cotton Mather, who had dabbled in medicine, advocated inoculation. The system of inoculation of that time caused the patient to have the disease in somewhat more obvious ways than are now apparent, after which mild seizure he was ordinarily immune. Franklin, with the intelligent tradesman's cold logic, thought it was nonsense to prevent a man's having a disease by willfully giving it to him; and he said so in his paper in no uncertain terms. He said further that if you wanted to find devil's work in Massachusetts, you had only to go to the Puritan clergy to get it.

Franklin's sentiments threw both the Mathers into a violent rage. Increase wrote to the rival *Gazette,* which was glad to get the letter and capitalize on the fight, that "In one of his vile *Courants* Franklin insinuated that if the Ministers of God approve of a thing, it is a Sign it is of the Devil; which is a horrid thing to be related." He went on to say that both Franklin and the whole colony would end up in hell if they did not behave themselves better.

Cotton wrote in his diary: "Warnings are to be given unto the Wicked Printer and his Accomplices, who every week publish a vile Paper to lessen and blacken the Ministers of the Town and render their Ministry ineffectual. A Wickedness never paralleled any where upon the Face of the Earth!" Sorry a man as Mather was, one had to pity him here, for that ministry was the beginning and end of his being. Besides, he was guilty of no moral error in his inoculation stand.

But James Franklin was not running off on a tangent. He had the collaboration of Dr. William Douglass, who was the only graduate physician practicing in Boston. Together they shared an intense hatred of the Mathers and all that their dynasty stood for; and together they teased and taunted and tortured them through the columns of the *Courant* until the populace was on the verge of an anti-Mather riot, for James Franklin was not above taking advantage of their ignorance in medical matters, and the Mathers were on the verge of an insanity more outright than that which dogged Cotton all his days. But Cotton Mather wrote furiously and preached fervently about the merits of inoculation. Whatever his sour sins, he believed earnestly and sincerely in it, and he had inoculated his own children. Still, fired by Franklin, the town as a whole opposed the measure, and Cotton wrote, in his perpetual agony: "It is the Hour and Power of Darkness on this Despicable Town." Then he scratched out "Despicable" and wrote in "Miserable." His son Samuel, whom he had inoculated secretly lest he die and the town accuse him, Cotton, of murder, contracted the disease seriously and was growing steadily worse. Throughout the town, houses were seething with fury and hatred against the Mathers and inoculation. Cotton paced his study floor, thinking up more vituperative phrases to heap on the town and the *Courant*. "The Town," he cried in his diary, "is become almost an Hell upon Earth, a city full of Lies and Murders and Blasphemies . . . Satan seems to take a strange possession of it." And Cotton was worried over what might next happen, for he sensed that his influence over his people was waning.

But Franklin had stirred up more trouble than he could control. As the epidemic progressed, and in colossal ignorance of what Mather was attempting to do, some roughs visited Cotton's house while a neighboring minister lay ill there. It was November now, the epidemic still raging, and the people were panic-stricken at the thought of the coming winter. For months Franklin's *Courant* had fed their fury, and they were on the point of explosion. The unknown rowdies had come to kill Mather and burn his house to the ground. To kill two birds with one stone, they threw a crude hand grenade, an iron ball packed with gunpowder and turpentine, through his window. His room, however, was occupied by the sick minister, and the grenade, by sheer luck, hit a piece of iron on the casement with such force that the impact jolted the fuse and the bomb then rolled across the floor harmlessly. Cotton picked it up, and found this note: "Cotton Mather, you Dog, Dam you: I'l enoculate you with this, with a pox to you."

Mather did not seem too unpleased at the incident, for it appeared to him testimony of his own standing with the "Angel of God," evidenced clearly by the miraculous deliverance from the explosion. He sat down and wrote a pamphlet in final damnation of the *Courant*. Then he turned to his domestic troubles and to reflections on his elevation to near martyrdom.

As for James Franklin, he got his first lesson on the power of the press which had hitherto been virtually nil. He well knew that another such disturbance would result in his paper's forced discontinuance. However, his circulation had gone up by forty subscribers, which was an increase of over thirten per cent on his list of three hundred; and being a businessman in the Franklin tradition, James thought it would be good business policy to keep up a controversy. He shifted his target from the clergy to the civil authorities. In the edition of June 11, 1722, he accused them of consorting with pirates by refusing to exert any effort to catch them and bring them to justice.

In high ferment the next day the General Court, which had never been so sorely tried since Goody Sherman's sow as it was by the introduction of the press, sent a courier after Franklin, had him brought into the assembly and fell to examining him. After he admitted his proprietorship of the offending paper, the court ordered the sheriff to "Commit to the Gaol in Boston the Body of James Franklyn, Printer," and to keep him there until the court's next session four weeks hence. In the heat of indignation, some members of the court tried to push through a bill of censorship, requiring every issue of any paper to be approved before hand. The bill failed of enactment, which was a victory for the press at a very embarrassing time in its history.

Jail did not agree with James Franklin. He became sick after a week's sojourn and begged the court, to which he had been rude and arrogant on his examination, for the privilege of walking around the jail yard. He called upon Dr. Zabdiel Boylston, whom he had insulted on the inoculation matter, to certify his illness was genuine. Puritan sternness was wearing out in Massachusetts. Dr. Boylston gave Franklin the certificate, and the court gave him the liberty of the prison yard.

While James Franklin was in jail, young Benjamin ran the paper. He had been a contributor right along, but nobody knew it. His official position was printer's apprentice, and he was bullied excessively by his brother, who set him to menial tasks about the office and to delivering the paper in Boston. But Benjamin had written an entire series of satirical essays under the

pseudonym of Mrs. Dogood and had slipped them under
the door of the shop at night. The Hell Fire Club read
them with admiration, and James printed them. Thus,
Benjamin was not the novice that the public fancied
him when he took over the paper for James. He was
not particularly anxious about the prospect anyhow,
for he considered himself rather young at seventeen
to mix in the court troubles that editing a paper apparently led to. And he was not overfond of James,
who had booted him about the shop mercilessly. But he
hated intolerance more, and crossed his Rubicon.

When James got out of jail, encouraged by the
court's failure to pass the censorship law and elated
at his own freedom, he twitted the government for first
condemning him to the devil and then, when the devil
refused to act, sending the sheriff instead. He used
Scripture to prove that the ministers were hypocrites
and the Magna Charta to prove that the authorities
were presumptuous. This time he made the mistake of
including the lower house of the General Court, which
had previously stood by him for the mere pleasure of
irking the upper house. The lower house this time con-
curred with the upper to appoint a committee to see
what could be done with the incorrigible Franklin.

The committee returned with the solemn opinion
that, as long as James Franklin ran it, the *Courant*
would probably continue to mock the ministers, insult
the government, and menace the peace. It proposed that
James be allowed to print nothing unless previously
censored and that he be put on probation for a year.
The court so ordered. It sent a deputy after James
again, but this time the warrant came back with a note

on the reverse side: "By Vertue of this Warrant, I made Diligent Search but cannot find him in my precinct."

Since the censorship order was directed only at the *Courant* and not any paper, and only at the *Courant* so long as James Franklin edited it, James published it thereafter under Benjamin's name. Then he got a baker and another printer to post bail for him and was later discharged from the contempt warrant that the General Court was holding for him when the sheriff had found him unavailable.

Benjamin prefaced his first edition with the ironic comment that the trouble with Boston papers was that they had stirred up too much trouble and that he proposed "to entertain the Town." He praised himself, saying that "There is no Man in Boston better qualified . . . to look two ways at once," for the double face of Janus graced the masthead, and describing himself as "clearly Christian . . . A Man of good Temper, courteous Deportment, sound Judgment, a mortal Hater of Nonsense, Foppery, Formality and endless Ceremony."

His amiable intentions were nipped in the bud by the influence of James, who soon had the paper attacking right and left again over Benjamin's name and protests. It attacked the clergy, the governor, other newspapers, the Church of England, the pope, and Mr. Ebenezer Fitch, who proclaimed, "You must have in the cavity of your calabash a viscid Juice!" Poor Ben got tired of it all, and one night slipped out on a sloop bound for New York, and the stormiest part of the *Courant's* history was over.

Nothing, however, that happened on the banks of the Charles led more to the freedom of the people who inhabited them than that comedy of paper versus paper

and paper versus Puritanism. And the *Courant,* wild as
it was, led all the rest. In the seven years of its history,
it gave America freedom of the press in seedling form,
and it gave her Benjamin Franklin. And that was sufficient for any four-page herald.

Part Five

Arms and a Ship

13

Siege

THE heritage of the first American printers to the New England character was not tangible. Newspapers long remained white elephants, and printing never did become a great and lucrative industry. But they fostered the spirit of independence which led John Winthrop and his little band to pit their consciences against the wilderness, and a deep love of freedom from oppression of any sort rooted itself more and more strongly in their posterity.

This independent spirit manifested itself repeatedly in the individual lives of the settlers of Massachusetts Bay, for someone was ever on the watch from the beginning for signs of despotism. Not until the reign of George III, however, did the river valley and all the colony rise up virtually as one man in defense of their liberty. And they did not quiet down again until the British army was sent scurrying out of Massachusetts for all time. What the Massachusetts militia, with their allies from the other colonies, actually accomplished was not from a military standpoint a momentous victory. But its effect was to sign the death warrant of foreign dominion over all the provinces. There was probably no man who knew that better than Thomas Gage.

Massachusetts was regarded by the North ministry, in London, as the perpetual bad boy of the colonies in America, and Gage's business was to administer the spanking. Accordingly, when the Port Bill closed Boston harbor as punishment for the colony's reaction to England's taxation policy, Gage assumed the dual role of governor and commander of the army occupying the town of Boston to maintain order. But he entered on his duties with limited enthusiasm and even more limited equipment. He landed in Boston in May of 1774, closed the port, and waited for the Americans to indicate that they would obey the laws of the British Parliament whether they liked them or not. He waited in vain. The Yankee character opposed him stubbornly by simply not giving in, leading Gage to the conclusion that he was playing a losing game.

For half of 1774 and until April of 1775, the Yankee character was at a deadlock with the British Parliament in a marathon of sheer stubbornness. The Yankees had no intention of accepting the taxation laws, and the Parliament had no intention of relaxing them. Gage, in his policeman's position in Boston, was acting as a referee, doing nothing more aggressive than keeping a military eye peeled to see that neither side was guilty of a foul blow in the contest. He had thirty-five hundred regulars encamped on Boston Common to back him up in any decision he might have to make. Beyond that, he did nothing.

But the Yankees across the Charles and deep back into the Massachusetts countryside were doing a good deal. They were amassing powder, smuggling some of it out of Boston under Gage's nose; they were forming themselves into militia, small home guard units that could be ready for an eventuality in short order; they were, in fact, beginning to feel the pinch of the port closing, but they had no intention of capitulating to the British demands in order to open it. Trouble was brewing.

Gage soon enough got wind of the military preparations going forward outside of Boston, where his army officers were having a pleasant time with Boston ladies and where the army itself was idling away the time in periodic fist fights with the civilian watch. Early in 1775 he knew that Sam Adams and John Hancock had long since passed the bounds of simple nuisances and were in sober fact leading characters in a movement that was spreading through the colony like wildfire. He knew that a militia was being schooled in the tactic of quick mobilization. He knew that powder was being collected and conserved with almost religious application. He knew it and was disturbed.

But he did not know what to do about it. The loyalists, who remained in Boston, entertaining the officers and calling Hancock names, were prodding him to action and calling him names too. His officers laughed behind his back at his inability to keep the peace among the provincials, and the loyalists openly branded him "The Old Woman." All through the winter of 1775 the town of Boston at the river's mouth was full of the idle soldiers, the critical officers, and the loyalists who wanted to know what Gage proposed to do to bring the rebellious provincials into line so that the port could be opened again. Meanwhile, all commerce had stopped. No ships were leaving the wharves, no cargoes coming in; trade with the farming country beyond the Neck had virtually ceased. An air of tense waiting hung over the town, and nothing was being done.

General Gage wanted to do something to relieve the situation, but he simply did not know what could be done. Essentially a good man, he was not brilliant, and his position was far from happy. He had married into an American family, but was conscientious enough in his allegiance to the king. Not the sort of man who could fire himself with hatred for these errant children in Massachusetts, he was hampered by a lack of diplomatic genius in handling them and by a total want of self-confidence in disciplining them. He was just enough the military governor to annoy them. His role, in brief, was that of a man with a colossal task to do and with neither the genius nor the insight to do it. By spring, however, he was determined that an effort at least would be made on behalf of the king's government. To appease the grumbling loyalists within the town and to teach the arms-conscious provincials outside a lesson, he would send a detachment of his army out to Concord to seize some military stores about which he had definite information.

It was probably a play to the grandstands; and he may have done it against his better judgment, for he was daily expecting reinforcements which he badly needed to get anywhere at all. Gage, to his credit, suspected the zeal and strength of the colonials from the start, but he was being goaded by the ministry at home into quicker action than he thought advisable. It seemed peculiar to those across the sea that a duly constituted military governor with a trim little army could not seize a few rebellious leaders and put down an insurrection before it started. But those at home did not know that, far from being governor of the colony, Gage was as a matter of fact merely the dictator of a tiny peninsula jutting out with the river on one side and the harbor on the other. So Gage, whose patience could probably have lasted some months longer, pondered the alternatives of seizing either the leaders of the stubborn provincials or their ammunition and decided that the latter was much the more effective course.

His decision made, he proceeded in no great hurry. He let the leaders slip through his fingers repeatedly. One night that winter when there was a patriotic meeting in the Old South Meeting House, the governor could have sent around a group of officers and taken into custody the whole crew of ringleaders. But he didn't. And on Tuesday, April eighteenth, the good general posted officers at all the outposts of the city so that no one could let word of the proposed secret expedition to Concord get out to the Middlesex militia. But he allowed word of it to pass around Boston freely. Moreover, while Hancock and Sam Adams had decamped for healthier territory, Dr. Joseph Warren, a more intelligent man than either of them and a more zealous patriot, was still in Boston, and Gage knew it. It was Warren who arranged the preliminaries for the code that sent Paul Revere racing across the river and over the Middlesex roads ahead of the British. Warren was always where he could be of use. On the night of the eighteenth, he was in Boston. Two months later, on the seventeenth of June, he was right on the hill when the Battle of Bunker Hill was fought. He entered the redoubt as an ordinary soldier on that day, and he died as an ordinary soldier.

While Dr. Warren was arranging a system to let

the provincials know what to expect, Old Woman Gage was making his final secret arrangement to get the stores at Concord. He had chosen a force of about seven hundred grenadiers and light infantry, the best of his little army of occupation, to cross the river and take over the military stores of the patriots. And he had also chosen the leaders. One of them, in twenty-four hours the unhappiest of mortals, was Lieutenant Colonel Francis Smith; the other was Major John Pitcairn of the marines. Major Pitcairn was a good officer, wise and humane. But Colonel Smith was fat and slow; he was always having difficulty in adapting his huge bulk to the demands of military precision, and he was consequently late when time was important.

Colonel Smith did not even know that night where he was going when he set out across the river. This was the harassed Gage's secret expedition, and he did not want anyone, not even the commanding officer, to know where it was headed, in spite of the fact that everyone else knew all about it. As the evening drew on, however, Gage could contain his secret no longer. He summoned Lord Percy and told him that he was about to send an expedition to Concord to seize munitions. Lord Percy wanted to know if anyone knew about it, and Gage answered that it was a secret so closely guarded that he had not told the commanding officers where they were to go or why and had not told the troops themselves that they were going anywhere. Gage thereupon swore Lord Percy to complete secrecy, and Percy departed from headquarters at the Province House for his home. To get there he had to pass the Common, and he walked along briskly, buoyed by his confidence with the governor. A little cluster of men were talking on the Common. As he approached them, his lordship overheard the words, ". . . the British troops have marched, but they will miss their aim." Surprised at the words, Percy joined the group and asked, "What aim?" One of the men, himself surprised at the newcomer's ignorance, answered, "Why, the cannon at Concord!" Lord Percy instantly wheeled about and hustled back to the governor's house, where he informed Gage that everybody apparently knew about the march except those who were to do the marching.

There was nothing to prevent Gage from canceling his plans then and there, but he had taken a long time to decide to do anything and he now intended to do it at any cost. Accordingly, he issued the orders for the night. A sergeant was dispatched to awaken the grenadiers and light infantry who were to go. The sentries themselves were not told of the expedition, and seven hundred of Gage's soldiers stole past them and out the rear of the barracks while the rest of Boston talked freely of the affair. A dog barked, and one of the soldiers, believing that the outside world knew as little as he himself did, ran the dog through with his bayonet. Silently the body of troops moved down to the river's edge, where small boats with muffled oars awaited them.

Dr. Warren meanwhile knew what the British were up to, where they were going, when and why. At ten o'clock, the same hour that Gage's troops were moving so stealthily toward the river, he sent for Paul Revere, a strong leader among Boston craftsmen. The only thing that Warren was not sure about was whether or not Gage intended to kill two birds with one stone— that is, as long as his men were going out to Concord, whether they were going to chase Sam Adams and

John Hancock out of hiding as well as look up the colonial military stores. Dr. Warren told Revere, therefore, to warn not only the minutemen but also Adams and Hancock that the British grenadiers and light infantry were on the warpath. William Dawes, a more obscure patriot, had already been sent on the same mission by the busy doctor. Dawes had the more difficult job, because the doctor sent him by land, which meant riding out over the Neck under the very noses of the British sentries. To get past the sentries, Dawes rigged himself as a farmer, slung a bag of meal over the rump of his horse and waited near the gates at the Neck until some soldiers marched out on a routine order. He marched out with them. Revere's commission was but to duplicate the trip of the British: to cross the river before them and to beat them across country to Lexington. A couple of his friends rowed him across the Charles right past a man-of-war, and he waited on the north side of the river until the lanterns were hung in the Old North Church.

Revere got across the river in good season, mainly because the sentry on the man-of-war had given up expecting anything to happen on the river and was half asleep. He waited on the Charlestown bank for someone to find him a horse. Then he set off on the main road but was halted by the sight of some British officers ahead. They espied him, and as one advanced to meet him the other waited to see what would happen. Revere dodged the first officer, changed his direction and shook off the other when the latter's horse got stuck in the mud. Then Revere raced through Middlesex County waking up the captains of the militia. But he did not bawl out, "The British are coming!" at every crossroad.

He let each village captain arouse his own militiamen. When he arrived in Lexington he went to Jonas Clarke's parsonage, where Hancock and Adams were hiding out. On hearing that the British were coming, Hancock was all for going out to meet them with muskets, but Adams was against it. He thought it would be wiser to move on. "We belong to the Cabinet," he told Hancock.

Revere stopped at Clarke's until Dawes caught up with him, and then both went to Concord in company with a young Lexington physician. The physician and Revere were intercepted by a pair of British officers, who were promptly reinforced by a couple more who sprang from behind a shrub. The officers directed the patriots to go off the road into a meadow. As they went, young Dr. Samuel Prescott rode out to the left, cleared a stone wall and got away. Paul Revere made for a clump of trees to the right, but when he got there six more British officers popped out and captured him. They took him back toward Lexington, commandeered his horse and then let him go. Revere, of course, went directly back to Jonas Clarke's, where Adams was still trying to prevail upon Hancock to put up his gun and run away to safety.

Back along the Charles, from that hour of ten o'clock when Revere was rowed across the river, the business of transporting grenadiers and light infantry was going on. The only success Gage had from the beginning was to keep his intentions from his own people, for the rest of the job was badly muddled from the start. The soldiers were rowed across at the widest point of the river and so that they had to disembark in a marshland. There were not enough boats, so that it took

until midnight to get the slight force across. But the
worst flaw in the entire expedition, and perhaps the
fatal error, was the delay in starting their march once
they were across. So badly was the thing bungled that
the wonder lies not in the failure of the march but that
any British soldier survived it at all.

It was mid-April and a clear night. Though the
days happened to be sunny and warm, the nights must

have been sharp and cool. Many of the regulars had
been landed on the Cambridge shore at eleven o'clock,
and all of them had to walk through water up to their
knees to get out of the marshes. Therefore, some huddled about in wet uniforms for three hours and all of
them for two, since the order to march was not given
until two o'clock on the morning of the nineteenth.

Not until Colonel Smith's army was some miles
northwest of their landing place did it occur to him
that the countryfolk were warned of his march. The

silence of the night was punctuated by the thin clang of distant church bells and the sharp reports of guns. Smith seemed to know instinctively then that he was in for no picnic in the country, for he sent word back to Gage that he would need support. His anticipation of a struggle can be seen in his reported words to his men not to fire unless fired upon and in his sending Major Pitcairn ahead with six companies to take the bridges at Concord. It was while Pitcairn's detachment was marching toward Lexington that the men who had captured and released Paul Revere came along. Revere had fooled them into thinking that five hundred militiamen were already waiting on Lexington Green, and Pitcairn immediately halted his march to address his troops. He ordered them to load their guns and gave strict commands not to fire on any provocation unless they had the order from him. Then he resumed the march toward the Green at Lexington.

What he found there was no imposing sight. There were two groups standing about on the Green. The first composed of about forty was made up of spectators, most of whom were minutemen who forgot to bring their guns. The second, seventy men strong, were the militia, and half of them were running back and forth to the meetinghouse to get powder which they had neglected to secure in all the time from Revere's alarm at one o'clock until the arrival of Major Pitcairn at dawn. When Captain John Parker of the militia saw the size of the British force, he immediately ordered his minutemen to disperse. Then trouble began.

A gun behind a rambling and low stone wall flashed in the pan. Some Britisher or some provincial, afraid of a sniper, opened fire on the Green. More shots, from both sides and ordered by neither commanding officer, were exchanged. Shots were finally barking from every gun, and Pitcairn shouted furiously at his men to stop. But they emptied their guns and when it was over there were eight dead Americans. The fault lay not with Pitcairn, whose orders were disobeyed all down the line, but with the irresponsible officers under him. They made no attempt to stop the ridiculously useless carnage. They urged the regulars in their yelling rush toward the minutemen. And they drove the latter to distraction by their curses and insults. Major Pitcairn's only mistake was that he did not march his companies right by the minutemen, for they did not attempt to block his path at all, and it would have been a simple enough matter for him to pass by the edge of the Green and continue to Concord. It was an inglorious day for the British. No battle was staged at Lexington, but merely a skirmish between an organized force and a few armed patriots. And nearly every man the British killed, they killed as he lay wounded on the ground.

By the time the incident was over, the fat and always late Colonel Smith was on the scene. He was there to hear the British regulars send up their cheer of victory, to help Pitcairn get them back into line and to go forth with the rest of the expedition to Concord while the minutemen of Lexington ran back to the Green to rescue the wounded and round up a few British troops who had not returned to the file.

Out in Concord the minutemen were preparing a reception for the British regulars, for they knew about the expedition before the march from the Cambridge bank of the Charles started. Throughout the early

morning hours they had scurried about in frantic
efforts to hide the provincial military stores before the
British got there. Reports arrived ahead of the regulars
of what had transpired in Lexington, and a couple of
hundred minutemen from Concord and the tiny village
of Lincoln decided to march down the road to meet the
British. "We thought we wood go and meet the Brit-
ich," one of them said; and they did, the farmers of
Concord and Lincoln. They got some drummers and
fifers, and under the rising April sun they marched
down the quiet Concord road to meet the forces of
King George.

As soon as they met them, they executed a wise
and immediate about-face and marched right back to
Concord. Old Amos Barrett was delighted with all the
music, for the little body of minutemen marched back
right in front of the British regulars in a strange procession. So close were the opponents that the minutemen mixed their music with that of the British. "We
march^d before them," wrote Amos, "with our Droms
and fifes agoing and also the British; we had grand
musick." The minutemen quickened their pace, however, and beat the British to Concord in sufficient time
to round up the "alarm" company, which joined them
to form the defense of Concord. The whole body of
minutemen, still numbering less than three hundred,
then chose their ground, picking a ridge that looked
down over the roadway leading to North, or Concord,
Bridge.

When they marched into Concord, the British
regulars, grenadiers, and light infantry were in full
force. Smith had caught up with Pitcairn at Lexington,
the light infantry had chased away a few minutemen

who threatened the line of march, and the whole British expedition paused at Concord Green to ponder the situation and parade formally while a few detachments hunted up the stores alleged to be in Concord. Then Smith remembered the bridges. He sent a small detachment to take the South Bridge, but six companies to take the North Bridge where the minutemen were waiting on the ridge. The North Bridge was the more important because the British had to cross it to get to Colonel James Barrett's house, where the provincial cannon were stored.

As the British approached the bridge, Parson William Emerson, who was part of the alarm company, was all for starting the war then and there, but men whose faith was weaker advised the holding of fire. Then Colonel Barrett himself arrived from his all-night business of hiding the stores and ordered all the minutemen to retreat across the bridge. The consecrated parson just said, "Let us stand our ground. If we die, let us die here." But Colonel Barrett gave a speech, a long speech, and long speeches have always been appreciated in Massachusetts. Accordingly, all the minutemen followed the old colonel across the bridge, but William Emerson stayed where he was. His manse was near by and he proposed to keep the British away from it.

The light infantry crossed the bridge and went on to poke about Colonel Barrett's farm for the cannon, while the grenadiers searched every house in the center of Concord. The minutemen were still biding their time and were gradually being augmented by companies from villages all over the county. The women were left in charge of the houses where the military stores were scattered about, and for the most part they got along famously with the British officers who were so courteous in some instances that they walked out of houses that had roomfuls of stores. There were only two slight fires set that morning. One was the town house, which probably caught fire from the British burning gun carriages. And the other was an inconsequential blaze in Reuben Brown's harness shop, where Reuben made various necessary items for the local militia. If these two fires hadn't sent whiffs of smoke into the air, there might not have been any Battle of Concord Bridge—although the war itself was inevitable.

But the minutemen saw the smoke and were ready to take vengeance, for what they assumed were their burning homes, on the British regulars. They were assembled then on a hill on John Buttrick's farm near the river and from which they could see the British swarming around the bridge. There followed a skirmish of but three or four minutes' duration. The British and most of their bullets went wild. But the minutemen scared them to death, sent them into a retreat more worthy of a horde of schoolboys than of crack companies and left two of them fatally wounded at the bridge. That was the Battle of Concord, but the great battle of the day was the long, grueling, and fateful running battle that Colonel Smith's retreat from the slender Concord River back to the Charles developed into during the endless afternoon and evening.

Colonel Smith was always late—late in starting from the Charles, late in getting to Lexington, and now, his forces thoroughly routed, he was late in leaving Concord in his retreat to Boston. For precious minutes that stretched into hours his officers and men loitered about Concord when they should have been making their way as fast as possible out of the hostile country. Moreover, every minute that the British tarried another minuteman was arriving from some distant village. The brief fight at the bridge took place around ten o'clock in the morning. It was noon, and the April sun shone down in unseasonable heat, when Smith's battered column set back down the road to Lexington. There were no fifes and no drums, unaccountably, for never was music more necessary. In total silence the regulars limped back down the road up which they had come in martial confidence but a few hours earlier.

The Concord minutemen were aroused and they were reinforced by militia from Reading to the north, Framingham to the south, and a dozen villages and crossroads between. All along the British road of retreat they shot from behind walls, trees, barns,—and then disappeared only to turn up again a few yards down the line of march. Before they were in sight of Lexington Green, whence they had marched so confidently that morning, the regulars were in disorder and almost without ammunition. The officers lost all control of their men. Pitcairn had his horse shot under him and joined the ranks on foot. Smith had his leg shot from under him. Soldiers, lacking either a target to shoot at or ammunition to shoot with, broke into disorderly runs. The only hope of Smith was that the courier he had sent back to Gage that morning when first he heard the country church bells had got back across the Charles and that Gage had listened to him and sent help.

Again there was delay, but this time it was not the fat colonel's fault. Gage had told Lord Percy, the man who had overheard the conversation on Boston Common, on the night before to have his brigade ready to march at four on the morning of the nineteenth. On that same night, the eve of the Lexington and Concord fiasco, the order was sent by messenger to the major of the brigade, who was not at home, and was left in writing. The major wandered home very late and went to bed, and his servant forgot to tell him about the letter. So at four o'clock the whole brigade, including the major, was sound asleep. It was almost six when Colonel Smith, alarmed by the church bells, could be passingly sure that his messenger to Gage had arrived in Boston. Accordingly it was slightly after six when part of Lord Percy's brigade assembled, and even then the marines had not appeared. At seven there were still no marines. Another messenger was dispatched, this time to find out where the missing marines were. He came back to report that the marines did not know anything about any order to march at four o'clock or any other time that day. The trouble was that the marines' order had been left at Major Pitcairn's quarters, and the major, of course, was on his way to Concord with Smith. That was Gage's penalty for taking the commanding officer of one detachment and sending him off with another. Anyhow it was nine o'clock in the morning when Percy's brigade finally got itself together. Before it was halfway to Concord, the forces of Colonel Smith were in danger of annihilation.

Lord Percy marched his army out over Boston Neck and proposed to cross the North Harvard Street Bridge over the Charles. When he got there, he discovered that the provincials had ripped up all the planks. However, instead of taking them away, the provincials had left the planks piled in a neat heap on the Cambridge side. So Percy sent over a few men on the narrow cross-stream timbers, which the provincials had forgotten to take up, and had the bridge rebuilt in quick time.

But it was midafternoon before he came to Smith's rescue at Lexington. There he found the sorry sight of the king's grenadiers and crack light infantry lying about on the Green, their bodies prostrate and their ranks shattered by a horde of back-country farmers. Percy planted his cannon to cover the rest of the retreat, gave his soldiers a half hour's rest and then ordered the whole expedition to resume the retreat. It was now a moving column of nearly two thousand British soldiers that hustled back to the mouth of the Charles, with any number of minutemen taking pot shots at them with every variety of crude blunderbuss and rifle. It was an unhappy spectacle, for houses were burned, innocents were killed, and disciplined soldiers acted like raw troops. Right down to the river's edge, where the British ran for safety under the guns of men-of-war, the Massachusetts farmers, tradesmen, and ministers chased the regulars of King George. When it was over, the Americans had lost forty-nine killed and five missing and had thirty-nine wounded. The British lost seventy-three killed and twenty-six missing and had seventy-four wounded. And the British never again ventured into the Massachusetts countryside. They stayed bottled up in Boston and only once more did they so much as venture across the Charles.

Who was the hero of Lexington and Concord? It was no one man—no great leader, for those minutemen were ill organized and had little need for a strong command. They fought according to their own judgment of circumstances at the moment they took aim and they wasted no bullets. The heroes were countless—men like the preacher Emerson, who stood his ground; like old Colonel Barrett, who did six young men's work in one day; like the couriers Dawes and Revere, who outrode and outtricked the British. And men like old Sam Whittemore, of Cambridge, the archetype of all Yankees.

The opening guns of the war did not catch old Sam napping. He lived in Cambridge, and he knew on that night of the nineteenth that Lord Percy's brigade would escort the retreat back through his town. Eighty years old, he grabbed his ancient rifle in one hand and his horse pistol in the other and went out and waited for the representatives of the king. At the first sound of rifle fire, he ducked behind a stone wall. As the British neared, he aimed his gun and shot a soldier dead. Then he cocked his horse pistol and shot another soldier dead. If he had not been discovered, he would probably have disposed of a couple more. But he was himself shot, half his cheekbone blown from his face. The poor old man was then rushed by a group of soldiers and was left with half a dozen bayonet wounds in his body and several thumps on his hoary head. His clothes were torn and full of bullet holes, his body broken and his head bleeding, but he did not die in spite of the ravages of war. Old Sam Whittemore died when he got around to it, and that was after the war was won and the republic established. He survived the historic day by thirteen and a half years, dying serenely at ninety-three.

After the day of Concord and Lexington, the British army was bottled up in Boston, and the aroused farmers and tradesmen kept it there. Boston was besieged. The patriot sympathizers within the city migrated out, and the loyalists in the country moved in for protection. Gradually, communications between the town and the rest of the colony became rare, and the British had no choice save to consider themselves fortified on a small peninsula in the midst of a thoroughly determined enemy. The patriots, full of confidence after their first engagement with the regulars, simply played a waiting game, made some awkward attempts to organize their militia into an army and planted what cannon they could muster around the besieged town.

14

The Genesis of an Army

THE late spring of 1775 was a deadlock in Massachusetts. The Charles, swelling to new breadth with the thawing of the brooks upstream, divided the colonials from the king's forces and alone prevented a meeting of the two. On their side of the river the colonial trops were idling away the time, a few men of disputed commissions trying to create order out of chaos but the potential army conducting itself for the most part with pleasant informality. Many of the soldiers went back to the farms whenever it pleased them; and other men drifted in to take their places.

At length the general staff, alias the Committee of Safety, decided that it was time to take steps against any possible move by the British. From their Cambridge headquarters, the deliberators cast an eye downstream to Charlestown and Bunker Hill, a high hill neatly situated on a peninsula and ideally suited for defensive fortification. It was decided, and with good reason, to throw up a strong redoubt on the slope of the hill facing the river, for the hill was too high for any attackers to overcome a reasonable defense. By way of backing up this timely order, it was also decided to plant a few cannon there, so that pot shots could be taken at the British across the river or at their ships in the channel—"to annoy the enemy," the order had said.

All this was the height of military wisdom, and it represented a judicious use of the limited equipment that the colonials had at hand. No one could get out of Boston to the north without being seen by whoever happened to be perched on Bunker Hill. It commanded an excellent view not only of the river separating Boston from the mainland, but also of Boston itself. It was high enough so that a redoubt could be built above the gun range of any men-of-war in the river. It could be easily defended against infantry attacks because its slope was sufficiently steep to interfere with both the march and the aim of attacking soldiers. And it could be a constant menace to the British in Boston simply by keeping them guessing as to the purpose of its fortification. As a site for a battle the colonials could not have picked a better place even if they could have reconstructed the topography of the river valley.

Then Old Israel Putnam came up from Connecticut with some companies of militia in tow. Old Put arrived in Cambridge with an overwhelming desire for activity. He was not a man given to pussyfooting around with a lot of fool strategy. You knew where the enemy was, didn't you? Well, all right, then, go ahead and smoke him out and annihilate him. That was Old Put's theory of war. And Old Put was a general with as much authority as the best of them. Already, since his arrival in Massachusetts, he had had one run-in with the British; and he thought himself pretty well acquainted with their limitations. It was up in Chelsea Creek, where a British armed schooner sailed upstream to stop the colonials in their retreat from some raids on British stores of cattle and grain on islands at the river mouth. Besides the schooner *Diana,* the British had sent a company of regulars marching up the other side of the stream. The raiders and the regulars swapped bullets. But no one was killed, and the schooner turned around and headed downstream to Boston. Along came Old Put out of the underbrush with a thousand of his soldiers and a couple of field pieces. He immediately decided that, by God, he was going to get that schooner. And, by God, he did. He put his heavy guns on the stream's edge, and then he waded out above his waist with his infantry to meet the armed schooner. By three o'clock the next morning his Majesty's armed schooner was blown to high heaven.

That was Old Put's method: no bother with military science at all, even if it involved a navy-infantry fight; just a matter of going ahead and doing what you wanted to do and getting it done. Consequently, in regard to Bunker Hill, the general's first thought was to hell with the general staff and also with Bunker Hill. To hell, too, with a lot of elaborate defensive fortifications. What he wanted was a fight, which was what one had an enemy for. At any rate, on the afternoon of June sixteenth, Colonel William Prescott set out with a thousand Massachusetts soldiers to perform some operations on Bunker Hill. Down the north bank of the Charles they marched on a clear, beautiful afternoon, right down past Inman's Farm toward Charlestown. Out into the roadway from the farm came no less than two hundred of Old Put's men under command of a captain. The twelve hundred marched on, picking up an engineer, a wagonful of tools, and then

Old Put himself. The whole expedition filed across Charlestown Neck and, except for a few sent to the beach for guard duty, climbed up to the top of Bunker Hill.

There on the top of the hill in the June twilight, with General Gage across the river unable to see the proceedings through his glass, Richard Gridley, the engineer, Colonel Prescott, commanding the Massachusetts soldiers, and Old Put, equipped with his general's commission and a hell-bent desire to send the British packing, entered into a long argument about the comparative wisdom of doing what the general staff told them to do to thwart Gage's anticipated move north of the river and of ignoring its instructions altogether. Old Put, because the general staff had the unaggressive title of Committee of Safety, was all for paying no attention to it. He himself was a general. It was true that he had no authority over the Massachusetts troops, but he was nevertheless a general. In fact, if Prescott had wanted to be technical about the affair, he could have told Old Put to do what he wanted with his two hundred Connecticut soldiers but that he himself would follow the wishes of the Committee of Safety. But Old Put fumed and growled and argued and swore, and the whole body of the colonial troops finally deserted Bunker Hill, marched down the river slope and up the little hill in front of it. That was Breed's Hill, the place where Old Put wanted to fight the Battle of Bunker Hill—and where the battle was fought.

Colonel Prescott put his Massachusetts soldiers, who were really farmers, to work with spades. Better acquainted with shovels than they were with military procedure, the farmers dug all night to make their redoubt. It was about forty feet square, but too large at that for the farmers to finish before the dawn revealed their activity to the British. The dawn, however, surprised the colonials more than it did the British, Prescott discovered that his redoubt, even if it had been finished, would not be much good, for the British could march right around it, without being within firing range, and thereby outflank it. Moreover, the British lost no time in making their discovery. The ship *Lively* signaled from the river that the rebels were up to some sort of inexplicable hell.

Thereafter the situation of the colonials was desperate. They were hungry and tired, for the lack of any military organization worth the name was responsible for the lack of both supplies and relief companies. Not even the fieldpieces were anywhere in evidence, and the engineer Gridley had disappeared altogether. Pretty soon the British opened fire on the works from a battery posted on a hill across the river. Cannon from the men-of-war in the river added to the rumpus. All morning the colonial farmers with Prescott encouraging them labored in the dirt of Breed's Hill, fashioning the redoubt which could never be expected to save them. Hungry, sleepless, thirsty, and dodging cannonballs, they worked frantically to get the thing finished. Then one of them was hit by the British fire and fell dead in his tracks. Without ceremony, for Prescott wanted no dead men lying about at this stage of affairs, he was buried in a shallow trench. Then Prescott, to prove that the British were bad marksmen and their cannon fire ineffective, walked up and down the parapet. "The Old Woman," Gage, peered at him from the battery across the river and asked a subordinate who the farmer in the rustic clothes was; he was informed that it was Prescott of Pepperell and that he'd fight "you to the gates of hell."

In spite of Prescott's brave faith, a number of his soldiers were slipping back over the hill and away to safety. No relief came, no water came, no food came, and no fieldpieces came. The men who deserted thought themselves deceived and in no way morally bound to stay. Even the British, except for the steady cannon fire which was as ineffective as Prescott claimed it to be, did not make a move toward them. There was obviously nothing to resist, therefore, and the Massachusetts farmers saw many of their number drifting away.

Where Old Put was all that morning no one knows. He was variously placed as running up and down the north bank of the Charles, trying to accumulate sufficient soldiers to go down and relieve those who had been working all night. He might well have been chasing up some fieldpieces, for they still had nothing on Breed's Hill but earthworks, a few hundred tired farmers, and one unyielding colonel. Later in the morning, when the redoubt was finished and Prescott was waiting for food and some fieldpieces to welcome the British, Old Put came charging up the hill full of loud talk. That was a hell of a place for a redoubt, he said; it should have been on the higher hill. In other words, the general completely reversed himself as of the previous evening. What, he wanted to know, did Prescott think of sending the men and the tools up to Bunker Hill to build secondary fortifications to fall back on? Prescott thought little of the idea and said so; he said, further, that once the men and tools had gone from

Breed's Hill they would never return, and the men were needed to defend it. Old Put then said he didn't give a damn what Prescott thought: he was general, and he was going to have a redoubt on Bunker Hill. So a goodly number of Prescott's men, glad enough to get out of range of British cannon, went up Bunker Hill with Old Put, and they were not seen again that day on Breed's Hill.

The most felicitous circumstance of that morning, as of the whole early phase of the Revolution, was that everyone took his time. War was unhurried, leisurely, peacefully measured almost. On the whole, too, it was polite enough, as polite as it was slow. The British, for example, could have opened fire on the little group of men on Breed's Hill at dawn, sent a swarm of regulars over early in the morning, and cleared the whole thing up before noon. But there was no such hurry in Boston. On the south side of the river, Gage was peering through his glass, making gentlemanly inquiries about the men on the other side. The brother-in-law of Prescott was at his elbow half the time, telling the Old Woman what fine men the colonials were. The Old Woman was merely a spectator in the proceedings anyway: this was General Howe's party.

Sir William Howe took his time too. He knew all about what was going forward across the river at dawn that morning of June seventeenth. Then he had gone up the hill facing Charlestown, with his glass in his hand; and the day being clear and beautiful, he could see plainly that there was nothing there but a bunch of upriver farmers, assisted by others of their ilk from farther afield, trying to make a fort from a lot of dirt and rails and hay. He could see that the whole business could be promptly stopped, but he did not want to hurry about it.

Nor did he want to make it too minor an action, for that matter. To cross the Charles was, of course, a matter of minutes; and to go from Boston to Charlestown could hardly be called a trip. But Howe made up his mind that he was going to have an expedition for his rusty troops. Accordingly, he spent the morning, while the colonials were completing their redoubt under his nose and dragging up the six fieldpieces that had worried them by their absence, in making all the preparations that might conceivably have been incidental to a march from Boston to Montreal against some crack Hessians. By one o'clock, when the colonials had had time to throw up some additional breastworks, he was ready to push off across the river with barges full of soldiers. They headed for the eastern extremity of the Charlestown peninsula. Prescott sent a couple of fieldpieces with some Massachusetts men and also Captain Knowlton and Old Put's Connecticut men down the hill to meet them. Howe took his time about crossing the river, so that Knowlton and his men had plenty of time to construct a little rail fort for themselves down within effective range of the landing place.

All this was at noon: the colonials, dog-tired but now wide awake with excitement and determination, were waiting to receive the British; the latter, brilliant in their scarlet uniforms and with their guns flashing in the high noon sun, were coming across in barges; Knowlton had his little company preparing a place suitable to meet them. Prescott was up on the hill watching the British move leisurely across the river. But where was Old Put? Possessed of the only horse in the colonial army of the hour, he was riding furiously up and down the north bank of the Charles, still trying to whip up enough enthusiasm to get some soldiers to help out Prescott's men. Finally he got John Stark to bring his New Hampshire regiment, which had been hovering around doing nothing, down to Charlestown. There were some other regiments there in Cambridge too, but they just marched around aimlessly, trying to appear occupied but having no anxiety to attend the festivities in Charlestown.

John Stark marched his regiment right down the river to the slim neck of land which one had to cross to get to the peninsula that was Charlestown. There he came upon an unorthodox military sight. The British, in a sudden burst of ingenuity, had made a couple of floating batteries of twelve-pounders out of heavy barges. These they had navigated into shallow waters that men-of-war could not reach and were keeping up a rapid bombardment of Charlestown Neck, over which any aid to the colonials on Breed's Hill must pass. Stark, on arriving with his men, saw this at a glance. He saw also that a couple of other relief regiments had come to a dead stop on the mainland side of the Neck and were standing around watching the British fire. Stark suggested that, as long as they intended to let a little cannon fire stop them, they get out of the way and let him bring his New Hampshire men over the neck. The intimidated regiments lost no time in getting out of the way, and Stark marched his men at parade pace right through the fire to Charlestown.

Old Put meanwhile had posted himself on Bunker Hill, which was where he had not, the night before, wanted the battle to take place. He was a busy man, like the miraculous Eddy Bigelow; and he immediately told Stark what to do. Stark paid no attention to him, even though he was a general. Technically, Stark was right; there was no law requiring a New Hampshire regiment to take orders from a Connecticut general on a Massachusetts battlefield. So Stark ignored Old Put, who would gladly have shot him dead were it not for the exigency of the moment, and marched his regiment down to support Knowlton. The latter was still waiting to receive the British before they got up the hill. Stark noticed that Knowlton's improvised fortification, the rail fence, did not extend beyond the beach, along which the British could march to flank it. He, therefore, sent a delegation of stout New Hampshire soldiers down to throw up a rock barricade, which they completed soon enough. The British, meanwhile, were still coming across the river at their leisure.

Old Put was up on Bunker Hill, while Prescott, who actually commanded the battle, was with his men on the smaller hill where the battle was really fought. Knowlton and Stark, having prepared their own defensive lines, were ready and waiting, even closer to the British attack. No one was in complete command, though Prescott accepted all the responsibility. New Hampshire men would not obey Connecticut's general; Connecticut refused to be bossed by Massachusetts; Massachusetts would be run by neither New Hampshire nor Connecticut. Disorganization, if ever it was any army's foe, was the foe of that small army of New England farmers turned soldiers. The foe of the British was their own tortoise pace.

In early afternoon Howe had his whole expeditionary force on the north side of the Charles. He lined them up, his twenty-two hundred regulars, split them into a left and a right wing and checked his six field-pieces, two twelve-pounders, and a couple of howitzers. He then proceeded to do everything wrong.

It was around two o'clock that Howe, his army disposed the way he wanted it, gave the order to attack. But here was no rude, hurried onset. The British regulars marched so slowly up the hill and toward the enemy's flanks that even the defensive farmers gaped open-mouthed. They just crouched there in their redoubt for a moment and enjoyed the spectacle of the oddly colorful funeral procession that was supposed to dislodge them. The day was hot by now, and every last British soldier was weighed down with full expeditionary equipment: three days' food supply (though they were a matter of yards from the home base), blankets for winter weather, and ammunition. They paced slowly through the tall grass of the hill, while the colonials, shirtless and ununiformed from the commander down, awaited them. Not a shot was fired by the Americans as the long lines of immaculate and heavily laden regulars advanced through the grass.

All of a sudden Prescott shouted the order to fire, just when the British were confident that they were going to take the redoubt without firing a shot. In a flash, muskets poked through holes and over the parapet, and a hailstorm of bullets was let loose on the lines of Howe. Scores fell in their tracks, their own guns totally unprepared to answer. Officers, who had been bored by the apparent fiasco, were killed among the very first. Nor did it stop with the shattering of the first line, for each successive charge was as quickly disrupted. Then the entire expeditionary force ran like mad back down the hill to the beach. Most of the farmers, transported less by their own effectiveness than by the British ineffectiveness, arose to scramble over the parapet and chase the redcoats into the river. But wiser hands held them back.

Howe's left wing, which was supposed to flank the hill and surround the redoubt, was having no easier time in the meanwhile. In the village of Charlestown, past which the wing had to go, many snipers were posted in attics and church steeples; and there were many casualties in the British companies marching by. Finally, the red-hot cannonballs that the ships in the Charles had been firing into the village took effect and the place was in flames. The left-wing gesture itself was so abortive that Prescott didn't know it even existed.

Back on the beach Howe was rounding up his soldiers by prodding them in the back with the point of a sword. Again and again he made a frontal attack, a blind forward uphill charge, and again and again whole companies were shot down in their tracks. The left wing, too, was in retreat. His officers advised him unanimously to ferry what was left of the twenty-two hundred back across the river, but Howe would not hear of it. He was furious by now, and fury paved the way for a measure of common sense. He decided to use his cannon. But some blunderer had sent over six-pounders with twelve-pound balls as ammunition, which rendered them useless except for grapeshot. Howe told them to move up and fire grape then. He also allowed his soldiers to divest themselves of the winter blankets and food supplies that were strapped to their backs. Finally, in a brilliant move, he sent back across the river for reinforcements. He re-formed his lines and then was ready for another attack.

But the colonials, impressed and surprised as they were at the turn of events, were not well prepared for yet another defense. Most of their ammunition was gone, and Prescott was running around smashing open cannon ammunition to mete out the powder to his men. Old Put was still on top of Bunker Hill, where many provincial soldiers loitered, unwilling to risk going over to the lower hill where the battle went on. There were soldiers who had not yet ventured over the Neck, though those barge batteries had been diverted. And many men were deserting still. One captain led his entire company away, until, met by another, the second forced him on pain of instant death to turn and go back. While the men fought magnificently under Prescott on Breed's Hill, artillery captains on Bunker Hill flatly refused to draw up their pieces to support them. This was what defeated Prescott that day, and not the fragment of Howe's army—for the latter never used the reinforcements.

Howe made his reorganized attack and won the battle by persisting, despite heavy fire, until his men were within a few feet of the redoubt and at last storming over the parapet as the colonials used their last gunpowder. Prescott fought bravely to the end, though he ordered a retreat. Many of his men, those who had started out on the evening before and done heavy labor all night and morning, stayed with him and fought the British hand to hand, picking up rocks or broken rifle ends or using their naked fists to answer the jabs of British bayonets. Prescott himself walked from that redoubt; he did not run. And well he might have won—

dered at the helpless host of his own countrymen behind him on Bunker Hill; they watched him fight to his last bullet while they stood in safe uselessness close by.

It was the last battle ever to be fought along the Charles. For the little cluster of New England farmers that surrounded Prescott and stayed with him, there is in its history much glory. And their stand there on the hill by the river's edge that hot June afternoon meant the opening of a way toward freedom and independence. Yet there was also something dark and gloomy about that summer battle: too many Americans died because of weak loyalty among their own number, and too many British soldiers paid mortal testimony to the tragedy of repeated error.

Bunker Hill was the greatest moral victory for an actual loser in all military history. The Americans lost the hill, commanding the town of Boston; and Charlestown lay in ashes. But the British loss in life was far greater and their loss of morale greater still. All through that summer, disease and starvation and malcontent drained the very soul from the town. Funerals were so frequent, after the effect of the colonial siege became more and more serious, that Gage forbid the tolling of church bells. The army, smarting under the repeated turning back of its prize companies by armed farmers and tradesmen, was defeated in spirit, restless, and totally indifferent to the eventual outcome. The loyalists lost all confidence in Gage and in their own destinies in the colony. Boston was full of miseries and was numbering its days as a British stronghold. The arrival of reinforcements from Ireland and the breezy entrance of Burgoyne with Clinton and Howe before the battle had proved a disastrous disappointment. The town of

Boston, from the British and loyalist point of view, was now worse off than it had ever been, and only time would tell how long the siege could be endured.

Across the river and upstream a few miles, George Washington arrived from Virginia to take command of the embryonic army of the patriots. He found good material but a pretty sorry mess as far as organization went. The British, having won Charlestown at such a heavy price, entrenched themselves there with Howe in command. The Americans were theoretically holding two hills facing their lines. Washington not only found the fortifications here "very insecure," but also discovered that the informal militia guarding the place were in the custom of walking over to the British lines and chatting for hours with their guards. Even the American officers saw no reason why they could not indulge in friendly conversation with the British soldiers. Washington's first move was to put an end to such congenial intercourse.

His second was to convert the "mixed multitude of people here, under very little discipline, order or government" into a real army. Hampered by lack of equipment, he could do little materially. There were no tents, so that the men continued to live in bizarre little huts of stone or brush, built according to their individual tastes, or in sailcloth cabins painted every hue of the rainbow. Nor were there any uniforms, so that they continued to wear their homespuns. But Washington created some order of rank by commanding the officers to wear cockades in their hats and ribbons on their shoulders, reserving for the generals the privilege of wearing a wide ribbon across the chest. He himself had the only uniform in the whole army: his blue-and-buff left over from his earlier military career.

Investigations of the cowardice at Bunker Hill, where Prescott's men could easily have been supported by reinforcements had the latter the courage led Washington to cashier every officer who could not vindicate himself. As soon as these were out of the way, he began his campaign to wipe out intercolonial jealousy. This took time and repeated exhortations in the orders of the day, but it eventually diminished to the point where the united army could function as one body. After some further quarrels among the generals, some of whom would not recognize Washington's command and others of whom declined to recognize the existence of the Continental Congress, the army settled down to the comparatively dull business of seeing that the British made no move beyond their lines.

The British never did. All through the rest of 1775 and into 1776, they huddled about Boston Common, eating salt pork, burying their long roster of dead, and hoping for a miraculous deliverance. In March, they woke up one morning to find that Washington had planted cannon on Dorchester Heights in a position from which the British ships could be blasted from the harbor. So the British army, together with the American loyalists who had remained under their protection in the town, boarded the ships and left the town as empty as the desert for the Americans to re-enter.

And that was the end to the first and last effort to subdue the Yankee spirit of independence by force of arms. The British had failed even to hold the town, and across the river the colonials had created an army capable of matching them wherever they went.

15

...and of a Navy

A<small>T</small> almost the precise point where the Charles flows into the sea, the Hartt family of Boston had been building ships for many years by the time the republic was founded and Washington inaugurated. There were four Hartts now: Edmund, the master shipwright who lived across the street from the shipyard; Edward, Zephaniah; and Ralph, the mastmaker. Twenty years had passed since the battle before Bunker Hill, but the Americans still possessed a genius for distributing authority. Almost as many men supervised the construction of the great frigate for the new navy in Hartt's shipyard as had assumed command at the battle. The four Hartts themselves, however, were taciturn men, not interested in being authoritative but merely in building good ships. If they had been otherwise, there might well have been more confusion than there was in the shipyard during the construction of the *Constitution*.

The designer of the frigate was Mr. Joshua Humphreys, who was close to the government at Philadelphia. He drew up plans and sent a model of the frigate up to Hartt's shipyard, where it was to be built. The naval constructor was Colonel George Claghorn, who took all the supervising out of the hands of Edmund Hartt and ran the shipyard himself. But the man with the money, without which neither Humphreys nor Claghorn could have accomplished anything, was General Henry Jackson. To confuse things further, the War Department appointed a captain of the frigate long before the ship was finished. Because there was nothing else to do with the captain, Samuel Nicholson, now that he had been assigned to the vessel, the department sent him up to Hartt's shipyard too. There were, therefore, excluding Edmund Hartt and his three brothers (who did most of the work), four high officials attending the *Constitution*. Before it was built, however, there were a good many more hands in the business.

As soon as Hartt had made room in his cluttered shipyard for constructing the frigate, another Boston shipwright, John T. Morgan, was appointed purchasing agent and authorized to pick some standing timber from which to build the ship. Morgan was out for the hardest oak he could get, and the people of Dedham said that he offered seventy-five dollars of the government's money for the Avery oak in that town. But they would not sell, and before Morgan got through he had gone all the way to Georgia to get his oak. He shipped it back to Massachusetts, where it was toughened in Hartt's shipyard while Washington dickered over a treaty with Algiers, the pirating of whose ships had started all the enthusiasm about building a United States Navy in the first place. When the treaty turned out to be no more valid than a pirate's promise, things began to hum in the shipyard, and work on the *Constitution* proceeded at a merry clip.

Except for the oak itself, the substance of the entire ship was taken from the region of its construction. The anchors were forged at Hanover of Massachusetts iron; the sails were made in the heart of Boston at Brimstone Corner. The Skillings Brothers, wood carvers of wide fame, carved out the figurehead and incidental adornments. Edmund Thayer built the gun

carriages in his workshop, and Paul Revere submitted a cautious bid to supply the copper. He said simply that he would do it "as cheap as anyone," and consequently was not underbid. After the failure of the Algerian treaty, there arose from Hartt's shipyard an unceasing clamor of banging hammers, ripping saws, and official yelling. Ironsmiths and wood carvers and sailmakers bustled in and out of the yard full of serious business and in a great hurry. Soon, although everyone was stepping on everyone else's toes, the frigate was completed, ready for launching and the admiring gapes of the populace.

The citizenry was properly enthusiastic about the unit of the new navy so close at hand. But Hartt would have no one wandering through his shipyard without any business there. Besides, the little yard was crowded to the gates with workmen and officials. Even after the ship was finished, therefore, he would allow no one within the gates unless they had something to be installed in the frigate. But Nicholson, the captain, and Claghorn, the naval inspector, and Jackson, the man with the money, were always inviting friends to come around to see the mighty *Constitution*. There was nothing Hartt could do about that, and he just peered up from his work and withered the visitors with a look. Sooner or later, he knew, the guests of the three officials would get on their own nerves. And on the day preceding the launching they did.

Early that morning Colonel Claghorn invited some friends to come and see the ship. The workmen were still eating breakfast, and the colonel thought it as opportune a time as any for these special friends to see how the United States Navy was about to take shape. Captain Nicholson, who had been captain of the vessel before it existed otherwise than on paper, was aboard the ship and told the ladies and gentlemen that they could not come aboard. This was a grave matter, not only because the pilgrims had risen at an unheard-of hour for ladies and gentlemen but also because Claghorn had told them they *could* see the ship. Nicholson said that he was captain of the ship and he didn't care what Claghorn had told them. So the visitors reported back to Colonel Claghorn and then departed without setting foot on the *Constitution*. That afternoon the colonel was aboard the ship and the captain was out in the yard. Some more visitors had somehow got inside the gates and sidled up to Captain Nicholson for permission to go aboard the frigate. Nicholson snapped viciously at them and told them to get out. Instead of going out, however, they went over to the ship. There they found Colonel Claghorn, and he invited them to come and look over the ship. Nicholson was extremely jealous of his ship and rushed aboard to reckon with the colonel. He damned the latter before the visitors, who stood there on the *Constitution's* deck greatly embarrassed before these formalities of the navy. Claghorn, who had been appointed supervisor and inspector of construction by the secretary of the navy, told Nicholson that he would stand no more back talk. Nicholson said that he would say nothing further but that it was a pretty pass when a captain could not have respect as the commander of his own ship. The colonel took exception to the remark and told Nicholson that, on the other hand, he was in command until the ship left the drydock. The visitors, duly impressed with the fine points of naval command, closed in around the disputing officers, who were presently exchanging blows. Nicholson happened to have a cane, which he threatened to use on the colonel's head, and the visitors intervened, apparently convinced that it was too early in the navy's history for any such scandal. Then they politely withdrew while the captain and the colonel swapped guarded apologies. That was the nineteenth day of September in 1797.

The next day was a great, if inglorious, day in Edmund Hartt's shipyard. President John Adams came up from Quincy to witness the launching. The governor of the commonwealth was there, too, and brought his whole Council with him. Besides the dignitaries, a host of citizens were present. Colonel Claghorn, who was an efficient and thorough man, had made adequate plans, however, and was sure that nothing untoward would happen to mar the occasion. He had written to all the newspapers, asking that public enthusiasm be kept within the bounds of public safety. He had roped off the safe areas of surrounding wharves, because, he said, a frigate of the *Constitution's* size would necessarily make a huge splash and probably flood the tide. He went around personally to inspect all the stagings that had been improvised by enterprising contractors as spectator bleachers for the launching. He even roped off the water to keep sightseeing craft at a safe distance, for he expected the frigate to slide off the ways with such speed that any neighboring craft would be in danger of inundation. He went so far as to make a little speech to the world at large through the newspapers, in which he said that the accidental injury "of a single citizen would mar the satisfaction and pleasure that the constructor would otherwise enjoy of building and conducting into the ocean a Powerful Agent of National Justice, which hope dictates may become the just pride and ornament of the American name." And that was no inconsiderable rhetoric for a naval man.

But the colonel, already tried by Nicholson's impetuosity, was destined to have his day in the sun marred by a worse calamity than the injury of a single citizen. Amidst a good deal of complimentary remarks and fanfare and before a patriotic host, workmen scurried around the underpinnings of the hull, removed the blocks and loosened the ropes, giving the frigate wide berth as it was about to slide down the ways into the water. But nothing happened. The *Constitution* stayed there untouched by water. Colonel Claghorn, mystified and mortified, raced up to give orders to apply mechanical aid to get the ship started. Then she moved slowly and grudgingly, while the crowd sent up a round of cheers. But the frigate moved only nine yards, and the ways settled comfortably into the dry ground under the ship's weight. Meanwhile the tide was ebbing, and pretty soon there would be no water to slide her into. Colonel Claghorn, laboring under the facetious observations of the spectators, hustled about directing efforts to move her farther. But no power on earth could get the *Constitution* to go her way. He called for the blocks again, reblocked the ship and shored her up. Then the President of the United States, the governor and his Council, and the public went home, leaving the colonel with his powerful agent of national justice stuck firmly in her stays like a wench in her corsets.

That night there was alternate joy and disappointment in Boston. Mr. John Hodgkinson, a local theater impresario, had already written and cast a musical sketch to celebrate the launching, and he, for one, had no intention of going back on his plans. It had taken him the considerable time of two days to write and direct the piece. In the full flush of patriotism, moreover, he had sold out the house of the Haymarket Theatre. So the *Constitution* was launched that night on the stage, even though in reality it rested high and dry in Hartt's shipyard up at the North End. But the verisimilitude of Mr. Hodgkinson's effort was preserved by its subtitle, for the piece was called, *The Launch, or Huzza for the Constitution*. And while Colonel Claghorn, his day of glory tumbling at his feet, paced his quarters in troubled concern over the ship, a minstrel named Tyler stalked up and down the stage of the Haymarket singing the glory of the frigate, her constructors, and her crew.

Mr. Hodgkinson had sold out his house and was triumphant. The public in general, however, was disappointed—so much so that the newspapers felt called upon to write philosophic editorials on the futility of being disappointed. The *Centinel,* which had taken a fatherly interest in the *Constitution* from the beginning, made a profound observation. "To indifferent, unthinking people," it proclaimed, "the disappointment is a disappointment." And as long as it was on the subject, it went on to take a passing shot at the rival *Chronicle.* "The Jacobins will crow, and the Chronicle, that speaking trumpet of the devil, will echo the tale of disappointment to the utmost verge of its pestiferous influence."

The day after the abortive launching found Colonel Claghorn a sad but undefeated man. In the empty shipyard, he examined the underpinnings of his proud frigate. Then he set to work raising the ship up a couple of inches, which he said took only fifty minutes after due preparation. The colonel now was inclined to believe that he made the ways too narrow in an attempt to ensure a safe speed for the ship's descent to the water. So he widened the ways and made the decline toward the water less gentle and announced that the frigate *Constitution* would be launched the following day. But he wrote no letters to the papers, and he did not care whether anyone came to witness the launching or not.

Not many did come, as compared with the previous launching, and it was a good thing. For once more the colonel gave the order for removing the supports, and once more the good ship lurched waterward for but ten yards—a gain of only one yard over the original launching. She was then partly stuck on a staging which was constructed only with a view to having her pass over it and not with sufficient strength to support her for any length of time. The colonel immediately called this second launching off, for if the ship proceeded any farther over that insecure staging and then got stuck again it would be in serious danger of paying a penalty for its capricious actions. Again Colonel Claghorn made an examination, and discovered that the ways had settled again, this time abaft the ship, so that there was no incline for it to slide down. By now he was justifiably determined to call the launching off entirely for the present, and begin all over again.

A month later, on the twenty-first of October, Claghorn was certain that he had ways down which the *Constitution* could glide gracefully into the water. A gun was fired at daybreak on that cold autumn morning to warn the public that the frigate would be launched. Captain Nicholson was there bright and early to take charge as soon as the ship touched the water. For himself he reserved one honor, which he was insistent no one else should usurp, and that was raising the first national flag on his ship. Before leaving the yard for his breakfast, he issued an unqualified order that no flag was to be raised aboard the *Constitution* until he got back from breakfast. But the minute the crusty old captain was outside the yard, a calker named Samuel Bentley, fired less by patriotism than by his share of the universal disdain of Nicholson, took it upon himself to raise the Stars and Stripes. When Nicholson returned, he was raging mad, but he could do nothing. It would be improper to lower the colors again.

All morning the yard of Edmund Hartt was filling up with citizens who were as determined to witness the launching of the *Constitution* as Claghorn was that it should be launched. The colonel, however, was going to take his time about matters this third launching day. So he kept the crowd waiting until shortly after noon, when Captain James Sever, who had an unfinished ship in dock at Portsmouth, hopped up on the heel of the bowsprit with a bottle of venerable Madeira from the cellar of Thomas Russell, a Boston merchant of unswerving patriotism. The figurehead of the *Constitution* was an image of Hercules holding a club menacingly, and Captain Sever made a strange contrast wielding his bottle of Madeira below.

He cracked the bottle. Claghorn ordered the shores pulled out. And the *Constitution* slid majestically, serenely and evenly all the way down the stays into the water—"a pleasing sight to those who contemplate her," remarked the ever-loyal *Centinel*, "as the *germ* of a naval force, which in no remote period of time will protect the flag of the *United States* from the depredation of piratical marauders." When the frigate was afloat at her moorings, the crew yelled wildly to those on shore, and then the latter yelled back. And that was all there was to a ceremony that had originally included the president of the republic.

The *Centinel* was still talking about it, however, the following week. With national pride equaled only by its rhetoric, it cried:

"May the 'hoary monarch' of the element, on

whose bosom she now reclines, protect her with his trident; and whenever her departure into the waste of his realm may be necessary, may propitious breezes waft her to the haven of peace, or aid her to hurl the vindictive thunder of national vengeance on the disturbers of our country's repose, or the depredators on the lawful commerce of our citizens. Though rated only as a forty-four, she can be made conveniently to mount sixty-four guns."

The launching of the *Constitution* was an end and a beginning. It was the end of the inspired contest for political freedom, waged in this river valley not only by soldiers and militia but also by craftsmen and workers, who fashioned their editorials in the free press as they fashioned the frigate in Hartt's shipyard, firmly and fearlessly. And it was the beginning, up in this far corner, of a totally undominated nation. The farmers of Middlesex had proclaimed that to the British. And the shipbuilders and sailmakers at the river's mouth, in common with those from Portsmouth to Baltimore, proclaimed it to the rest of the world.

Part Six

Bridges and Progress

16

The Great Bridge

P ROGRESS, in both its idealistic and its materialistic sense, is founded on dreams of freedom. Practically,
and especially to hard-thinking Yankees long before
New England's halcyon days, it was also involved somehow with the improvement of old ways and the devising
of new ways to make money move.

Since the Charles, flowing with quiet regularity
over its meandering course to the sea, was never an eminently useful river in the industrial sense, no realistic
businessman bothered much about its value as spur to
a water wheel. The river had started the wheels of
small mills turning in the inland villages of Massachusetts, and there its commerce with industry stopped for
the present. And the possibility of its making money in
any other way for the men who inhabited its banks was
considered limited enough to be fantastic. Many an extravagant scheme was discussed in the alehouses of Cambridge and Boston by men who tapped their imagina-
tions with as zesty appetites as they did their ale kegs.
Plans to make the Charles a great waterway to the West
were advanced sufficiently to reach the public in print,
until more conservative and sober men pointed out
that, while the Charles was a mighty river at its mouth,

it tapered down to a stream before it went three leagues to westward. Nevertheless, they, too, had fond dreams of the day when revenue from cross-river traffic would compensate for the obvious impracticability of upriver traffic. And eventually they were right.

The first bridge to span the river, however, and the first considerable bridge in America, had nothing to do with money, except on the losing end. When it was conceived, the colony was young; and exhibiting all the impatience of youth, the colony committed itself to visions far beyond its immediate ability to realize. Thus, for a quarter of a century, "A Great Bridge over the River" lingered as an official dream among the settlers. Because it was official, it could not go the way of most youthful dreams, which is but to fade into memory, but was constantly resurrected to taunt to the minds of a second generation.

Five years after the *Arabella* had sailed into the bay and at about the same time that the Hermit of the Charles was seriously considering moving upstream to less exposed haunts, the townspeople of Cambridge, probably in a surge of unwarranted enthusiasm, gathered together one December day and forthwith fell to the wholesale passing of all sorts of orders designed to foster the public weal—but with little or no respect for the public treasury. "It is further ordered," they went on bravely, "that there shall be sufficient bridge made down to low-water mark on this side the River, and a broad ladder on the farther side the River, for convenience landing; and Mr. Chaplin, Mr. Danforth and Mr. Cooke to see it made."

The perplexity of these three men on the next morning, as they stood on the freezing north bank of the Charles and looked across the wide expanse of current and marshes that separated them from the opposite shore, completely effaced any satisfaction they may have felt in being named to supervise such an enterprise. At any rate, surveying the wilderness around them, Messrs. Chaplin and Danforth lost no time in dropping out of the scheme entirely. Though they were men of vision, they not only could not imagine a great bridge in that lonely spot but also were totally incapable of foreseeing any roadways through the forests to lead to it. So they turned their thoughts from the whole affair and went about their own business.

Mr. Cooke, on the other hand, was more intimately associated with the river. The idea of a bridge arching it did not appall him. But he had other plans. Something of a realist in surroundings more amiable to realists than to others, he quickly realized the remoteness of the possibility of bridgebuilding and hoped that his townspeople on the Cambridge side of the Charles would also come back to earth. His hopes were vindicated, for they made an abrupt descent not a month after they had caused that dream of a great bridge to be inscribed forever on their records. Moreover, they voted, "That Mr. Joseph Cooke shall keep the ferry, and have a penny over, and a half penny on Lecture days."

The river gave Mr. Cooke, in return for his hard sense about the fancied bridge, a comfortable living. His ferry was the only means of crossing the Charles, unless one wanted to go downstream some miles, which was, of course, foolish. And there was a good deal of shuttling back and forth on Lecture Days, the popular taste for lectures in those first years being pretty near insatiable. The river valley has always been comparatively good territory for lecturers, but it was a paradise for them in the beginning. Some attended the lectures for the creditable purpose of steeling themselves against a callous and laborious life by listening to the elaborate harangues of the clergy; others, for the more understandable purpose of enjoying the company of widely

scattered neighbors. Whatever their purposes, they all flocked down to Mr. Cooke's ferry on Wednesdays and Thursdays, "Lecture Days," to cross the river for a lecture. Mr. Cooke beamed on them, collected his especially reduced fare, and propelled his well-laden ferry over to the south bank. As his passengers went their way, he may well have sighed for those first two years of the settlement of the river basin, when lecturers held forth four days each week instead of two.

It was not long, however, before the balmy days of more and more lectures returned. Throughout the years of the history of man's life along the Charles, the river has flowed to the perpetual accompaniment of the frequently monotonous and occasionally melodious and often vehement voices of the lecturers. The people of this valley have long been a lecture-loving race. And thereon depended even such an apparently unrelated thing as the pecuniary success of a seventeenth century ferry. Nevertheless, it may have been that Mr. Cooke's very thirst for more lectures was the killing of the goose that laid the golden eggs. Governor Winthrop, deeply concerned over the pouring of his people into the meetinghouses, was genuinely alarmed in 1639 at the ever increasing activity of the lecturers and the unabating following of the populace. In his journal, he sounded a note of grim warning: "There were so many lectures now in the country, and many poor persons would usually resort to two or three in a week, to the great neglect of their affairs and the damage of the public." It was growing to be, far from an encouraging aspect of Puritan life, nothing more than a social evil—a precursor of penny bingo and with every indication of undermining the new society. To cope with the situation, emergency legislation was attempted in the Great and General Court, but the voice of the people, strengthened by ministerial Amens, promptly killed it. And still collecting his halfpenny per head, Mr. Cooke blissfully ferried the inhabitants of the north bank across to the lectures, a latter-day Charon bringing his boatload from the superficial world of rugged living to the nether world of forebodings, admonitions, and threats of hell.

Still, too, that early vision of a great bridge persisted in the minds of the embarkers. And twenty-one years after the first courageous order had been passed, it was resurrected from the heavy files of unfinished business and paraded before the town meeting. This time the townsfolk went so far as to commit themselves "to pay each one their proportion of a rate to the sum of 200 pounds towards the building of a bridge over the Charles River." Again they sent a committee out to effect their order; and although the committee boldly selected a location for the structure, they shrank from the overwhelming prospect of executing the public whim. There followed six more years of prosperity for Mr. Cooke before the bridge was erected. And then the good people of Cambridge found that they had a gigantic white elephant on their hands. It was the first "great bridge" in America, and it was also the first great drain on the public treasury.

Soon after it was opened, the bridge began to crumble in spots, so that the anxious community, like midwives to that pioneering construction, solicitously ordered that "the bridge shall be layed in oyle and lead, provided that it exceed not 40 pounds charge"— a sum representative to them of the height of human sacrifice for the salvation of a fond dream, which, having once been made real, daily threatened to disintegrate. The story of that great bridge was an ignoble one —best passed over, for it was merely the struggle of the hopelessly unfit for existence. Completely discouraged with the whole affair more than once during the following century, the sponsors of the bridge and their descendants often threatened to aid the natural processes of disintegration. Already the New England character was changing. Less given to ecstatic action motivated by young dreams, it was proceeding to rear itself on sound practicality in the administration of its affairs. Accordingly, it was fast losing patience with this childhood creation that was rendering so poor an account of itself. If the bridge could not be satisfactorily financed, then it would have to go and the ferry, which had paid its own way and more, be restored. But that, whatever else it might be, was not progress.

The Great and General Court, sitting in conclave and fearing signs of retrogression, was solemnly aware of that fact. Moreover, there seemed to be something faintly immoral, because faintly wasteful, in allowing a great bridge to revert to the elements. The proposal to go back to the faithful and self-supporting old ferry did not please the legislators. Sadly and with a heavy tone of reproach to everyone in general for not appreciating the bridge, they officially declared that a ferry was by no means "so safe, convenient or useful, as a bridge, for a ferry is altogether useless in the winter, and very inconvenient to transport horses, and not at all accomodable for carts or droves of cattle." From there the court, fully comprehending the nature of progress, hung the fate of the bridge on cold, monetary considerations: anyone who had the public spirit to repair the structure would be permitted to collect tolls for his trouble. Even this was insufficient to restore faith in the old bridge; and the upshot of the matter was that all towns north of Boston that had roads which ran, however vaguely, in the general direction of the Charles were required to contribute to a fund for supporting the bridge in its senility. And the fruit of that youthful dream of a few visionaries was condemned to a pauper's death.

The Great Bridge was clearly a mistake, so clearly indeed that no other bridge was attempted for well over a century. The concept of progress itself changed in that time, and the utter lack of activity in bridge-building had nothing whatever to do with a lack of progress. The trouble was solely that some people, who were reputed to rate far above others in deciding such matters, regarded the building of any more bridges as a step backward. In other words, it was felt by them that the existing mode of crossing the river by ferry had proved as profitable as could be expected and that any alteration would necessarily be a change for the worse. It was further felt by these same people that, since Boston was rapidly approaching the size of a metropolis, it would do the surrounding towns no good, morally or otherwise, to become too closely allied with it.

Those who returned these judgments were the president and fellows of Harvard College; and from the financial point of view, at least, they knew what they were talking about. For the river Charles literally fostered higher education on this continent, as the learned and honorable petitioners frankly pointed when, in 1738, a group of progressive businessmen saw an opportunity to make quick money by throwing a toll bridge across the river. They quickly and definitely nipped the progressive idea in the bud with this impressive document:

To his Excellency Jon^a Belcher, Esq., Capt. Genl and Govern^r in Chief in & over his Majesty's Province of the Massachusetts Bay in N. England, the Honble his Majesty's Council, & the house of Representatives in Genl Court, assembled,

The Memorial of the Presid^t & Fellows of Harvard College in Cambridge humble sheweth,

The Whereas We are inform'd there are now lying before the Honble Court Petitions from Sundry Gentlemen referring to a Ferry & Bridge, over Charles River and inasmuch as that Affair, must necessarily very much affect the interest of the College, Wee therefore as we think ourselves in duty bound beg leave to make the following Representation wth respect thereto, Viz^t

That our Fathers in the Earliest Days of this Country, out of their pious care for Religion & Learning were pleased to give the revenues of the Ferry over Charles River,[1] to the Use & benefit of the College wch have been a very Considerable part of the Support of s^d Society, and it is as Yo^r Excellency & Hon^{rs} are Sensible, in Some proportion to the increase of the Country a growing interest, and upon wch the College very much depends, for defraying its growing Charges.

We beg leave also further to represent to Yo^r Excy & Honours, that we apprehend, that any nearer and more ready Passage, over the s^d River and especially by a Bridge, will cause such an increase of Company &c at the College, that thereby the Scholars will be in danger of being too much interrupted in their Studies and hurt in their Morals. But if this Honble Court shall see cause to grant any of the Petitions relating to a bridge or another Ferry; Yet we hope & Trust yor Exc^y & Honours, in Yo^r wise & tender care for the s^d College, will prevent its receiving any Detriment; by making such provision as you shall in Yo^r great Wisdom, judge proper for the Securing an Equal interest & One that may be equally growing; And will also consider wt Methods may be taken, for preventing so great a Resort of Company to the College, as Such a Short and Easy Access to it may Occasion.

But we are perswaded that this Honble Court are so sensible how much the whole country is interested in the flourishing of Religion & Learning in this Society, that We doubt

---

[1] This ferry was four miles downstream from Joseph Cooke's which had, of course, passed out of existence.

not, but We may depend upon Yo^r Wisdom & care in a matter of so great Importance to it, & Yo^r Memorialists as in duty bound shall ever pray &c.

Edwd Holyoke Presd^t in the
Name of the Presd^t & Fellows
of Harvard College

Cambridge June. 26. 1738.

This very emphatic, although somewhat sycophantic, communication put the problem squarely up to the governor and court: it was either the toll bridge or "Religion and Learning." The court, just as the college expected, chose Religion and Learning and let the toll bridge go.

The college cannot be blamed for its highly militant spirit in the matter. The financial standing of the institution was precarious enough in those days that knew nothing of generous drives and opulent alumni. For one hundred years Harvard's life and prestige were ingloriously dependent in no small measure on the number of people who wanted to cross the river downstream. And Dr. Holyoke and his confreres, although their judgment in involving the Charles River in the issue of student morals leaves something to be desired and more to be clarified, nevertheless acted with prompt wisdom in putting an energetic damper on those sundry gentlemen who would sell learning with the ferry down the river for a mess of pottage.

17

Lemuel's Masterpiece

AFTER the Revolution, Progress became the undisputed national religion (so intensely that the word itself was popularly held to be synonymous with Americanism). Even the corporation of the vigilant and paternally anxious college on the riverbank could do nothing to impede its onward march. It is doubtful that the college wanted to, for progress is highly contagious in nature and the college itself, despite a slight Puritan hangover in some quarters, was progressing in its own right. When independence was a reality, moreover, and the seeds of democracy were safely planted, though sprouting with no great promise, many of the most practical men of affairs within hailing distance of the Charles—men who had previously been too busy baiting the British to think of making money—turned their activities in some degree from the arena of politics to that of commerce. And just as the river had played an important if passive part in the strife to establish democracy, it played a no less important if equally passive part in the strife to establish prosperity. One of the first to see its possibilities in this connection was John Hancock.

Hancock was a man of amazing adaptability. Both

himself and his private affairs he invariably adapted with extraordinary readiness to the public affairs with which he went out of his way to identify himself. When the Revolution came along, Hancock, whose hide the admiralty courts were long hounding because of his persistent habit of landing rum under cover of night, combined patriotism with discretion by quickly embracing the cause and immediately making himself scarce at the river mouth. When he was accorded the opportunity and honor of serving spiritual matters by accepting the treasurership of Harvard, he did it and lined his own purse with a few thousands of the college's funds, which he let his heirs pay back. Both Hancock and the Great and General Court survived the Revolution; and as Hancock's influence in the free commonwealth mounted, he readily adjusted it to his private business.

John Hancock had his eye on the Charles. He petitioned the court for the privilege of building a bridge across the river and for the right to collect tolls from those who used it. His petition was granted. Andrew Cabot, in the same year, also petitioned the court for a similar privilege and right. His petition was not granted. Hancock quickly saw the enviable value of a monopoly on spanning the Charles, and he did not intend to have it molested. The only flaw was that in his petition Mr. Cabot had tactfully offered to pay Harvard two hundred pounds annually so that the college would not feel so badly about losing the income from the old ferry. Whether from academic pressure from across the river or merely from its own sense of the fitness of things, the court punctiliously ordered John Hancock's new corporation to go and do likewise. Hancock figured closely, found that he could not possibly lose, and went out to sell some shares in the venture to his friends, chiefly on the very firm basis that the bridge was to be their private property for forty years before being turned over to the commonwealth. When he had collected enough money, he went to see Lemuel Cox.

Lemuel Cox was one of the unsung heroes of the American odyssey to economic greatness. Born in Boston in 1736, he modestly described himself at maturity as an artisan. His contemporaries, on the other hand, called him "a masterpiece of ingenuity," though the term was probably better suited to his work. Lemuel, nevertheless, well deserved a less general characterization than artisan, for he was first in many things: he was the first projector of a powder mill in the colony, the first to invent a card-wire cutting machine (which invention the commonwealth duly rewarded by giving Lemuel a thousand acres of land in Maine that no one else wanted), and the first to make the practical suggestion that prisoners in tax-supported institutions be put to some useful employment if it was only making nails. Foiled by nothing in his career, he welcomed the chance to try a new field and set to work on short notice at designing a bridge of the required specifications of forty feet in width with a draw opening of thirty feet. It was probably the draw that intrigued Lemuel, for he liked to devise ways and means of doing such things as lifting a segment of a bridge. Anyway, he so interested himself in the assignment that he had the bridge not only designed but constructed within a year. It was an unheard-of accomplishment, the pioneering engineering achievement on the continent.

It was a milestone also in the career of Lemuel

Cox, who, although now describing himself more pretentiously as a millwright, was made internationally famous as a bridgebuilder. Four years after his Charles River Bridge, he was summoned to Ireland, where four English engineers had declared it was impossible ever to construct a bridge over the Foyle at Londonderry. But Lemuel, looking over the situation and having in mind his own bridge back home, not only said that he could do it all right but went so far as to make an estimate of the probable cost. His offer accepted, he came back to New England to get the only lumber he would trust for such an undertaking and the only men he would trust to use it. Again he sailed for Ireland, this time with a load of lumber and twenty skilled workers. In five months a bridge of fifty-eight arches of American oak, built by American workers, was jubilantly thrown open to the use of the astonished people of Londonderry. The corporation of the City of London, hearing of these things, unanimously invited the Massachusetts artisan to take a look at Wren's famous bridge over the Thames, for it was in grave danger of collapsing. Lemuel told them how much the restoration of the bridge would cost. When the corporation haggled over the price, he indignantly left their city and came home. He lived on the southerly bank of the Charles but he crossed his bridge to die on the north side, so that the river ran both literally and figuratively through his life.

Most of John Hancock's enterprises were characterized by singular success, and the Charles River Bridge was no exception. He combined business and advertising acumen with patriotic sentiments and scheduled the opening of his bridge for June 17, 1786, a date historically important as the eleventh anniversary of the engagement at Bunker Hill. It was naturally a day of unbridled jubilation on the banks of the Charles, jubilation over what was fast fading to a memory. Himself greatly responsible for the original significance of the date, Hancock was happy to have the opportunity of adding to the general celebration this new reality of a bridge with a draw. A broadside published expressly for the occasion waxed so hysterically ecstatic that it confused the issues somewhat but did not fail to increase the rampant excitement.

"This elegant work," it shouted in reference to the new bridge, "was begun on the first of June, 1785, (a date remarkable in the Annals of America as the Ports of Boston and Charlestown were unjustly shut up by an arbitrary *British* Administration) and was finished on the seventeenth of the same month 1786, the ever memorable day on which was fought the famous and bloody Battle of Bunker-Hill, where was shown the Valour of the undisciplined New England Militia under the magnanimous Warren who gloriously fell in his Country's Cause! Blessed Be His Memory!! And All the People—Say Amen!!!"

Long after the festivities of the opening, the Amen was echoed month after month and year after year by the scuffling of feet and clattering of hoofs over John Hancock's private bridge. For the original investors, most of whom had gone into the bridge business with less faith in the venture than regard for an association with its promoter, it was proving a veritable gold mine. The Charles, doing nothing more active than flowing continually into the sea, was making them rich. Those were still the years of the Confederation, characterized in the social and economic centers by the emergence of a new aristocracy. The Tories, former incumbents of the highest chairs in society, were dead, ostracized, or ruined. With the passing of this traditional patriciate a new one arose, founded not on polite traditions, for the aristocratic traditions brought over intact from England went out of Massachusetts Bay in the wake of Gage's ships on St. Patrick's Day, but on enterprise and commercial prosperity.

All this fostered a new spirit of competition, which in turn became the agent of progress. It served also to kindle the fire of Yankee imagination and vision, both of which were in close danger of being snuffed out after the long lassitude of the Revolution. It granted a boon, too, to that delicately balanced combination of stubbornness, shrewdness, and craftiness called "Yankee ingenuity." Thus progress itself, for all its nakedly materialistic implications, evolved into a sort of positive tradition. There was no material progress here in this valley without dreams and a faith in them that was often far from practical during the struggle for their realization. Before his dreams were vindicated, a man was a visionary; to his fellows, he was very often worse, a crackpot, probably, or an idler. It was only afterward, after the years had proved him, that he was called a success, a realistic fellow whose undertakings were built on solid common sense. He was a practical man, then, a materialist. His visions and his dreams, somehow culpable in their conception, were then entirely commendable under this new guise of ingenuity.

That first Charles River Bridge was built by visionaries, like the Great Bridge long before it; the tolls were collected by materialists. A good many people had watched John Hancock enter the bridge business with misgivings about the soundness of his mind. Some thought it was due to the war, others to deeper difficulties. He had been through a good deal and was even then going through another political ordeal. And he had always been weak and ailing physically. Accordingly, his running off on a tangent was pardonable and understandable. What was not quite so understandable was the gullibility of those who backed his proposition. Hancock was probably only slightly unbalanced, but those who esteemed his name so highly that they were willing to pay for it were specimens to be watched closely. Little more than five years passed, however, before all those visionaries and crackbrains were being envied, which is the first step toward emulation. The Charles River Bridge, it was readily perceived, succeeded from its having been planned with a cold regard for figures and based on common sense. The proprietors were practical men, whose soundness in their affairs had returned them the double dividend of an increased income and a creditable position in society. Thus automatically there was created the first tradition of that new, awkward society—the cardinal one of competition.

By January, 1792, Hancock's bridge was among the most lucrative projects in all New England. This being true, other men lost no time in organizing themselves to build another bridge upstream to break Hancock's monopoly. Hancock was then governor of the commonwealth; and since permission to span the river was subject to his veto, the new builders inserted an advertisement in a popular journal so that any such veto by the Governor would look suspiciously like an attempt to exploit the river at the expense of the public convenience. "As *all* citizens," they wrote with no vague intimation, "have an *equal* right to propose a measure that may be beneficial to the public or advantageous to themselves, and as no body of men have an *exclusive* right to take to themselves such a privilege, a number of gentlemen have proposed to open a new subscription for the purpose of a bridge from West Boston to Cambridge, at such place as the General Court may be pleased to direct. A subscription for two hundred shares in the proposed bridge will this day be opened at Samuel Cooper's office, north side of the State House."

This confident announcement, making the bridge —with orthodox Yankee strategy—a foregone conclusion, left the General Court nothing to do except to state exactly where the bridge was to be built. The shares were all sold within three hours after the appearance of the advertisement—a fairly certain indication that no Bostonian had any intention of giving Hancock, governor or not, a corner on the Charles.

Neither did Hancock have any intention of relinquishing his virtual monopoly, and he used two official weapons to protect it. The first was to arrange that the General Court order the new bridge to be undesirably "near the Pest House." And in case the proximity of the pests did not keep away traffic, his second device was to require the new corporation to pay Harvard three hundred pounds per annum, which was a hundred pounds more than he himself was paying. Francis Dana, the proprietor of the new bridge, rose to the occasion. He did not mind the Pest House location at all, because it was the nearest point to Cambridge, the town from which he had intended to attract his patronage anyhow. And he lost no minutes in protesting the rate he was ordered to pay Harvard and getting it reduced to two hundred pounds. Furthermore, he constructed a better bridge than Lemuel's masterpiece.

Dana's bridge was opened in November of 1793. The *Columbian Centinel*, which from the beginning seemed partial to Dana at Hancock's cost, was triumphant. "The elegance of workmanship," it stated, "and the magnitude of the undertaking are perhaps unequalled in the history of enterprises." The brave journal went on to express a tactless and impudent hope that the government would not be so ungracious as to boycott the bridge.

Both Hancock and Dana's bridges continued to make money. The public was served efficiently. The president and fellows of Harvard College were happy with their four hundred pounds annually. After a while the two bridges were no longer rivals. Hancock's had the Charlestown clientele, and Dana's served the people of Cambridge. In a few years the two became not only partners in the business of getting people over the river but also partners in a protective alliance, for a new threat arose to darken their rosy future.

The new threat was Andrew Craigie. In the very year that Hancock's monopoly was broken by Dana, Craigie bought the impressive house overlooking the Charles that Washington had used for his Cambridge headquarters. Craigie liked the Charles. Not only did he want to live out his years on its banks, but he diverted himself by buying up all the land on the Cambridge side that he could lay his hands on. He apparently wanted to build a privately controlled city someday and amuse himself by running its affairs to suit himself.

In 1808, Mr. Craigie owned three hundred acres of Cambridge, most of it close to the river. In that year, too, he decided to build his own bridge. When he filed his application with the immortal Great and General Court, Francis Dana's company voiced vigorous protests, but it did no good. Craigie had Harvard behind him. Already Harvard had perceived the direction the bridge industry was taking and the very surprising beneficial effect it was having on the academic exchequer. If every bridge across the Charles was to mean a 200-pound annuity to the college, then Harvard would lend the weight of its influence to any bridgebuilder who came along. At any rate, Mr. Craigie got his bridge. Moreover, because he owned so much of Cambridge, he was able to construct several roads leading to it.

Craigie's bridge, like Hancock and Dana's before it, was a financial success, though Mr. Craigie himself became swamped in money troubles. There seemed to be no end to the profits that could be made simply from people going back and forth over the Charles. During the next fifty years the General Court was constantly besieged with requests and petitions, humbly praying for permission to build a bridge across the river. At last, in 1858, the court put a stop to the craze. It was done simply by taking all the profit out of the bridge-building business. And to do it, the court resorted to Yankee ingenuity again.

In 1846 the court gave Isaac Livermore, who was then the largest holder of all that remained of Hancock's corporation, the right to build another bridge, midway between those of the now late Mr. Dana and Mr. Craigie. The right carried with it the requirement that Isaac Livermore buy both the Craigie and Dana bridges and present them to the commonwealth, together with his own two (the Hancock bridge and the one he was about to build), as soon as he had made $150,000 for his pains. Twelve years later, however, the commonwealth bought the former two in its own name and made a gift of them to the city of Cambridge.

That was the end of the Charles's earning power in the field of transportation. On a Monday morning in

February, 1858—seventy-two years after Hancock had opened his bridge—the directors of the surviving corporation met with the Cambridge municipal officials and congratulated themselves on the progress made in those years. Then they were loaded into carriages, suitably preceded by a brass band and followed by half the population of Cambridge. The whole procession moved joyfully down to the north bank of the Charles. At noon the bells in all the churches rang out; military companies fired salutes; and everyone made a speech. All Cambridge was rejoicing that the Charles could henceforth be crossed without the payment of a penny.

But the president and fellows of Harvard College turned down an empty glass for the days when crossing the river meant promoting learning; and they bravely faced the new order of things.

18

The Merchant Princes

T HE importance of John Hancock's bridge and Lemuel Cox's engineering masterpiece lay not so much in their significance as long strides in the development of transportation as in the fact that they both represented commercial triumphs over culture in their relation to Harvard College. Nor were they merely isolated examples of a transition of the region from the first fruits of Puritan thought to the first fruits of Yankee commerce. They were, indeed, characteristic of a similar transition all through the valley. Things of the spirit were fast becoming secondary to things of the flesh as the eighteenth century faded into the past.

In this period, Emerson has wisely written, "there was not a book, a speech, a conversation or a thought in the state of Massachusetts." That was a broad indictment, and a severe one. But it was as true as Emerson himself was.

After the Revolution and all through the early half of the century following, the story of the Charles River valley is a story of sheer commercial expansion —and expansion often at the price of things more important than commerce. The high ideals of the founding fathers that had created Harvard College on the riverbanks to perpetuate learning were frequently ignored or forgotten. Education in Massachusetts and in Boston itself fell to its lowest standard in the entire history of the commonwealth. It was not only because men preferred early in life to make money rather than to learn, but also because teaching was an almost ludicrously paid profession. No one could teach and make a living at the same time. The result was that no schools were worth opening, and the General Court relaxed its education laws, no longer requiring towns of a couple hundred families to maintain grammar school teachers.

This laxness could not, and it did not, go on long without dragging the standard of living down to a slave depth for some and raising it to the skies for others. In the commercial mania that spread like wildfire through the valley in the early nineteenth century, there were strains of the most sordid forms of exploitation of women and children. The former turned from the spinning wheels and the looms in their homes to spinning and weaving in the factories. In the 1830's they spent long working hours six days each week for an average wage of forty-two cents a day. The factories were ill equipped in their infancy to handle their employees so far as the latter's physical comfort was concerned: there was ventilation too poor to permit proper breathing in the crowded rooms, light too meager to see by, and no sanitary conveniences at all. In the inland towns, where the houses had been scattered through the countryside, housing problems arose, and the solution was found in "corporation boarding houses." These houses meant merely the prolonging of the conditions in the factory itself through the few hours of leisure afforded the women by a hard schedule of working hours. It was not uncommon for the rooms to contain half a dozen sleepers, and the meals were ill prepared and hastily eaten. The very appearance of the poorer class women changed after the introduction of woman labor in the mills. They were flat-chested, stoop-shouldered, and squint-eyed from the endless hours of bending over the looms in the dark factories, so that one of their contemporaries arose at the first convention of the National Trades Union in 1834 and exclaimed, "We talk of the rising generation! What must that generation be, coming from such a stock of disease and deformity!"

The generation already rising in that first half of the nineteenth century was badly enough treated. As far back as 1789, however, George Washington, then President of the Republic, took occasion to compliment highly a Boston factory in which sails were made according to a sort of chain labor system in which young girls were employed. The president was much interested in the system, for the girls worked at their spinning with both hands free, with the flax fastened to their waists and with other girls employed to turn the spinning wheels for them. Up until the middle of the next century, the practice of employing young girls at a pittance grew from bad to worse. The day was lengthened to twelve hours, the age limit dropped as low as eight years for eligibility as a factory employee, and schooling vanished almost altogether. Finally even the child's home life became a thing of the past. Corporation boardinghouses were opened for the child laborers, and social conditions in the region sank to a level lower than that of the Dark Ages.

One would think a crusader would have arisen before that to protest conditions. But Emerson, as he so often was, was right: in the first part of the nineteenth century there was not a thought in Massachusetts. Everyone was too busy.

Out of all this arose that new aristocracy, the caste of the merchant and manufacturing princes, which was seen in its incipiency shortly after the Revolution in the careers of men like John Hancock. The religious leaders no longer were the important men of the region, as so long they had been. And the printers, the editors, and the almanackers found their influence rapidly declining in a society that was beginning to concern itself primarily with making money. It is not to be wondered, therefore, that a new sort of culture began to replace the simple intellectualism of the Puritans and the free, aggressive philosophy of the Revolutionary period. Culture began to be associated with wealth. Harvard was becoming the wealthiest university in the world. The most respected homes in the region were not the manses of the clergy but the mansions of the commercial princes. The professions yielded in influence to the merchants. It was not long before eastern Massachusetts became the latter's world. Artists painted the merchants' portraits; the poets sought their company; colleges, slipping out of the grasp of the clergy, courted the favor of the merchants.

The rise of the merchants was apparent both in Boston and in the valley. The town at the river's mouth grew into a flourishing port, its harbor teeming with square-rigged ships which brought in cargoes of raw goods and carried away loads of finished materials. Soon the merchant princes became a class within a class, and the term was limited to those men who were merely shippers, exporting and importing goods with which they had nothing to do beyond loading them at one wharf and unloading them at another. Often one such merchant prince owned a fleet of over a hundred great ships that radiated from Boston to every corner of the globe; and if Boston was ever the hub of the universe, it was so more literally in this sense than in any other. And it is only in the same commercial sense that Boston has ever been anything but provincial.

The merchants of Boston changed the tenor of life there so thoroughly that European travelers whose visits were spaced a quarter of a century apart hardly recognized the city. Even the stern theology of the Puritans was forced into the background. The merchant princes, whose minds were entirely unfettered by doctrines, never thought much about either salvation or damnation during the week. And on Sundays they turned their backs on the meetinghouses that were the survivals of Winthrop's days and of Mather's to indulge themselves in the genteel worship of Episcopalianism, carrying the whole denomination to a material prosperity that not even the pre-Revolution Tories had been able to bestow on it. Stained glass and altars and a liturgy became commonplaces in Boston, and the episcopate was established in the very seat of Protestantism with a security that was never again shaken. Christmas, long ignored as a popish conceit, was openly and widely celebrated as a festival. Candles beamed across the snow from the small-paned windows of the new houses on Beacon Hill, and mistletoe and punch bowls and Yule logs brightened the drawing rooms. It was the era of the merchant princes, and Boston was drawing back toward the traditions of England.

It has never really drawn away again. Visiting Britons call it the most English of American cities, but its Anglican aspect dates not from its Puritan period or its Revolutionary period. It is English in a Regency sense, because the rise of the merchants with their stamping of their own tastes on the town coincided with the Regency in London. When dinners became an institution in Boston, no longer merely meals, they followed the pattern of the English dinners; and the sole survivals of simpler fare were the bean and the cod. Ale and cider yielded to Bordeaux wines and rare liqueurs. Pork was replaced by roast beef. The homely family meal of the Puritans passed away, and the brightly lighted dinner table surrounded by guests came into being.

The club life that took on the proportions of an epidemic in the London of Dr. Johnson's time and continued unabated through the Regency became a characteristic of Boston society, and remains so to this day. The *Transcript*, modeled on the London papers, started publication in the merchant prince era. Private schools, modeled on the British public schools, were founded. Great retail establishments developed, catering not to the mass of Bostonians but to the new aristocracy, and they have remained as unchanged as the Common in all but their physical equipment. There is a story that Messrs. S. S. Pierce and Company, purveyors of food and liquors to Beacon Hill and to the Brahmins who inhabited the Back Bay later, still have on file the favorite blends of coffee and tobacco of their first customers. . . . All this, it is true, was less representative of a newly rising culture than of a far-reaching and enduring change in a way of life. The simple necessities of living, spiced none too palatably by the intellectualism of the Puritans, were no longer enough; and a certain graciousness of living which bordered upon sensualism in its more limited sense was the substitute of the merchant princes.

The outward changes created by the era of commercial expansion throughout the valley southwest of Boston were not so happy. For all its economic limitations and despite its exacting toil, life in the towns and the country had achieved, during the quieter days before the factories came, an opulence that the partial industrializing of the valley did not have in its power to replace. Life was sordid and hard, and the youth who left the land to make quick money in the factories were bitterly disappointed. A family's cash income may have been two or three times what it had been before any of its members turned to the factories, but its standard of living was far below its earlier level, even if the family was not broken up altogether. And if the farm with its endless chain of chores from the rise of the sun to its setting had left little time for leisure, the long sunless days in the factories left as little energy when the workers walked the few rods to the corporation boardinghouses at the day's end.

The living habits of no region on earth can be changed radically within one generation without serious results. Consequently, the merchant princes soon found themselves faced with the responsibility of organizing charities to relieve conditions among the workers to which their own genius for trade had given rise. The charities of Massachusetts that have become venerable by today date from the early nineteenth century. Before that, cases of pauperism, owing to whatever causes, were scarce enough to be handled as individual items of business on the agenda of the town meetings. With the coming of the factories, the tough physical fiber of the Yankee was weakened, early sicknesses among women increased seriously, and orphaned children became so numerous that the commonwealth saw the necessity for assuming responsibility for them. The great public hospitals of Boston were founded, and smaller hospitals and almshouses were distributed throughout the valley. And the sad significance of this was that one group of people, among whom self-reliance had been a common trait for close to two centuries in the valley, was becoming dependent upon both the economic leadership and the charity of another.

Part Seven

Painters, Poets,
and Immigrants

19

Palettes

THE hard years of the Revolution and the period immediately following were not without their reward, although no miracle happened. Life along the Charles, when the yoke of the British exploitation of the colonies was removed, had undergone changes with the passing of the years. We have seen how a small aristocracy, headed by men like those who built the first bridges and later the merchant princes, arose to take the place of the exiled Tories. They were for the most part hardheaded, calculating men bent on the founding of great commercial dynasties and not much concerned with building a national culture or even a provincial culture. They had strong tribal feeling, however, which may have been an element in their dynasty building, for it was important that a man add ". . . and Son" to his business firm's name. It was this dynastic tendency that eventually exposed the new aristocracy to the arts, and it was first apparent in the almost wholesale rush to have family portraits painted and duly hung in the drawing rooms of the town and country mansions. No post-Revolutionary house was of any great consequence without at least one portrait in oils.

All this accounts for the fact that the first men to achieve a degree of lasting fame in the arts in the valley of the Charles were not writers or musicians, but painters. Gilbert Stuart, the leading American portrait painter of the eighteenth century, heard about the land-office business a painter could do in Massachusetts; so he brought his temperament and his talent to Boston and established himself as, by appointment, portraitist to the great of the self-conscious petty aristocracy. And he gave them a taste also of what it means to have a famous artist at large.

No man presents a more difficult problem of appraisal than Gilbert Stuart, for it is almost impossible to decide what he valued in life. He liked money, according to some evidence; according to others, he was almost completely indifferent to it. At times it appears that his painting meant the world to him for its own sake, but other things indicate that he merely regarded it as a way to make a living. Friends are usually of some importance in a man's life, but Stuart valued his snuff more highly. He was without roots, a drifter, a grouch, tactless, rude, and unfeeling. It was almost incidental to all this that he was an artist.

Stuart came to Boston with no intention of bowing down to the aristocracy that lured him here. He equipped himself with a system designed to make life as miserable as possible to the sitter. He was very demanding in time and more demanding in money. If possible, he insisted on receiving every cent of his fee in advance. In case he got it all, he took his time about starting the painting and spent all the money long before it was finished, when he was very apt to lose interest in it. If he was not paid in advance, or if the sitter gave him only a small retainer and a promise to pay the balance when the portrait was done, Stuart rushed through the work at high speed and then demanded twice the original fee before delivering the finished canvas.

One would think from this that what Gilbert Stuart was after was the almighty dollar, but such was not the case. Repeatedly he showed marked indifference to money. The Philadelphia Academy of Fine Arts offered him the prodigious sum of fifteen hundred dollars for a portrait of Washington, to say nothing of the honor of hanging it in the Academy. Stuart was so phlegmatic about it that he never bothered to answer the letter—even though he happened to need money badly at the time. The immortally great Florence Academy fared no better in its overtures to the master. A self-portrait of the artist was requested and commissioned by the Italian archcritics, but Stuart threw the letter aside and never gave it a second thought.

Stuart's chief pastime was baiting his sitters until he had either driven them away with insults or cowed them into silent submission. There was not an ounce of gallantry in Stuart's character. He used his tongue to insult his clients; and when it did not prove sufficiently effective, he used his brush also. One woman sitter, who had sat for him through long, tedious hours, whiled away the time with small talk to keep herself awake. When the ordeal was over, she approached Stuart's easel in profound gratitude that she had had the patience to pay the price for the rich privilege about to be given her. The poor woman's high hopes paled, however, when she saw the master's portrait of herself. He had painted her with her mouth opened as wide as a barn door.

"Mr. Stuart," she gasped, "you have painted me with my mouth open."

"Madam," the gracious master replied, "your mouth is always opened."

Such a malicious distortion of a hard-earned portrait was no temporary reprimand on the part of Stuart. A client either took the picture rendered by the master or it was sent up to the great Stuart attic, which overflowed with unfinished or willfully disfigured portraits. The lady who talked too much was fortunate to get away with any picture at all and equally fortunate that it had a no more unorthodox feature than a well-opened mouth. Once a woman, less talkative but more pointed in her remarks, arose from her final sitting, peered over the artist's shoulder at the picture and at once fell to criticizing his work. Stuart called upon St. James: "A man beholdeth his natural face in a glass," he quoted, "and goeth his way and straightway forgetteth what manner of man he was." He then rang for his servant and sent the portrait away to the garret and the subject home to her husband.

One suspects that the chief satisfaction Stuart derived from his work was catching and recording the personalities of his subjects. Whether he derived any such pleasure from it is immaterial, for that was his achievement and it was what placed him above such a popular artist as Copley. Perhaps, too, that was why he had no patience with some sitters. There is the story, which is certainly not apocryphal, of Stuart's rendering the portrait of a sitter who fell asleep with a pair of full-grown ass ears. The explanation is not too in-

volved: the slumbering fellow's countenance was entirely devoid of expression and the closest that Stuart
could come was the vacant visage of the ass.

It is a strange truth that the first of Boston's great
men in the arts—that is, the first to become a living tradition in the province—should be distinguished by his

Bohemian habits and curt manners. For that sort of
living has never flourished much along the Charles. For
all the region's alleged high standards of perfection in
literature or any other art, it was infinitely more eager
to welcome the indifferent and second-rate so long as
the practitioner was polite than the truly good and first-
rate when the practitioner happened to be sloppy and
careless in his way of living. Longfellow was a polite

man and a bad poet and he came from Maine; but he became the great poet of the Charles. Whitman was a rough fellow and a good poet and he came from Brooklyn; and literary Massachusetts was as ready to recognize his genuine merit as it would be now to concede that the state of Illinois is not made up one-third of unregenerate savages, one-third of stranded gold rushers, and one-third of cattle dealers with pearl-studded revolvers. The remarkable thing about Gilbert Stuart, then, is that he could come into the province with his atrocious manners and Bohemian ways and make his patrons like it.

Politeness, not so much in the sense of courtesy as in that of moderation and restraint, was, even as far back as Stuart's time, becoming the criterion of culture along the Charles. But Stuart smashed the ideal into a million pieces. He branded the habit of snuff-taking as "a pernicious, dirty, vile habit and like all bad habits to be carefully avoided"—and took a daily minimum of half a pound. When someone told him of the old Boston sea captain's habit ("I have always a nostril in reserve. When the right becomes callous after a few weeks' usage, I apply for comfort to the left; which, having had time to regain its sense of feeling, enjoys the blackguard until the right gains its senses."), Stuart counted the information the richest reward of his long habitation in these parts. He had painted the Adamses from the top of the list to the bottom and all the rest of the province's notables, he had mixed freely on his own terms with any group that attracted his attention, and he had breathed the rare Yankee ozone in spite of his snuff. But none of these things impressed him. The old captain's remark on taking snuff was probably the only thing he found worth remembering. "It's a great discovery," he exclaimed. "Strange that I should not have made it myself when I have been voyaging all my life in these channels."

Gilbert Stuart was an artist who lived near the Charles. An artist who lived with the Charles was Washington Allston, a native Southerner who first saw the river when he came to Harvard to study. As friendly as Stuart was antagonistic and as gentle as Stuart was savage, Allston went to Europe to study his art and, when he returned after the death of his young wife, left behind him a trail of friends from the poet Coleridge to lowly fruit vendors. In 1830 he built a studio cottage in a sparsely settled section of the north bank of the river, married again and lived out his years in peace, executing several minor commissions while he worked steadfastly on the great dream of his life, a huge Biblical painting to be called "The Feast of Belshazzar."

Nearly everyone who knew Allston was attracted to him by his extraordinary countenance. He had a mass of long white hair, which framed his pale face and seemed to accent the deep blue of his eyes. It was probably his eyes, set deep under his brow and looking out sadly and sympathetically at everything that passed, which first commanded the attention. There was something about those eyes that made people like him and trust him instinctively.

William Wetmore Story, the sculptor, wrote: "I used to see him when I was a boy at Cambridge, and always had the highest admiration for him, gazing at him with wonder, delighted whenever he came across my path and now and then being admitted to his studio where he delighted me with his conversation and his reminiscences of poets and artists whom he had known." Lowell wrote long, long paragraphs too, in praise of Allston, for he was an artist all the best people (as well as the worst) on both sides of the river loved. "The beautiful old man!" the poet said. "Here was a genius with no volcanic explosions (the mechanic result of vulgar gunpowder often), but lovely as a lapland night; not sought after nor worn in any cheap French fashion as a ribbon at the buttonhole, but so gentle, so retiring, that it seemed no more than an assured and emboldened modesty; here was ambition, undebased by rivalry and incapable of the sidelong look; and all these massed and harmonized together into a purity and depth of character, into a tone, which made the daily life of the man the greatest masterpiece of the artist."

Allston was thus approved by one who, for all his balking at much of his own heritage, expressed pretty clearly what this river valley expected of its artists. Let them be polite, gentle, restrained, moderate (all that Lowell could find wrong with Washington Allston was his habit of smoking cigars without pause, "a single incongruity" in his character). And let there be no volcanic explosions of the Stuart variety! Because Allston had all those desirable characteristics, the people on his side of the river always went to great pains to point out his studio to visiting friends, and the people from the other side of the river crossed and recrossed over John Hancock's bridge to wait upon the kindly old man and look at his paintings. Some of the new aristocracy even bought his paintings, departing from their custom of investing only in family portraits. They never cared much about them, to be sure, but there was an artist in their midst and they resolved to support him. Yet, as Lowell said, "As a race we care nothing about Art." So Washington Allston—he who had traveled in Italy, who was born in the warm South, and who was a follower of the richly sensuous Titian—withered and wilted on the bleak bank of the Charles.

As for the artist himself, he was quite happy. He knew what he wanted to do. He wanted to finish the great "Feast of Belshazzar" and then he would be content to go his way. But he came to the wrong corner of the globe to do it. Washington Allston liked the Titian glow of life, the richness of the Venetian school, warmth and color. Even if he had been able to keep the memory of all these things alive in the shadow of Harvard Hall, he could never have found sufficient models in Boston or its environs. The first ice had not chilled the river before his own warmth grew cold, and the Massachusetts frost touched him. He spent too much time writing bad poems and doing bad paintings that would be understood and appreciated by his neighbors. And he worked on Belshazzar spasmodically and amid interruptions. Though even the chill New England climate could not kill his love for that masterpiece for which he lived and dreamed, there were things in his environment beyond his ken that crippled him in its execution. This valley is rich in many things and productive of near greatness in many fields and of greatness in a few; but painting Biblical pictures after ye Italian manner is not among them.

Why, then, did Washington Allston come to live at a lonely spot on the banks of the Charles? He did not know exactly: it may have been because he identified the happy memories of college days with the place rather than the time of their enjoyment; or it may have been that, slender and empty as it was, the incipient culture in this region was at least an incipient culture; or it may have been merely that, since the death of his first wife, Europe was a torture to him and that he had more friends, the survivals of his Harvard days, here than anywhere else in America. It was without doubt a combination of all these reasons that led him and rooted him here. "A snug, commodious little mansion," he called his home on the river bank, "commanding a pleasant view of the adjacent country, taking in in a part of the river and a picturesque little pine wood, which used to be the favorite haunt of my younger days, to which I used to saunter after college hours and dream sometimes of poetry and sometimes of my art. These youthful associations have an indefinite charm, peculiarly pleasant to me at this time; they seem to bring together the earlier and later portions of my life, mingling them as it were into one, and imparting to the present some of that eloquent quiet of the past which my nature has always most loved."

From this, it will be seen that Allston was willing to part with much for the sake of old memories. He evolved a way of life here that satisfied him. It was leisurely, slow and easy. He never saw much of the morning and as a rule preferred night to the daytime. He went into his studio at around one o'clock and started his day's work, beginning with mixing paints and having previously fortified himself with a day's supply of cigars and a huge pitcher of water. He mixed his paints until one-thirty, when it was time to throw away the first cigar and light a new one. For a half hour, after the work of mixing paints, he sat back, serenely puffing his cigar and contemplating the easel before him. Then at two he rose, lit another cigar and went to work at his easel. This third cigar usually went out during his labors, and he just chewed at it, occasionally relighting it, until the sun set. Then he sat down again, lighted one more new cigar and contemplated his easel. He made an elaborate affair of dinner and occupied himself for three or four hours with it, after which he devoted another couple of hours to conversation. Then he went back to the studio and worked through the early hours of the morning. He liked wine and talk and bright colors and the Bible and poetry and cigars. He preferred the common people to the aristocracy, and the longest house guest he ever had was an inmate of the Cambridgeport Poor House. One night the Poor House burned down, and Allston, being fond of glowing colors, went out to see the fire. He came home with the old lady, whom he established in his own house.

Washington Allston was seized one summer day in 1843 with an inexplicable desire to get "The Feast of Belshazzar" done. He rose earlier than was his habit and set to work, forgetful even of his necessary cigars. The great painting had been hanging fire too long, and it was still far from completed. He worked at it all day and in the evening sat down for a well-deserved glass of wine and a cigar. He contemplated his easel for the last time, looked upon the unfinished Belshazzar, and then died. They buried him in the little churchyard a few rods from the river he loved and close by Christ Church.

The palettes of these two men, Stuart and Allston, were not those of geniuses approaching the stature of a Rembrandt van Ryn or of a Michelangelo Buonarroti. But they awakened the sons of the Puritans to the beauty of color and introduced a measure of it into the plainness of their lives. The Tories, those who fostered what there was of art in Massachusetts before the Revolution, had been gone since the departure of the British in 1776. Stuart and Allston, neither native to this region, came to take up where they had left off, and their work was one as much of enlightenment as of achievement. The people of this river valley, particularly surrounding the basin of the Charles, are lovers of art and of music. And no small debt for that is due to the two men, the roaring, snapping Stuart and the lovable, gentle Allston, for their coming here and practicing their craft amid surroundings far from congenial to their profession, however personally satisfying it may have been in Allston's case and however trying in Stuart's. Though his reputation is slighter now, Allston's was probably the richer gift. As Lowell said, he went to Europe with "a nature open on the southern side and brought it back so steeped in rich Italian sunshine that the east winds (whether physical or intellectual) of Boston and the dusts of Cambridgeport assailed it in vain."

20

Three Houses and Three Poets

Tory Row runs vaguely parallel to the Charles.
It begins a little west of Harvard Square, where the sons
of the Puritans begin to live, and it ends at Mount
Auburn cemetery, where the sons of the Puritans end
their lives. At one extreme of Tory Row is, suitably
enough, the Episcopal Theological Seminary, and the
Chapel of St. John. At the other extreme is the cemetery itself, which is richer in its accumulation of bones
and dust than Westminster Abbey. Between are proud
houses set far back from Brattle Street in the sedate
shade of old elms, and in bygone days conversation so
heavy with classical allusions that you could feel its
pressure in the street rolled out over the marshes of the
Charles on winter evenings until its polite, mellow rumble echoed through the drawing rooms of Beacon Hill
downstream and across the river. The great men, the
poets and the philosophers, had taken over Tory Row,
and what they lacked in fiber they made up in their
inheritance of the Tory politeness that once had ruled
their roosts.

Before the Revolution, Tory Row represented the
most gracious way of life that ever came into being
within sight of the river. The Cambridge Tories were

wealthy, refined in their tastes, and catholic in their pleasures. They built for themselves a church which outlasted the sectarian meetinghouses in the sheer physical dignity of its beauty, and which still stands, and they named it Christ Church as a pleasant departure from the numerical nomenclature that distinguished the others. They reared fine houses with great square rooms where they dined in simple state and listened to chamber concerts. They toasted his Majesty the king under brilliant chandeliers, they entertained the royal representatives, and they took steps to have a bishop of their own duly consecrated by the episcopate of the Church of England. Then the Revolution came. Estates were confiscated left and right, and the Tories were run out of their homes into exile.

Right in the midst of this Tory village, John Vassall, the heir to a fortune amassed in the West Indies trade, built his house in 1759. He had probably the best site on all Tory Row, for his house faced the Charles and was separated from it only by a wide green meadow. Vassall was but two years out of Harvard when he built his mansion, and he expected to live there in comfortable security for the rest of his days. But he was one of the most stubborn of the loyalists, and when 1775 came John Vassall went. His family motto had been, from time immemorial, "Saepe pro rege, semper pro republica." So fiercely loyal was John Vassall that he would not use the motto at all; he held that it was disrespectful and compromising to the king. John Vassall was not often for the king and always for the state. He was always for the king, and the state did not matter. A mob visited his mansion one night, after kings had become unpopular, and Vassall was sent packing to England via Halifax, whence he never returned.

After Vassall's departure, the provincial government, with quaint informality, took his house and turned it over to the use of George Washington, who came to Cambridge after Bunker Hill to weld the motley assortment of militia into an army. Washington lived there during the British occupation of Boston, treating the mansion with respect and upholding its traditions. His wife insisted on reopening Christ Church, in spite of its association with the Church of England, and the Cambridge gentry who had run out the loyalists and were bent on using their church for a barracks found themselves in the awkward position of having a commander in chief who himself was a strong adherent of the loyalist church. With Mrs. Washington issuing orders and the general established in the Vassall mansion, Tory Row, which might well have been annihilated during the early months of the Revolution, survived.

In April, 1776, after the British had evacuated Boston, Washington and his retinue left Cambridge to meet them elsewhere. The Massachusetts government finally confiscated the mansion and sold it for about ten thousand dollars in 1781 to a Newburyport pirate named Nathaniel Tracy, who had made a fortune by sailing as a privateer. Tracy had more money than was good for him and entertained lavishly in the Tory Row mansion until 1786, when the house passed into the hands of an even richer owner, Thomas Russell, Esquire, the man who gave the wine to christen the *Constitution*. Russell used the house for a summer residence, living in Boston during the winter. Russell was so rich that he allegedly had for breakfast one morning a sandwich consisting of two slices of bread and a hundred-dollar bill. He kept the house for six years, and then Mr. Andrew Craigie, the man who had built the bridge and bought up all the land on the north bank of the Charles downstream, purchased the mansion.

Mr. Craigie was one of the beacon lights of this valley. His house had been occupied by Washington and it was to be occupied by Longfellow. But even today no one refers to the mansion at 105 Brattle Street as either "Washington's Headquarters" or "Longfellow's House." It is always the Craigie House, and both the general and the poet seem incidental, strangers who wandered into Andrew Craigie's place.

One of the shrewdest Yankees in history, Mr. Craigie was an apothecary of very moderate wealth at the beginning of the Revolution, and he emerged from the war as one of the richest men in the commonwealth. He was apothecary general of the Continental Army and made so much money that he went around buying up the promises of the shaky government which he confidently believed would someday be able to meet them. And he was right. By the time the war was over, the heaviest debtor of the new government was Andrew Craigie, the apothecary. Unlike most shrewd Yankees, Craigie was as willing to part with his money as to get it. So he made certain changes at Craigie House. He erected a large ell, so that he could have a bigger kitchen to prepare food in, and enlarged and glorified the great dining room, so that he would have more space to eat it in. He also built a greenhouse east of the mansion and an icehouse close by. This latter business was evocative of a great deal of adverse criticism in Cambridge, for the Tories had gone now and Puritanism reaffirmed itself. Prophecies were freely made that Mr. Craigie would come to grief for his presumption in attempting to match God by growing flowers in his greenhouse in winter, when God meant there to be no flowers, and for storing ice in his icehouse for the summer, when God meant there to be no ice. Craigie was not susceptible to criticism, however, and he answered the charges by sending a communication to his Philadelphia agents, in which he asked them to get prices quoted on the erection of a private brewery. And he had china imported, furniture built to particular specifications, carpets especially woven, maps drawn and prints searched out to adorn his mansion. He then laid down a store of venerable wines and was ready to live.

Andrew Craigie lived a high life there in his mansion overlooking the river. He had so many guests that he was constantly sending emergency orders to England for more of his privately designed china. He bought horses whenever it pleased him. He bought carriages, "riding chairs," and fancy sleighs until his coach house overflowed. He imported fowl from Philadelphia, which served as his chicken coop. He imported a wife from Nantucket, taking advantage of the absence of the girl's poor fiancé, who had gone to sea for the express purpose of making enough money to marry her. Mr. Craigie had been living a lordly bachelor's life before that and apparently he was irresistible.

As a matter of fact, Mr. Craigie had the distinction of being instrumental in breaking two engagements in one day. He gave a lavish garden party, and all the fashionable world of Boston went across the river to see for themselves what the extravagant bachelor's establishment was like. It was a warm and beautiful day; Craigie had spared neither money nor pains in arranging the entertainment; and the cook had outdone himself in preparing the refreshment. Mr. Craigie strolled about his lawns in the wake of a pair of lively-looking girls when he was delayed by a close friend. "Craigie," the friend said, "what can man desire that you have not got? Here are riches, friends, a scene of enchantment—and you the master of them all!" Craigie registered as wistful an expression as is possible in an apothecary prince and sighed. "I am the most miserable of men," he said. "If you doubt it, you shall know my secret. Do you see those two young ladies just turning down the walk? Well, they are both engaged, and with one of them I am desperately in love."

Craigie's friend soon disappeared among the guests in the garden. In a few days he returned to Craigie House to wait upon the master. "Craigie," he shouted in high excitement, "I have come to tell you glorious news! The coast is clear! Miss Foster has broken off her engagement."

"What the deuce is that to me?" Craigie snapped.

"Good heavens, man," his friend answered, "don't you remember telling me that you were desperately in love with one of the young ladies you pointed out at the garden party?"

"To be sure," Craigie said. "But unfortunately I referred to the other young lady."

The friend intended to make amends and somehow did, for he was back again in due time with the astonishing news that the other young lady, daughter of the Reverend Bezaliel Shaw of Nantucket, had also broken her engagement. Her parents were ambitious for her, and the father had intervened in her romance with a young Southerner who had been studying under him as a boarding student. The minister shipped the student back to the South and cleared the way for Mr. Craigie. Miss Shaw could not do much about it. Aside from his money, Craigie was no magnet to women of her young age. He was described as "a huge man, heavy and dull; and evidently looks upon his career as the high lyric of Nathaniel Tracy's [the earlier privateer owner of the mansion] muddled into tough prose." But the young Mrs. Craigie lived a happy enough life with him until her young Southerner sent her a letter out of the blue one day to tell her that his father had died and that he was coming north to marry her, assuming that she had been as faithful to their love as he had been. The letter threw poor Mrs. Craigie into deep regret. She lived in the same house with her husband and aided in the management of the household, but she kept entirely to herself forever after. When Craigie died, she fired ten of the servants, moved into the back part of the house and leased the remainder.

But Craigie did not die for a long time. First he wanted to make more money. He was entertaining such celebrities as Talleyrand, Prince Edward, the father of Victoria, and visiting notables to Harvard College. So Craigie started to buy up all that land down near the river mouth at Lechmere Point. He bought acre after acre secretly, so that no one would know who was behind the boom and try to edge into it. For twelve years Craigie bought land, planning secretly to develop "The Pint" into a thriving trade center when he got around to unloading the property. He built the bridge, as we have seen, in 1809. Then he started to sell his property.

But his plans miscarried. In spite of his bridge and his reputation for business acumen, no one bought his lots. In three years he sold only ten. In desperation he gave Middlesex County land for a courthouse and jail, which he offered to build at an expense of twenty-four thousand dollars, just for the sake of starting some activity in his deserted acres. But even that gesture did not succeed, and Mr. Craigie found himself in very embarrassing circumstances. His resources gone, he lost everything but Craigie House, to which he clung stubbornly long after he could afford to finance it. "Mr. Craigie," a visitor of those latter days said once, "I should think you could lose yourself in all this spaciousness." And Mr. Craigie replied, "I have lost myself in it."

The development at the Pint, with its nice new courthouse and jail, looked like a vacant lot full of unsold Christmas trees on the Feast of Stephen. "I can remember in my boyhood the scanty population of the lower port," wrote John, the brother of Oliver Wendell Holmes, "outside of the main street, with the brick blocks planted here and there in the solitude, like seed for new settlements. Concord Turnpike and Craigie's Road, also, each offered a retreat to which the austere recluse, shunning the face of man, might retire with no fear of intrusion. The toll which was to repay the building was found represented only by the funeral knell of departed funds."

And the chief mourner was Andrew Craigie. The sheriff, operating from the courthouse that Craigie had built for the county, dogged his steps wherever he went.

Soon Craigie had to shut himself up in his mansion to keep beyond a warrant. He used to disappear from Monday through Saturday of every week. But on Sunday, immune to any sheriff under the law, he marched grandly from Craigie House to Christ Church. Then he returned to spend the rest of the day in the blessed out of doors, sunning himself in the garden. But through the weekdays, wrote Holmes, from his window he "looked with longing eyes at the free and solvent Charles carrying his punctual dues to Ocean."

On a September day in 1819, Andrew Craigie, the great man of Cambridge, died. A half dozen people attended his funeral, and those days when Craigie House was overflowing with princes and diplomats and the great of the world were forgotten. Speculator, bon vivant and lover of life, Mr. Craigie had maintained his inner mansion in relative splendor until his death. But afterward the now practical and once romantic widow scaled her way of living down sharply. She fired ten of Craigie's twelve servants and leased the greater part of her house to genteel roomers from Harvard. She herself lived a quiet life among her books, her plants, and her singing birds in the back parlor. Cambridge did not approve much of her reading. It was whispered in dreadful confidence that she was never beyond an arm's length of Voltaire and that Spinoza was one of her enthusiasms. But the widow Craigie let the rest of the world go by and stuck to her books. Draped in a gray silk gown and wearing a white turban, she sat at her window and read Voltaire to her heart's content. James Russell Lowell, who lived down the street a few paces, said, "I used to wonder, as I saw her sitting always alone at her accustomed window, whether she were ever visited by the reproachful shade of him who had died broken-hearted for her in her radiant youth."

Mrs. Craigie had lived in her back rooms with Voltaire for eighteen years when a Harvard instructor approached the house in the summer of 1837 in quest of

rooms. Longfellow, a young widower, had been in the house but once, to visit a law student, and having glimpsed the "waters of the Charles gleaming in the meadows" through the slits in the closed blinds, he went away full of the hope that one day he should live there. Longfellow was a romantic and a dreamer, and he was never happy unless within sight of moving waters. Accordingly, when his law school friend gave up his quarters at Craigie House, the poet made up his mind to get them.

Mrs. Craigie, ever since receiving that letter from her lost suitor, had been on the defensive. So when young Longfellow, polite as he always was, knocked at her door and inquired about the vacant rooms, Mrs. Craigie snapped that he could not have them. She was sick and tired of students in the house, and that was all there was to it. Then Longfellow explained that he was an instructor and the author, to boot, of *Outre-Mer*. Mrs. Craigie capitulated. "She then took me all over the house and showed me every room in it, saying, as we went into each, that I could not have that one. She finally consented to my taking the rooms mentioned above, on condition that the door leading into the back entry should be locked on the outside." Mrs. Craigie was through with romance.

The house was otherwise occupied that year by a young Southerner, who was a friend of Mrs. Craigie's and whiled away the hours playing on a flute. "Like other piping birds," wrote Longfellow, he disappeared with the first snows. Mrs. Craigie had also a couple living there, a gardener and his wife. The latter acted as cook and housemaid. The gardener was a small, humble man, and his wife was a huge, belligerent woman who was always challenging Longfellow on theological grounds and overcharging him for his meals. No one else lived in Craigie House.

"The winter was a rather solitary one," Longfellow wrote, "and the house very still. I used to hear Mrs. Craigie go down to breakfast at nine or ten in the morning and go up to bed at eleven at night. During the day she seldom left the parlor, where she sat reading the newspapers and the magazines—occasionally a volume of Voltaire. She read also the English Annuals, of which she had a large collection. Occasionally, the sound of voices announced a visitor; and she sometimes enlivened the long evenings with a half-forgotten tune upon an old piano-forte."

Longfellow was content with his quarters. He liked physical comfort and an atmosphere of peace, and he got both at Craigie House. He could see the river from his window, and his imagination could float along with it. The only thing that disturbed him was Mrs. Craigie's indifference to the cankerworms on the elm trees. Craigie House was surrounded by tall and graceful elms, which since Craigie's death had been eaten by the cankerworms. The latter, when they got through eating the trees, used to drop down in sheets on the house and lawns. But Mrs. Craigie just sat by her open window and let the little worms crawl all over her white turban. When the poet, concerned over the elms, asked her why she did not do something to protect her trees, she said, "Why, sir, they are our fellow worms; they have as good a right to live as we have."

Mrs. Craigie outlived her husband by twenty-two years. In that time she never went to Christ Church, and she never entertained at Craigie House. She told Longfellow that she preferred to conduct her relations with God direct; she would have no mediator. She liked birds and cats and flowers and worms. She knew when she was about to die and would have no physician. She hustled about Craigie House, burning all the papers relating to her lost lover, and then took to her bed. Longfellow came to her room, but she advised him strongly against it. "You'll never be married again, because you see how ugly an old woman looks in bed." Longfellow gave her some counteradvice. He suggested that she have a doctor in quick time. Each neglected the advice of the other, for Mrs. Craigie would have no doctor at this late stage. Her system, she said, was not "adapted to medicine." And within twenty-four hours she died.

Joseph E. Worcester, the lexicographer, took the house for the following year, and Longfellow stayed on in his rooms. In 1843, Longfellow married again, after eight years of loneliness to which his gregarious spirit could never adjust itself. Nathan Appleton, his new father-in-law, bought Craigie House and the five-acre meadow separating it from the river and presented it to the Longfellows. And there Longfellow lived out his days. His life was pleasant for the most part and serene; for though personal tragedy within his home did not pass him by, it left him unscarred. As for the outer world, it did not bother Longfellow in the least. Perhaps his only touch with reality was the river that flowed past his door. For the rest, it was always Spain and the lovely Germany of old Heidelberg, Dante and Norse poetry, and kindred remote things that were close to Longfellow. No man who wrote poetry in that time separated himself more cleanly from the world in which he lived than did the poet within the high, thick walls of Craigie House.

There was something ever childlike about Longfellow; perhaps it was in the way he set his mind so free, perhaps in the way he accepted personal sorrows with calm resignation, or perhaps in the way, while the rest of the nation was in the throes of great political struggles, he found importance in simple legends, boyish dreams, an open fire, the river flowing by him on its way to the sea. He never liked twilight, which is understandable, for in no place in the world does twilight have such a melancholy character and vest itself in such sad grayness as in Cambridge during the autumn and winter. Longfellow would sit by the fire in his study and write long letters to George W. Greene in Rome, where he wished himself to be, until the night came.

Lacking the profound mind of Emerson, the quick wit of Holmes, and the poetic mind of Lowell, Longfellow's quiet nature responded more readily to the little world in which he sequestered himself than did any of theirs. His house meant more to him, his books more, and that meadow and the river more. The great ideas of all time, the great episodes of history, and the great new thought formulated in his own corner of the world meant little to him. He was like a child in a roomful of adults as he lived in nineteenth century Cambridge. Though he was a professor of modern languages, he knew little of literary criticism. Though he was a translator of Dante, he never really understood great poetry. Though he wrote poetry for years, he never advanced far beyond his initial efforts. Yet he was content, and he probably knew his limitations. Gentle, polite and kindly, he wrote his verses in peace and trusted the world would like them. The world did, and whether it was justified did not much concern him.

He was the Poet of the Charles, and he loved the river. It was his companion and his teacher, his escape and his frequent goal. He liked to walk along its banks or linger over its waters on a bridge. Certainly he was one of those to whom the river had brought peace;

and though it collapsed right in the middle to doggerel, his poem "To the River Charles" tells much of his feeling toward the stream:

> Thou hast been a generous giver:
> I can give thee but a song.

Hostile critics might add, "And an indifferent song at that." But at least it was sincere.

His journals and letters tell more. Although he did not recognize it as such, he perceived a likeness in the waters to his own verses, as he stood on the bridge after seeing *King Lear* performed. Ice cakes in the current were dissolving as they came in contact with the salty water of the flood tide. Longfellow heard "a low and musical sound, a gentle simmering"—which was exactly what his poetry was. Longfellow was always standing on the bridge at midnight. He came upon Jared Sparks and William H. Prescott, the historians, there one night, and confessed perhaps his own failing when he said, "Prescott was brimful of his book; glorious in young fame. He is a striking example of what perseverance and concentration will accomplish." Longfellow could neither persevere nor concentrate. He was always restless, always too unconcerned to do anything really well, always too much the dreamer. "The blue river runs in front, and the wind roars loud in the trees, and it is all spring-like . . . But I think spring a most restless season. I cannot possibly sit still."

But it was not seasonal. It was the same in the winter. If Longfellow was not dreaming, he was walking up and down the riverbank. It was in December that he wrote, "I like to go to the mouth of the Charles and see the tide-waters spreading out sea-like, flashing and freshening the air. Then I walk with the sun at my back; and when he sets, return with all the glory full upon me."

That was Henry Wadsworth Longfellow, professor and poet. If he had wanted to, he might have schooled himself to be a great scholar. But he was content to live his life calmly and easily and write his simple verses. He was elevated to great fame through the sheer partiality of the people for indifferent poetry; but if freedom was still the goal of each individual who lived in this river valley, Longfellow's life was a noble success. His spirit was free, and his heart was happy even as it hungered. "The glimmer of golden leaves in the sunshine; the lilac hedge shot wtih the crimson creeper; the river writing its silver S in the meadow; everything without full of loveliness. But within me the hunger, the famine of the heart!" Yet Longfellow's life was, measured by most standards, the happiest of any man's in this valley. He was happy in his work, happy in his home, and happy in his heart. It is no wonder that the children of Cambridge and the world loved him, for he was in sober truth one of them until the end. Wrote Lowell, who was a much better poet:

I need not praise the sweetness of his song,
    Where limpid verse to limpid verse succeeds
Smooth as our Charles, when, fearing lest he wrong
The new moon's mirrored skiff, he slides along,
    Full without noise, and whispers in his reeds.

Down the Old Road to Watertown, some yards from the Craigie House and nearly at the end of Tory

Row, Thomas Oliver built a palatial home in which
to start married life with the daughter of Colonel John
Vassall. Oliver was the son of a West Indies merchant
and a good loyalist. He was lieutenant governor of the
province and was rewarded for his loyalty by George III
with an appointment as president of the Council. Since
the patriots contended that members of the Council
should be elected and not appointed, Mr. Oliver was as
popular as a freethinking Republican would be in the
Cathedral of St. Philip, Atlanta. Accordingly, several
hundred provincials surrounded his house one September morning in 1774, and forthwith demanded his resignation. They had the resignation all written out and
merely wanted Thomas Oliver's signature. Oliver talked
with them, promised that he would do what he could
to get the governor to stop the troops' marches to Cambridge, and was relieved to see them leave.

But the troops marched again that same day, and
in the afternoon the crowd once more visited Oliver's
house on the edge of the river. Oliver went to his car-
riage, but four thousand people had surrounded his
house and there was no escape. Shouting threats of his
signature or his blood, they forced him to sign the
resignation, to which he added the following message:

"My house at Cambridge being surrounded by
four thousand people, in compliance with their commands, I sign my name, Thomas Oliver."

Oliver left the house among the elms on the river
on that same day, never to return. His house was confiscated by the patriots. After the Battle of Concord
Bridge, when Benedict Arnold brought up his company
from Connecticut, they were given quarters at Oliver's
house. Then when Bunker Hill left the colonials with

some wounded, the house was converted into a hospital. When the Revolution was over, the commonwealth sold the house and ninety-six acres along the river edge to Arthur Cabot, who sold it in turn to Elbridge Gerry, vice-president from 1813 to 1814, when he died. Gerry was extremely unpopular on Tory Row for his political shenanigans, which are still periodically denounced as "gerrymandering." Four years after that statesman's unlamented passing, the Reverend Charles Lowell, of the West Church in Boston, bought the house for a permanent home. And there James Russell Lowell, the youngest of six children, was born on Washington's Birthday in 1819.

Much of what Lowell was he expressed in his statement: "I have but one home in America, and that is the house where I was born and where, if it shall please God, I hope to die. I shouldn't be happy anywhere else." That was provincialism, but Lowell was a provincialist. Elmwood, as he called his house by the river, was his introduction to the world. The acres bordering the wilderness were full of oaks and elms, flowers and birds, grasses and shrubbery. He explored it carefully in his youth, and early in his life nature took on great meaning to him. He has been blamed by migrant critics of today for his insistence on extracting a moral lesson from the small things of nature. But he was a part of his times and his region, and moralizing was in turn a huge part of both. What is important is not that Lowell was a moralist in his poetry, for all poets worth much are moralists of one sort or another, but that his moralizing was warm and genuine.

Had Lowell never met a Watertown farmer's daughter, he might have taken a leaf from Longfellow's book, although he would inevitably have written better poetry for the simple reason that he had deeper poetic feeling, and let his life go at that. He was never anxious to concern himself with the world outside his beloved Elmwood. Having been graduated from Harvard, he studied law and left it. He took a position in the business world and left it. Then he returned to law again, and again he left it. "I don't know what to do with myself," he confessed; and later added, "I even begin to doubt whether I was made for anything in particular but to loiter through life and then become manure." The trouble was, of course, that if he was destined to anything "in particular" it was to be a poet. Shut up in a business house or poring over dusty lawbooks, he was bound to be miserable. He was by nature a potential poet. A dandelion was more important to him than law; the turn of the river more significant than monetary figures; men were more precious to him than their institutions. "I go out sometimes with my heart so full of yearning toward my fellows," he wrote, "that the indifferent look with which even entire strangers pass me brings tears to my eyes."

He was sensitive to a point that no Puritan would have countenanced in himself. As Longfellow had contemplated flinging himself from a bridge into the Charles when it had seemed he could bear no more sorrow, Lowell at twenty pressed a pistol to his forehead and confessed that only a lack of physical courage stopped him from pulling the trigger. He was retiring and at times despaired of the world at large. He was, in short, the very man to dodge all the weight of the world's problems (and it was to be heavy before his life was done) and shut himself up within the solid walls of Elmwood. But Abijah White, "the most perfect specimen of a bluff, honest, hospitable country squire you can possibly imagine," had chanced to send his son to Harvard in Lowell's class, and through him Lowell met Maria White.

Maria White supplemented the quiet, almost shy personality of Lowell perfectly. She concerned herself militantly with the life of the nation, and she gave Lowell the incentive to express himself. He became one of the first true poets of America, in that he was one of the first to represent the voice of humanity in this country. The little world of Elmwood paled for a while, and Lowell wrote of his people and for his people. He stood out against imperialism and slavery. He repudiated his Federalist heritage. There were serious fears in Cambridge that young Lowell was on the road to perdition; but before the Civil War his wife died, and the poet entered into a long period of lethargy. The body of Lowell's works, therefore, are a strange mixture of quiet pastorals, strong hymns, militant in their plea for freedom and humanity, and then trifles. He gave expression to the salty New England character of Hosea Biglow; he gave expression to the New England abolitionist spirit; and he gave expression to himself. His poetry, to a great extent, gave this valley a new type of freedom, for Lowell—though he may have regretted it in old age—revolted against the chilly element of his heritage and set poetry on the way to being an art instead of an artifice. And he did more than any of his fellows to make the Puritan's son take himself with less dreadful seriousness than was his wont.

"Bostonians (I am not a Bostonian)," he wrote,

"seem to have two notions of hospitality—a dinner with people you never saw before nor never wish to see again and a drive in Mount Auburn cemetery, where you will see the worst man can do in the way of disfiguring nature. Your memory of the dinner is expected to reconcile you to the prospect of the graveyard." Lowell himself, if his poetry is not the greatest in the language, did much to release his art from two kindred ordeals: the barren, repetitious business of "making" poetry and the empty pastime of "fashioning" poetry.

"Yankee Jont" was the nickname of Jonathan Hastings, who lived in a gambrel-roofed house on Cambridge Common. Yankee Jont was the steward of Harvard College and a patriot of no mixed sentiments. Consequently, when the British were occupying Boston and it became unhealthy for the Committe of Safety to meet there, Yankee Jont invited them to hold their sessions in his house. When affairs grew even more serious, he went the whole way and turned the entire house over to the use of the provincial army. General Ward used it as his headquarters, and Benedict Arnold was commissioned a colonel there.

Yankee Jont took all this in his stride and probably housed himself in the barn with no ill grace, for he had always been a hospitable man. There was once a poor beggar in Cambridge named William Marcy, a man who was pushed around a good deal. No one wanted him on his property, and the unfortunate Marcy was homeless. So Yankee Jont put him up in his own barn. Nevertheless, the selectmen passed the following order in 1770: "Voted, to warn out of the town William Marcy, a man of very poor circumstances; he for some time hath lodged in Steward Hastings' barn; the Steward paying the charges." Apparently neither William Marcy nor Steward Hastings paid any attention to this enactment, for William Marcy was still around in the historic year 1775, when he died a hero's death.

William Marcy was a man of somewhat undeveloped mental equipment, and his hobby was sitting on the fence watching the British troops make their periodic exercise marches to Cambridge. Marcy loved a parade; it excited him and made him happy. When the British troops came tearing through Cambridge at the reception end of Middlesex muskets, therefore, happy Marcy assumed that the red-coated soldiers were out on parade again. So he ran up to his pet fence and sat down to enjoy the show. He was transported with delight when he saw that not only was there an unexpected parade but also a sham fight. Nothing could move Marcy from enjoying the sight. When the British got within shooting distance, however, one of them mistook harmless Marcy for another of the ubiquitous minutemen and shot him dead. Marcy toppled off his perch on the fence. A century later the City of Cambridge erected a monument over him, in common with five others who fell that day. It immortalized William Marcy for dying "in defence of the Liberty of the People." "O, what a glorious morning is this!" it added.

After a post-Revolutionary interlude as the home of a humdrum professor of Hebrew, the title "Hastings House" passed from the gambrel-roofed dwelling and it became the "Parsonage" when the Reverend Abiel Holmes bought it. A spindle-legged little boy with a tiny body and a tinier head was romping about the house within a few years, and Oliver Wendell Holmes was on his way as the god of the Brahmins. He trooped his playmates through the house, showed them the diamond-scratched names of Revolutionary heroes on the windowpanes, fought the Battle of Bunker Hill over again with apples stolen from the pastoral study closet, and had terrible nightmares in the ghost-infested house. Then he grew up to graduate from Harvard and to write poems at the drop of a hat and essays at the drop of a pun. More properly he did not write his poetry, but—despite the example of the younger Lowell—fashioned it. If anyone wanted a poem to celebrate an occasion, he went around to Dr. Holmes, who was always willing to oblige. He was probably the worst poet of all those who lived within sight of the Charles, but it did not bother him much. He did his bit in spite of it. Lowell's *Biglow Papers* made the sons of Puritans smile. Holmes achieved the impossible and made them laugh out loud.

So far as the River Charles was concerned, it was merely one more facet in the doctor's talent for enjoying life. When he returned to Boston after two years of teaching in Hanover, he established himself in a house overlooking the river, where he maintained a "fleet" of various sized rowboats. Rowing, like writing, was one of Holmes's successful hobbies. He had a fiddle too, and liked to practice on it with horrible scraping sounds in the privacy of his study overlooking the river, but he never advanced far with it. He also tried photography, with no happier results. But he was a master oarsman.

He always had at least three boats moored at his back door. "A small flat-bottomed skiff of the shape of a flat-iron, kept mainly to lend to boys. A fancy dory for two pairs of sculls, in which I sometimes go out with my young folks. My own particular water-sulky, a 'skeleton' or 'shell' race-boat, 22 ft. long, with huge outriggers, which boat I pull with 10 ft. sculls,— alone, of course, for it holds but one and tips him out if he does not mind what he is about."

It was in the latter shell that the wiry, Lilliputian professor of anatomy skimmed up and down the river. He used to linger under bridges, dodge around schooners, and make a nuisance of himself in the Navy Yard. And he liked to fight against the rip tide until he had to slump in his chair as soon as he reached home. If he had had his way, moreover, the river basin would have been thick with boats, and he would have been surprised if the country would not be better off if all the relics haunting the Athenaeum haunted the river instead. "I am satisfied that such a set of black-coated, stiff-jointed, soft-muscled, paste-complexioned youths as we can boast in our Atlantic cities never before sprang from loins of Anglo-Saxon lineage."

It meant nothing that many who sprang therefrom were bent on more serious business. Holmes himself had hit upon a happy combination of pleasure and usefulness, and he had little patience for those who did not follow in his train. He was the high priest of the polished people of his times. As such, albeit in jest, he felt called upon to point the way for them. And that was the way: be polite and witty, useful and happy, superficial and polished. Perhaps his good-natured, sparkling ghost comes back to haunt his favorite riverbank today. If so, it might confront other medical professors who have done much with the pen. Dr.

Merrill Moore is one such, and a far better poet than Holmes. And another was the rich, calm, and truly great mind of Hans Zinsser, who was a far more opulent writer of prose.

21

The Annals of Mike O'Shea

U P to the era of the merchant princes there was little new blood among the inhabitants of the river valley, and Massachusetts was the most homogeneous of the states that formed the new republic. The reason for this was, of course, that a century and a half was not enough to dispel the notion that the colony was the home of the elect. With the sole exception of a little band of French Huguenot refugees, therefore, none but English immigrants were admitted to the colony; even the Huguenots were here for half a century before they were naturalized.

From the beginning, however, there was one country from which immigrants seeped into the colony despite the vigilance of the General Court. And that was Ireland, which finally took over the General Court itself.

Apparently the first of the Irish began to trickle into the sacred precincts as early as the first quarter of the eighteenth century, for the General Court took official cognizance of them in 1720, chastising them for "presuming to make a settlement" and promising to prosecute them as trespassers if they did not get out within six or seven months. But the Irish had a genius for politics that left the General Court far behind, and they must have talked themselves out of any prosecution, for there were nearly four thousand of them here by the time political parties in the new Union were ready to function. Excepting those from Great Britain, they thenceforth led all the foreign-born of Massachusetts in numerical strength in every census. They led also in political strength, but not until they had adjusted themselves.

Before the merchant princes' day, nevertheless, the Irish had been regarded by the posterity of the founding fathers as a wild race, and they were frequently referred to as "the wild Irish" even in official records. The Irish didn't bother to revolt. They were used to that sort of thing and they merely bided their time. Then in the second quarter of the nineteenth century, their time came. The factories needed hands, and there were thousands of Irish who, as always, found it desirable to get out of Ireland. The result was a veritable swarm of Irish immigrants during the thirty-five years that preceded the Civil War. And it was they who settled themselves so permanently and comfortably, completely unmoved, beyond reciprocal ravings, by the condescending attitude of the natives.

What the Irish were mainly in search of was a degree of economic security and a place where they could assert themselves. Thus, although most of them were from peasant stock, they settled in the towns and cities and rallied around the Democratic party. They came as empty handed of goods as of plans. But they lost no time in sensing the situation: they knew that to prevail against the natives they would have to cling together, settle in the cities and towns and push themselves forward relentlessly.

Mike O'Shea, the typical Massachusetts Irish immigrant, probably looked too often upon his father's back, bent from digging potatoes from the old sod, not to resolve that as soon as he saved up enough money he would sail for America to escape a kindred fate. By 1840, when he had enough cash tied up in a sock, he boarded one of the ships that were bringing the Irish over in herds and landed at Boston. Boston was the landing place of the Irish not because they had any partiality for the city or because it was the nearest port to their ultimate destinations. As a matter of fact, Mike O'Shea did not know anything about Boston except that it was the first port the ship touched in America and therefore the least expensive place to which to buy passage. Nor did he have any ultimate destination. Once in America, he drifted around to the nearest factory and told the foreman that he wanted a job. So Mike settled down in Boston or in one of the factory towns near by and went to work bending his back over a machine or a bench instead of over the potato fields as at home. He was probably disappointed by his low status in the promised land, but he was resigned about it for a little while and just waited.

Mike O'Shea could not be in his new home long without discovering that there were quite a few others just like him, with some female counterparts thrown in for good measure. As a consequence, he and his peers, indulging a craving for organization that they have not yet satiated, promptly organized themselves into a social club. The function of the social club was to take Mike O'Shea's mind off his relatively poor estate. He had no money, no more influence than he had had at home, and no particularly promising future. But he refused to weep into his beer, and joined a social club instead. Within the club he could argue and engage in an occasional fist fight. Outside the whole club could be used as a defiant weapon against the ostracism which

the natives tacitly agreed was the best treatment for the Irish.

The early Irish clubs were full of Mike O'Sheas: young immigrants of peasant stock who dreamed of liberating themselves from the yoke of poverty and social inferiority that had weighed down their fathers. But they rarely achieved much more for themselves on coming to the new land, and the young dreams did not last long. Mike O'Shea sought out a likely lass from among the army of Irish housemaids who worked in Boston and turned his mind to finding a comfortable rut in which to settle for the rest of his days. And Mike did. The tenement, previously unknown, came into being, and Mike found a flat for his colleen and himself.

The years and the days gradually took on a pattern for Mike O'Shea. He drank his mug of ale every night and two on Saturdays; he turned over his pay to his wife, who gave a respectable sum to the mission priest who followed the mass immigration of Irish to these shores. He argued politics, about which he knew very little, with his bosom friends, cursing them roundly for being "thickheaded Irishmen." He went to mass once a week, and worked six days a week, cursing his boss and the owners and the material that passed through his hands. He thus continued unbroken the tradition of picturesque expletives that had begun with the pious but alarmingly explosive utterances of the Puritans themselves. Mike O'Shea and his friends, however, could curse steadily without resorting to repetition, and they were always finding something to curse about.

Mike never advanced his lot very far and, aside from the material value of his man power as a worker, his main contribution to his world was his progeny, of which he had many. He did not attempt to exercise much influence over them, for poor Mike always felt inferior and left their training pretty much to his wife and the parish priest. He went his own way, growing white and stooped from the years of hard work, drinking an occasional glass too many at the wake of a friend, where local politics made the air heavy with arguments over the indifferent body of the blessed departed, and getting sentimental about the old sod that he had so gladly left in his youth. And old Mike probably died with all his family around him and a pang for what might have been had he only had a job on the horse cars or the police force.

But the second Mike O'Shea carried on, coming to maturity after the close of the Civil War. He inherited his father's taste for politics and political debate, but he got further with them. He found himself a better job than his father's, and he probably realized the latter's ambition by getting on the police force. There he achieved an independence beyond any that his father had possessed, and he was able to pick a likely lass from the mass of Irish housemaids who served the prosperous Yankee homes as their mothers had, and he raised a family as large as his father's, thereby giving the Irish a strength of numbers that the natives might well view with alarm. But the pattern of his life did not differ from his father's. Politics and a mug of beer, wakes and mass, a large family, and once in a while a sentimental thought of the old sod of his parents were his lot. And he died in the faith, knowing full well that his children would get somewhere.

The third Mike O'Shea did. He probably became mayor, and he saw to it that the children's children of his father's friends became schoolteachers and policemen and street foremen and representatives to the Great and General Court. Nothing in the political history of America strikes one as more phenomenal than the definiteness with which the second generation of Irish in Massachusetts took over the politics of the towns and of the commonwealth itself. They did it because they early recognized politics as the one field in which they had an equal opportunity with the native stock, because they knew the strength of numbers and because they welded themselves into a solid block.

The Irish thus established themselves so firmly in eastern Massachusetts and so entrenched themselves within the civil organization of the state that, even when political squabbles among themselves lost them the higher elective offices, they had more of their num-

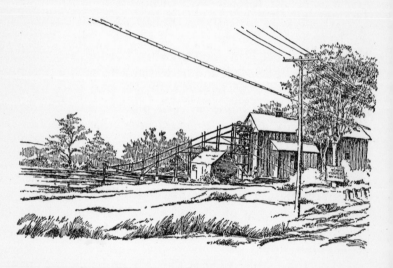

ber in life-tenure positions than the Yankees themselves ever held. The Irish influx created more jobs, and the Irish filled them as soon as they were created. Moreover, they organized themselves against the Yankees in other fields: they sold insurance to each other, bought groceries from each other, built their own schools and their own colleges, and hired help all along the line from among their own numbers. But it all started from their political talent. Only circumstances and never another man can beat an Irishman in local politics.

The other immigrants to the river valley never achieved what the Irish did. The only group that approached them in numbers were the French Canadians, but they fought too much among themselves to come anywhere near political unity. For a while, the Yankees and the French Canadians tried to team together to stop the Irish, but it did not work. Not only were the French Canadians splitting the party among their own factions but they were fighting with the Yankees too. And out of every such mess, the Irish emerged doubly triumphant. The sons of Mike O'Shea threw caution to the four winds once they were in office. But during a campaign, for sheer political strategy, they left the Yankees and everyone else so far behind that not even their dust could be seen.

Part Eight

The Valley at Evening

22

Downstream

"IN my thought I seem to stand on the bank of a river and watch the endless flow of the stream, floating objects of all shapes, colors and natures; nor can I much detain them as I pass, except by running beside them a little way along the bank. But whence they come or whither they go is not told me." Those are the words of Emerson, and they reflect a state of mind as much that of the Charles River valley downstream as the sage's own. In Emerson's day, the odyssey of the Puritans was done. Channing and his Unitarianism set free the Puritan soul from the chains of Calvinism. Emerson and his profound optimism set free the Puritan mind from its alliance with the powers of darkness. The soldiers and the farmers and tradesmen set free the Yankee character from an outmoded principle of political despotism. The poets and the artists, limited as they may have been in their powers, set free the Puritan heart from the frigid restraint that had chilled and withered it into a hard core. And now the inhabitants of this valley had achieved maturity. The noon of their day had come with Emerson, and they were entering the long afternoon.

Many things happened then, but those things were

merely witnessed, they were never explained and never probed, by those who lived on the riverbanks. Boston grew into a metropolis from its place as a provincial capital. "The College" across the river grew into a university of huge dimensions. The Cowley Fathers reared a monastery on the riverbank within yards of the Harvard buildings. The Irish migrated in swarms to spread out over the entire river valley. The Italians took over the whole North End peninsula of Boston where the *Constitution* had been built and where Revere had lived. Elevated trains shuttled back and forth across the river at a pace that would have startled the stoutest of the pioneers. The Great and General Court's rolls underwent changes, and more Gaelic, Slavic, and French-Canadian names appeared than the *Transcript* reporters could decipher. The rolls of Harvard underwent similar mutations; registrants appeared from such foreign countries as Ohio and even other planets such as Wisconsin. New journals appeared, dispensing news of the activities of new people and new organizations. The Gaelic, concentrated in South Boston, took over Evacuation Day, anniversary of the British departure from Boston, and celebrated it noisily as St. Patrick's Day. The Italians, concentrated in the North End, took over Columbus Day. Legislation was enacted changing the names of public squares from such prosaic names as Suffolk to such poetic ones as O'Flaherty or Zimbolski.

And Boston or Cambridge did not even run along the riverbank to catch up with these things that flowed past. As Arnold Bennett was quick to point out, this region was beyond a process of becoming anything. It simply was. The lower Charles today is Symphony Hall

on Friday afternoons, when the female population of
Boston's old self adjourn as one woman to a session with
Bach or Beethoven. It is the Boston *Herald* at the breakfast table and the *Transcript* at twilight. It is the used
bookshop under the Old South Meetinghouse in winter
and the used bookshop in the Old South churchyard in
the summer. It is Thompson's Spa, noontime mecca of
the professional and businessmen, many of whom would
go without lunch rather than trust the menu elsewhere.
It is Beacon Hill on Christmas Eve, when choirboys
from the Church of the Advent walk through the narrow streets singing hymns from an English hymnal. It
is the Athenaeum, the private library in which one can
buy a "share" only when an old member or his heirs
offer one for sale, and where the ghost of a woman lost
among its shelves still walks in a bewildered state of
resignation. It is Commencement along the Cambridge
bank, when the faint glow of lanterns gleam in the
college houses' courtyards and the illuminated towers
of Harvard are reflected in the river. It is Gilbert and
Sullivan at the Colonial Theatre. It is beans on Saturday night and Back Bay churches on Sunday morning,
swanboats in the Public Garden and squirrels on the
Common, students on the Esplanade along the river
basin, and respected citizens dying in Phillips House
overlooking the river.

Except in the instruments of life, the dominant
characteristics of life at the river mouth remain unchanged, so far as the inhabitants themselves are concerned. New peoples and new institutions they pay no
attention to, and there is less absorption of new blood
here than at any other spot in this land. Cabots don't
marry Murphys, and the Harvard Corporation does not

number among its fellows any French Canadians. Philadelphia scrapple is Colonial Breakfast Food, and New York's letter *R* exists only in words that have no *R* in them. The river basin looks inward and not outward, and life here feeds on itself. Best sellers in New England are books about New England—not about the rest of the world, which doesn't matter much except as a curiosity. Mark Twain was a disturbing element from the West, but Howells, who came from Ohio, achieved the impossible and became a Bostonian and a resident of Massachusetts in the fullest sense because he was prepared to make certain concessions.

Life at the river mouth, therefore, has taken on a certain immutable pattern. There are three cycles; like three varieties of old wine, consecrated with age, ripe and sacred. There is the daily cycle of life, the seasonal cycle, and the cycle of the years. The daily cycle begins with the *Herald*, even though there are three other morning papers in the city; but the *Herald* is conservative and knows how to make up the obituary page. It proceeds with walking to State Street, in the case of city dwellers, or entraining on the Boston and Maine or New Haven, in the case of country dwellers. There is some semblance of commercial activity in the morning, but there is no wild hurry about it; and for the volume of business transacted therein, State Street is probably the quietest street in the world. At noon there is Thompson's Spa, where the financial structure of New England eats lunch at a long counter on stools. In the afternoon, commerce resumes, but on an even less hurried plane than in the morning. Late in the afternoon the *Transcript* appears and the clubs show signs of slow life. A cigar, a whisky-and-soda and a polite word of conversation, and the social interlude is over. Boston club life is not intricate. There is a legend that a man died once in his chair at the St. Botolph Club and was not discovered for three days, because club members did not have the effrontery to speak to him unless spoken to first. The Somerset Club has not yet conceded the 1932 election to Roosevelt, and the Tavern Club has not yet conceded that the electric light is any improvement over gas, which is still used for illumination. The Harvard Club has just officially recognized the existence of women; but in providing room for the wives of members, the club has also provided a separate entrance for them. The Boston Opera House did the same thing for second-balcony frequenters; the latter have to sneak in ignominiously through a side portal while the great use the main entrance.

After the club interlude, Boston goes quietly to sleep. No city of over half a million population in the world so silences itself after sundown as does Boston. Many of the hotel dining rooms are totally deserted at nine o'clock, and to eat in one of them after that hour is a rare experience in asceticism. There are some cocktail rooms that stay awake, but they are patronized largely by strangers who have lived in New England for only a century or so. The lights of the city are not glaring, but twinkle politely across the river like diamonds on a dowager's black velvet.

People at the river mouth eat lunch in public places, but dinner is a private affair and is eaten at home. If Gilbert and Sullivan is playing at the Colonial, there might be a busy night at the theater, but as a rule Boston is not currently theater-minded. Producers no longer present the right things. Old H. T. Parker, the music and theater critic of the *Transcript,* with his great staff and flowing cape, is dead.[1] Philip Hale, the *Herald's* critic, is dead. Theater criticism in Boston is dead too, and a candidate for a doctorate across the river may someday emerge from the depths of the Widener Library to produce a capable paper on the need of good criticism if one is to have good drama.

Boston can no longer recognize a good play, although it will patronize an indifferent musical comedy.

Concerts fare somewhat better, perhaps because the music critics still function. The *Herald* and the *Transcript* will pounce on bad music as a cat pounces on a mouse, and there is no toying with it. Music is a large part of life at the river mouth. At regular inter-

[1] Now the *Transcript* itself is dead, too. Since these pages were written, it died slowly and quietly of old age and sclerosis of the advertising columns. Its readers sighed, and turned to the conservative, moderate *Christian Science Monitor* for their evening news.

vals the Boston Symphony orchestra leaves the city and goes across the river to play for the Cantabrigians, though Symphony Hall in Boston is about ten minutes from Harvard Square. A score of little halls around Copley Square are filled with music daily, the soaring voices of sopranos, the sparkling notes of the piano, or the wistful strains of a violin. Spring comes officially with the Pops, when patrons sit about little tables drinking pale drinks and listening to a delicately blended program of light classical and popular tunes. Summer comes officially with the open-air concerts on the Esplanade, when the sad strains of Sibelius float out over the river.

Aside from music and the theater, night at the river basin brings out more lecturers. Boston and its environs have never given up their enthusiasms for lectures, and the reason for the success of Christian Science in Boston suburbs is often held to be the frequency with which it has been extolled in lectures. There are lectures all day in Boston: morning, afternoon, and night. The Lowell Institute provides the best lectures free of charge, though one must read the *Transcript* to get to them, because tickets must be sent for in advance and the trustees assume that anyone worthy of a ticket would necessarily read the *Transcript* and accordingly announce the lectures only in that paper. Lectures are held in the hotels, in the libraries, in the clubhouses, in brownstone homes, in churches, and in theaters. Some are sponsored by endowments, some by clubs such as the Browning Society (which was founded to probe the mysteries of that queer poet and, having long since failed, continues to probe deeper mysteries), some by society matrons, and some just happen.

The lecturing spirit is infectious, and even the drifters on the Common lecture; some of the patricians of Boston will stop on the way from State Street to the Back Bay and give them as courteous attention as they would give the president of Harvard.

But lectures and concerts and plays are over early, and the few who venture out regard them as something of an event and get back home in good time. Night clubs do not flourish. There may be somewhere a drearier spot than a night club at midnight or any other hour in this area, but it has not yet been discovered. There was a salesman at the Parker House one year in the roaring twenties who felt the need for some convivial entertainment. He ventured out into the city in search of some. They found him ten days later in Mount Auburn Cemetery, entreating the marble statues of John Winthrop, John Adams, James Otis, and Joseph Story to please, for tradition's sake, be quiet.

The seasonal cycle of life at the river basin is fixed by gentle signs rather than by exciting events. In the autumn, the swanboats disappear from the Public Garden, the sightseeing boats from the river, and the *Herald* has a long column of notes relating to the wholesale migration of Harvard professors back from the White Mountains. Black-mustached Italians and florid Irishmen remove the plants from public parks, maintenance men lay out boardwalks in Harvard Yard, and Goodspeed's Bookshop moves its annex out of the churchyard of the Old South back into the basement. In Cambridge autumn is gray and sad, when the elm leaves fall down on the brick sidewalks and a bleaker wind comes up the river. On the river itself, it is an in-between season with only the shuffling of feet over the bridge on a Saturday afternoon and the uninspired "regular Harvard cheer" drifting out over the river and dying upstream at Mount Auburn. In Boston the janitor of Symphony Hall puts his charge in order, the Book Fair fills the Boston Garden, and Tremont Street stores dress their windows in accordance with the Harvard football schedule. If it is election year, Old Tinkham, the perpetual congressman from the longest Congressional district on the Charles, goes to Africa to shoot big game and returns in November to find himself safely elected, having completely ignored the whole campaign. If it is not election year, he may stay home.

Winter brings hand-bell ringers to Beacon Hill, candlelights (not the electric facsimiles) in windows, skaters on the river, huddling transients to the Common, a brave and short-lived stock company effort, female clerks to the male-dominated Old Corner Bookstore, and more slush in the streets than the Street Department could remove even if it did not consider an attempt to do so a sacrilege. Winter in Cambridge means the climax in the Charles Eliot Norton series of lectures on fine arts and poetry, the universal playing of squash, swimming across the water surrounding the Yard, revolt against some censorship across the river in Boston, and complaints by the ward heelers of Cambridge that what Harvard University is trying to do is to capture the city government of Cambridge.

When spring comes, old men sit down and take their pens in hand to advise the papers that a crocus was observed on Beacon Street, hurdy-gurdy men play weird versions of popular airs on street corners, the Harvard crews row up and down the river, the boardwalks are taken up from the Harvard Yard, the Cathedral Church of St. Paul is full of late Lenten worshipers at noontime, the Harvard students riot and march to Radcliffe, the Technology students riot and march to jail, the Boston papers editorialize against student riots, three or four people attempt suicide in the river, and Eleanor Sears walks to Providence. Spring on the south bank of the Charles is tulips in the Public Garden, the spelling bee in Faneuil Hall, chintz covers in the Touraine lobby, weddings at Trinity Church, speechifying on the Common, and the elaborate election rights of the Ancient and Honourable Artillery. On the north bank spring means the restless walking of Harvard freshmen longing for girls back home, burying the dead that have accumulated in the vaults of Mount Auburn, green leaves on the elm trees, avowals by Cambridge landladies that never again will they have students in the house, and an old lady who sells shoelaces on the steps of the First Church.

Then the summer comes, full of Commencement, summer schools, the sightseeing skipper on the Charles who believes that everything bordering it is the "greatest" thing in the world, the Esplanade concerts, Goodspeed's in the churchyard again, putting shutters on the Back Bay town houses, letters to the papers from ladies who resent the nude urchins' swimming in the Frog Pond, letters from liberals asking why the ladies can't stay away from the Frog Pond, flower vendors on Boylston Street, and the man who sells catnip on Brimstone Corner. Summer brings the highest temperature (in the nineties) in forty years just as winter brings the lowest in fifty. It brings bathers to the river in front of the Suffolk County jail, yachts to the basin, and light pleasure craft upstream, canoes at Norum-

bega where the Norse were supposed to have built the
Lost City in some versions of the affair, and the heavy
odor of burnt flesh at the Brighton slaughterhouse. It
brings long cool evenings, when there is a spell of
quiet happiness all along the river, the soft flowing of

the water and the sweet distant music from the "Shell"
on the Esplanade.

There is something permanent and aged about all
this downstream. It is immune to politics, to innova-
tions, and to history. Things unexpected happen but
such things flow by as the waters of the river, and life
goes on the same as it did before.

23

Upstream

It is three centuries now that white men have been settled along the Charles and two since the last village at its source was founded, the village where Sir Harry Frankland established his Marblehead mistress in splendor. Through those centuries there have been changes far more apparent than those at the river mouth, and it is only beyond the towns and into the country that there is evidence of a permanent pattern of life. Nor in many cases have the upriver families held to their ground as have those downstream. The river mouth impresses one with the age and enduring quality of its civilization. But the towns and villages upstream impress one with the fleeting quality of human affairs. Life downstream is like the waters of the river in its permanence; but life upstream is like the trees that abide their season and then fall to the ground.

When the Charles begins its way on the surface of the earth, it is a thin ribbon of a stream and it trickles, nearly hidden by a woodland undergrowth, past the old, forgotten graveyard of a deserted village. It is amplified a few rods farther along by another streamlet, which has its origin in a deserted quarry. Then it flows down past what was once a thriving little village and where now even the ancient cellars are filled up with earth and blossoming with dandelions. There was a granite quarry there in the nineteenth century, and the settlement at the headwaters of the river boomed. Men first came to work at the quarry; and then, when both

the granite and the market for it alike looked inexhaustible, they sent for their wives and children. A scattering of temporary homes appeared, and an inn was erected close to the quarry. For a few years the slim riverlet flowed past the busy scene of horses hauling huge blocks of granite on stoneboats, of men sweating at the quarry all day and downing beer at the inn at night and of promoters who worked the quarry as if its resources might dissolve before their eyes. And after

all this came a sudden departure of workers and promoters and horses from the village. The inn fell to
pieces, the little houses tumbled down, and the village
has disappeared almost completely. Nothing remains
but the tiny graveyard with its brave inscriptions and
the quarry pit deep with water and feeding the Charles
from its seemingly bottomless reservoir.

The little quarry village at the riverhead has vanished from the earth, and it has been fortunate in that
there are no sad traces left of an abortive dream. The
other upstream towns are not so happy. In early times
they were settlements with a water mill grinding away
in the heart of the community and the workers huddling close to it. Then the nineteenth century brought
the mad scramble for bigger mills and cheaper workers.
The Poles and the French Canadians and the Irish
flooded into the valley, courageous, longing people who
had vast hopes. Money was flowing freely. The mills
erected long rows of boxlike little houses, which the
workers could rent. The executives built splendid mansions, according to the bizarre architectural standards
of the day, farther away from the mills. Main Streets
grew up overnight from a dusty road with a general
store and a post office to a paved street lined with one-
and two-story buildings. Lodge halls sprouted up all
along the street, the hall one rickety flight up and two
or three stores underneath. School buildings were
erected to give the millworkers' children a fleeting ac-
quaintance with a larger world before they went the
way of their fathers. Where one church had struggled
along since the founding days, three more flourished
under the auspices of the millowners. Racial groups
clustered about defensively after hours on the front

stoops of the mill houses, and they talked about the mill. All their lives were centered about the mills, and even the towns themselves, Milford and Millis and City Mills had the mills in their names.

The daily cycle of life meant little in the nineteenth century mill town upstream; it was empty and barren and hard. People seemed to live not for the joy of living but in the perpetual hope of better days, when they could move out of the mill-owned houses and the shadow of the great smokestack and have a plot of land somewhere on the edge of town. Immigrants, to whom this life was itself the last frontier, were slow to give up hope of all those things they had dreamed of in the old country, and they believed in the future of their children. They sat about on summer nights, hating to attempt sleep in the hot little houses, and talking of this strange new land, of its promises and its disappointments. Their sons found haunts on Main Street to pass the time, and their daughters, the first lost generation, took top honors in the public schools and were snatched out at fourteen to go into the mills.

There was scarcely time for a single generation of immigrant millworkers to complete their lives close to the mills before calamity came. Having arrived late in the nineteenth century, they saw the towns spread from tiny communities to sprawling boroughs, new railroad sidings and new way stations, new and higher ells on the factories, Carnegie libraries, atrocious "blocks" on Main Streets, ugly pseudo-Gothic frame churches, better Gothic stone churches that never rose higher than the basement, electric street lights, "opera houses" featuring first the strolling melodramas and then Fatty Arbuckle, streetcars and the World War. They saw all this, but they never became part of the communities. They had their own churches, since the church followed them wherever they settled on the wrong side of the river and close to it, for the mills were close. Otherwise, they were a people apart from the old town, and they spoke their own language in the markets and took possession of Main Street only on Saturday nights.

They saw, too, without apprehending, changes in the mills and among the millowners. The expansion and the rise of the mills themselves can be traced even today from the shade of the bricks with which they were built. The little building in the center, a century old perhaps, is darkened to a deep brown and covered with ivy. Surrounding it are various ells somewhat larger and deep red in color, and the ivy is up to the first-story windows. And behind all this are the larger buildings, the brick in their walls still bright red and no ivy in sight, for they were built in a boom era when there was no time for such things as slowly creeping ivy. The millowners, meanwhile, moved farther away from their mills. They built great wooden houses on the other side of town, houses with towers and many bay windows and rambling piazzas. The times were good. There were croquet sets on front lawns and stereoptical paraphernalia in libraries, and iron stags in the front yards. There were gas chandeliers, which could readily be adapted to electricity within, dark walnut and horsehair furniture and double doors all over the place. A close clannish life was led, and four or five of the town's hugest homes stood in a row, with the residents of each cousins to the residents of the others. At whist parties and victrola concerts in the evening, the future of the town was decided, because the cousins were all church wardens and bank directors and hospital or library trustees and rulers of the press, since the banks financed and the mills supported the stores that advertised in the press.

The millowners sent their sons to the local public schools in most cases, and the second generation of millowners and millworkers, therefore, knew much more about each other than their fathers ever did. Democracy worked in the public schools, and in due time the Yankee stockowners and the Continental-sired workers may have achieved some sort of social synthesis. But the first generation of millowners frowned on extracurricular associations between their children and those of the workers. So the slight, brief school-day intercourse of the two groups was broken when the last bell rang and severed completely when the high school diplomas were given out at endless ceremonies on a hot June night in the opera house. The owners' sons went away to Harvard, and the workers' sons went to the mills.

As the years went by, nothing came to heal the breach. Most of the owners' sons came back to take up their fathers' management jobs, but they married their cousins' children or brought wives home from fac- similes of their own families in other towns. Their con- temporaries among the workers were already married and reproducing down in the dreary rows of mill houses. Then the South beckoned to the textile indus- tries, and many of the mills reduced their production. Economic changes came too, all through the structure of New England industry. Larger and larger portions of the mills were used exclusively for "storage" pur- poses, which meant that they were not used at all. Families in the mill houses that had three or four work- ing in the mills found themselves with only one em- ployed there. Local banks lent money for a while, but the sums were too small; and Boston banks would not lend any more. Railroad sidings grew rusty and hidden by weeds. The factory whistles blew less and less often. Some mills closed down completely, and they were the wise ones. Others struggled on stubbornly, attempting to resist this thing that none of them understood, and they were courageously foolish. The railroads closed the little way stations, the paint peeled from the walls of mill houses and mansions alike, and the sun set on strangely quiet industrial towns.

Some of the thrifty immigrants had saved enough to move out of the rows of mill houses and into the surrounding country, where they bought a few acres of land and worked it unendingly. Truck gardeners planted the land closely and wisely, and made a better living than they had in the mills. Many of them had never seen the soil, but the peasant love and knowledge of the earth was in their blood. So they lived on closer terms with it than they ever had with the mills. But they were the few and the fortunate. The countless others are still living in the shadow of the great

smokestack and close to the mills that are as quiet as death. The banks own their houses now, and they are beyond redemption. The second generation, many of them young parents of unwanted children, drift through the years aimlessly, themselves unwanted and themselves beyond redemption. They play bingo once a week and go to bank night at the successor to the opera house once a week. They look to the Democratic party for some sort of salvation, but they are not surprised when they do not get it. They are surprised by nothing, embittered by nothing, hopeful of nothing. They were born in places where they do not belong by heritage; moreover, they know it. It was not they but their fathers who were lured to the industrial towns along the upper river, but it is they who must pay the price for all those beautiful dreams. They understand, too, that this region was never made to be cosmopolitan, that it is far too inbred for that. They know that it is a provincial country.

The middle Charles valley is a happier region, for it has never attempted to be something beyond or aside from its destiny. It has remained provincial. Suburban settlements for Boston businessmen have arisen, but they are not American suburbs. They are Boston suburbs. Like life at the river mouth, suburban life there has taken on a pattern that is far from rapid or exciting but is richly satisfying. Conformity is still important; yet there is a marked absence of community prying. Absorption of new strains of blood is far more evident than either downstream or upstream. In the suburbs, Irish and Jews and Yankees live together not only in concord but on terms of friendship, and that is one thing which makes living there good. Traditions have not lingered as they have at the basin, but neither have there been the uneven and disrupting upward and downward trends that left the mill towns lying about the river like decaying corpses. Where life at the river mouth defies time and life in the upstream towns has been conquered by it, life in the suburbs moves along with it at a serene and measured pace.

The path of the river valley down the years to

come is a provincial path. The work of this region has long since been done, and this corner of the nation is like the oldest ell on an ancient house. It is the part where the visitors are taken, the part that served its practical function generations earlier. People from the rest of the country, whose fathers were born here, will return to see the scene of their heritage. But there will be no greater industries here than there have been, and no greater farms, as there will be elsewhere.

It is September along the Charles, and the day grows old. The sun sinks slowly in the west. Evening comes, quietly, peacefuly, to the river basin and the Cambridge elms, under which the poets walked in the afternoon of their content; to the suburbs around the bends in the river, where old Judge Fuller had bawled protests against desecrating the waters of the Charles and where the almanackers wrote of time the omnipotent; and to the deserted village and the little graveyard which is all that remains at its source. The river itself flows unimpressed to the sea. On moonlit nights little children, who understand such mysteries, see the ghosts of their poets and their heroes along the banks. And old men, mindful of their Puritan ancestors, never stop to regard the moon.

Sources and Tributaries

Sources and Tributaries

IF a river can lure men at its mouth to venture upstream to seek its source, it has achieved no small thing. Any book worth its salt should accomplish a similar mission and invite its readers to look into its sources. This bibliography is, therefore, not primarily an author's credential but merely a guide or a map to help the reader in further explorations of the river and its valley. There are some things, however, that you can never find out in books, things as yet unwritten that you can see in the valley or perhaps only feel. Other things you can learn by talking with those who have lived near the river all their lives. But each of these books that I have consulted and have listed here is like a tributary of the river itself and leads you into lands worth knowing more about.

The valley of the Charles has undoubtedly produced more books than any other river valley in this hemisphere, and it has probably had more written about it. In preparing this book, therefore, I have limited myself in various ways. I have, for example, not bothered much about repeating the happenings that belong to history in general, but have confined myself to their local or regional beginnings. This led, early in the work, to more extensive concern over the lesser lights of history, whom I found to be surprisingly important in their own rights. The men who challenged autocracy, the men who toiled in lowly printing shops, and the men who hammered for liberty in the infant newspapers seemed to me characteristic of early life in this valley, and as significant as the political leaders, the college presidents, and the generals. It has been the same way with things as with people; and I found such things as almanacs and wooden plows as consequential as government decrees and heavy artillery.

All this is responsible in some measure for a bibliography which would not meet the requirements of formal history but which will acquaint the reader with what living in this valley through these centuries has been like and with the sort of people who have known the Charles.

The standard and the best history of Massachusetts is the *Commonwealth History of Massachusetts,* under the general editorship of Albert Bushnell Hart and published in five volumes in 1927-1928. Of immeasurable value have been the *Collections* (Boston: 1792-1940) and the *Proceedings* (Boston: 1792-1933) of the Massachusetts Historical Society, as well as the *Publications* of the Colonial Society of Massachusetts and the *Proceedings* of the Prince Society and those of the Bostonian Society. Another work of general interest is the *Memorial History of Boston,* edited by Justin Winsor and published in 1880-1881 in four volumes. Samuel Adams Drake's *Historic Fields and Mansions of Middlesex* (Boston: 1874) is a pleasant tour of the river valley, although many of the more interesting parts of the river flow through the adjacent county of Norfolk.

Professor Kirtley F. Mather, of Harvard, furnished me with a bibliography of the geologic history of the river so far as it was obtainable. Bulletins 839 and 760-B of the United States Geological Survey are, respectively, *Geology of the Boston Area*, by Laurence La Forge, and *Physical Features of Central Massachusetts*, by William Alden. More helpful than either of these, however, is an article in the *American Geologist*, Vol. 29, entitled *The Geologic History of the Charles River*. More readable than any of these but with less particular information on the river itself are *New England Acadian Shorelines*, by D. W. Johnson, and *Rivers of North America*, by I. C. Russell.

The best work on primitive life near the Charles and anywhere else is E. B. Tylor's *Primitive Culture* (New York: 1877); the two volumes indicate a deep understanding of primitive man and are both authoritative and beautiful in tone. *The Myths of the New World*, by D. G. Brinton (Philadelphia: 1868), is well written and of great interest as American folklore. The following have firsthand accounts of the Indians: *New England Prospect*, by William Wood (London: 1634), *New English Canaan*, by Thomas Morton (London: 1637), and *Historical Collections of the Indians in New England*, by Daniel Gookin (Boston: 1792). George E. Ellis has a valuable chapter on the Indians of the Charles region in the above-mentioned *Memorial History of Boston*.

The best books referring to the Charles prior to the settlement of the valley are those of Captain John Smith himself. *The Works of John Smith* (ed. Edward Arber, London: 1884) are inclusive. Smith's particular works on New England were his *Advertisements for the Unexperienced Planters of New England* (London: 1631) and his *Description of New England* (London:

1616). E. Keble Chatterton's *Captain John Smith* (New York: 1927) is an entertaining biography. The best general book on pre-Calvinistic colonization is C. H. Levermore's *Forerunners and Competitors of the Pilgrims and Puritans* (Brooklyn: 1912). Various and numerous books have also been written to prove that Norsemen settled along the Charles years earlier, but most rivers of America enter like claims and there is no valid evidence that any of them were ever seen by the Norse.

There have been several books on William Blackstone, most of them rather colorless biographies. The best are Thomas C. Amory's *William Blackstone* (Boston: 1877), H. S. Ballou's *William Blaxton* (Boston: 1931), and B. F. De Costa's *William Blackstone* (New York: 1880). A novel of wide interest as a reconstruction of the Puritan scene and containing much about Blackstone is John Lothrop Motley's *Merry Mount* (Boston: 1849).

For the Puritans' duel with the devil the best material is their own works. Winthrop's *Journals* were published as a history of New England by James Savage in Boston, 1853. His *Life and Letters*, of less general interest but of value in a study of the man, were published in Boston, 1869, edited by R. C. Winthrop. Cotton Mather's *Magnalia Christi Americana* (London: 1702) is the only authority for some things and, for Matheriana, is exceptionally readable. The diaries of both Cotton Mather and Judge Samuel Sewall are fascinatingly illuminating and are published within the collections of the Massachusetts Historical Society as separate volumes. Mather's extensive diaries, amounting to two large volumes, make the biographies of him of secondary consequence, for the man fairly leaps out from the pages of the diaries very much alive. But Samuel Mather's *Life of the Very Reverend and Learned Cotton Mather* (Boston: 1729), although it is little more than an extensive eulogy, has some arresting details about Mather's daily life. Of the several other biographies, Barret Wendell's *Cotton Mather, the Puritan Priest* (New York: 1891) is still the best if one remembers that Wendell was a sort of apologist for Mather. Of contemporary writers on the Puritans, Samuel Eliot Morison represents the healthiest point of view. He is tolerant and realistic, and his book, *Builders of the Bay Colony* (Boston: 1930), combines a thorough understanding of Winthrop's settlement with an active sense of humor. *The Founding of New England*, by James Truslow Adams (Boston: 1921), is critical history of a high order in which Mr. Adams brings down the ax sharply on Puritan leaders. Sydney George Fisher's *Men, Women, and Manners in Colonial Times* (Philadelphia: 1900) is the best history of manners for the period. The state of the Boston mind in its strife with the devil is, of course, best reflected in the types of sermons delivered there and in upstream towns, but they are all of a piece and any picked at random would do for the curious.

John Eliot is a man worth reading about, but much of that written about him is not worth reading. *The Life and Labors of John Eliot*, by Robert B. Caverly (Lowell: 1881), is biography at its very worst, but it contains information. *Eliot of Massachusetts*, by David Chamberlain (London: 1928), is a little better; it is brief and prosaic, but sound. Eliot himself wrote a

Description of New England, an edition of which was published in Boston in 1886.

The chapter on Harvard's first year is based primarily on Winthrop's account in the *Journals,* which contain also the elaborate confession of Eaton's wife. Professor Samuel Eliot Morison's *Founding of Harvard College* (Cambridge: 1935) offers nothing further on the college's first year but has an interesting series of chapters on the background of the college, both as regards its heritage and in regard to the cowyards surrounding it. Supplementary reading of an entertaining variety, because of Morison's style, and of informative value, because of his studies, is the same author's *Harvard in the Seventeenth Century* (Cambridge: 1936).

The origin of the upstream farms and the beginning of the inland towns are, of course, most readily traced through the local histories, which do not, however, offer especially entertaining reading and are uniformly flat. The best of towns in the Charles valley are L. R. Paige's *History of Cambridge* (Boston: 1877), Francis Jackson's *History of the Early Settlement of Newton* (Boston: 1854), and Herman Mann's *Historical Annals of Dedham* (Dedham: 1847). The Dedham Historical Register is also of value, and so are the Records of the town of Watertown. Charles Francis Adams wrote an important paper on *The Genesis of the Massachusetts Town,* which is in the Massachusetts Historical Society *Proceedings,* 2nd Series, Vol. 7. Another work of interest is Anne B. MacLear's *Early New England Towns* in the Columbia University Studies in Economics, History, and Public Law, Vol. XXIX, No. 1.

John Josselyn, whose works are mentioned in the text, wrote two books of interest for the light thrown on early agriculture in the valley of the Charles: *New England Rarities* (London: 1672) and *Two Voyages to New England* (London: 1675). Captain Edward Johnson's *Wonder Working Providence* (London: 1654) is another early account, but Johnson would not seem as likable an author as Josselyn.

There are two good books on the almanacs. One is *Notes on the Almanacs of Massachusetts*, by Charles L. Nichols (Worcester: 1912). Another, which is about the Ameses in particular, is *Essays, Humor and Poems of Nathaniel Ames, Father and Son*, by Samuel Briggs (Cleveland: 1891). To know the almanacs as they were, however, one should look up a few originals, which are still preserved in various eastern historical societies.

The adventures of the early water-mill proprietors along the river I have pieced together from court and town records. There are some good histories of American and New England industry for the student of economics but few from the angle that I wanted. The most useful was W. B. Weeden's *Economic and Social History of New England* (Boston: 1891). All the rest are so dull that I would not suggest anyone's trying to read them for pleasure.

The chapter on early printing in the colony is indebted to a group of assorted sources. Paige's *History of Cambridge* (Boston: 1877) mentioned above and the *Supplement and Index* to the same, edited by Mary Gozzaldi (Cambridge: 1930), are helpful. The most authoritative *History of Printing in America*, by Isaiah Thomas (Albany: 1874), constitutes two volumes of aging vintage, but they are still the best work in the field and quite readable. In the Massachusetts Historical

Society *Proceedings* (2nd Series, Vol. XI) there is an historical note on New England printing by S. A. Greene, a Cambridge historian and physician. *The Development of Freedom of the Press in Massachusetts,* by Clyde A. Duniway (New York: 1906), is worth reading as a work of importance and worth rereading as a fascinating story.

For early newspapers, in addition to the foregoing works, the following may be consulted: *History of American Journalism,* by James M. Lee (Boston: 1917), *History of Journalism in the United States,* by George H. Payne (New York: 1920), and *Literary Influences in Colonial Newspapers,* by Elizabeth C. Cook (New York: 1912). The *Diary of Cotton Mather* (Boston: 1911-12) and Samuel A. Greene's *History of Medicine in Massachusetts* (Boston: 1881), together with such biographies as Bernard Faÿ's *Franklin, the Apostle of Modern Times* (Boston: 1929) and Carl Van Doren's *Benjamin Franklin* (New York: 1939), contain much of interest concerning the Mather-James Franklin feud and the association of Benjamin with his brother's newspaper. The Massachusetts Historical Society has the most complete files of the newspapers mentioned in the chapter.

The first year of the Revolution has, of course, produced a mountain of books. I am suggesting here only two outstanding authorities and a few books that deal especially with the first days of the actual hostilities. The authority on the occupation of Boston is still Richard Frothingham's *Siege of Boston* (Boston: 1849), but Allen French's *The First Year of the Revolution* (Boston: 1934) is the most complete study of the Revolution in Massachusetts. It is the soundest history written in an evocative style, as are also the same author's *Day of Concord and Lexington* (Boston: 1925) and *General Gage's Informers* (Ann Arbor: 1932). Harold Murdock's *The Nineteenth of April, 1775* (Boston: 1925) is a brief but keen analysis of the happenings of that day. Murdock also edited Lieutenant John Barker's diary under the title, *The British in Boston* (Cambridge: 1924). Another good diary is John Rowe's, published in the *Proceedings* of the Massachusetts Historical Society, 2nd Series, Vol. X.

There are three or four histories of the frigate *Constitution*. I liked best Ira N. Hollis's *The Frigate Constitution* (Boston: 1901). *On the Decks of Old Ironsides* by Elliot Snow also is interesting. Volumes VI and VII of the *United States Service* (New Series) contain an excellent history of the *Constitution*, by Captain H. D. Smith.

If anyone wants to read more about old bridges I don't know where it could be done. I could find no convenient references to draw upon for my chapters on bridges. I gathered my information from the records of the General Court, Harvard College, and various newspapers; and for much of it I am indebted to the publications of the Colonial Society of Massachusetts and of the Massachusetts Historical Society.

The best books on the literary life in the river valley are, of course, Van Wyck Brooks's *Flowering of New England* (New York: 1936) and *New England: Indian Summer* (New York: 1940). To find out much about Gilbert Stuart, you have to take a rather devious route. There are three books about him: *Gilbert Stuart,* by William T. Whitney (Cambridge: 1932), *The Life and Work of Gilbert Stuart,* by G. C. Mason (New

York: 1879), and *Gilbert Stuart*, by Lawrence Park (New York: 1926); but none of these are absorbing reading. *The Rise and Progress of the Arts of Design in America*, by William Dunlap (New York: 1834), is, despite its formidable title and mature age, much more interesting. There is also a good deal about Stuart in Dunlap's *Diary* (New York Historical Society: 1929-1931), which is first-rate reading.

Much the same situation exists in regard to Washington Allston. There are three biographies of him: J. B. Flagg's *Life and Letters of Washington Allston* (New York: 1892), Moses F. Sweetser's *Washington Allston* (Boston: 1879) and William Ware's *Lectures on Works and Genius of Washington Allston* (Boston: 1852). All three are extremely dry. The journals of various Cantabrigians, as those of Lowell, suggest much more clearly the sort of person Allston was. In Lowell's *Fireside Travels* (Boston: 1864) there is an essay called "Cambridge Thirty Years Ago" with some paragraphs on Allston.

My approach to the three poets, Lowell, Longfellow, and Holmes, has not been that of the biographer or of the critic. To me they have been men who lived on the banks of the Charles, who knew the river, and who loved it. I have, therefore, approached them through their homes, the houses in which they lived near the river. My very brief estimates of them are consequently based on their lives as men and not as professor or poet or physician or diplomat. There have probably been better poets who walked along the Charles, either in student days or after, than those three; but the moderns do not seem to have had the roots of those of the last century, whose lives had a richness and a fullness not now found. Good poets or bad, Lowell, Longfellow, and Holmes lived in intimate association with the Charles; and there is repeated evidence that the river meant much to them as a companion. *The Complete Writings of James Russell Lowell*, in sixteen volumes (Boston: 1904), contain also the *Letters* edited by Charles Eliot Norton and the *Life* by Horace E. Scudder. Ferris Greenslet's *James Russell Lowell* also is of interest (Boston: 1905).

While on the whole the prose writings of James Russell Lowell are inferior to his poetry, the prose of Longfellow reveals more about him than does his poetry. If the latter is consistently childlike, there was in fact something consistently childlike about Longfellow himself, and this is best expressed in his letters and private papers. You can learn little of the poet himself through reading the poems, for he always went far afield in his poetry and the number of stanzas which he really wrote poetry in the sense that he h self was there in the poem are pitifully few. H too polite to be a poet. *The Complete Poetical ar* *Works of Longfellow*, in eleven volumes 1886), tell as much of him as does any biogr ever; the definitive biography is the three by Samuel Longfellow (Boston: 1891) readable is probably H. S. Gorman's *A ican* (New York: 1926).

The poetry that Holmes wro reflects nothing of the man excer as the "Wonderful One-Hoss S The truly delightful Holmes have been, is in the *Autocr* papers. *The Writings of C* teen volumes (Boston: 1891), are complete. The definitive biography is J. T. Morse's *The Life and Letters of Oliver Wendell Holmes* (Boston: 1896).

The last section of the book has been written from a personal knowledge of the river valley more than from anything else. I have talked with various people, ranging from the chief of police of the little village of Hopkinton at the river's source to Harvard professors at the river's mouth. I have driven all over the valley with a friend who has lived in the region all his life, and we have spent many afternoons going about aimlessly and talking over what we have seen and trying to penetrate the future. We were not enheartened by certain upriver sections, and we were aware of a certain sadness, an emptiness, in the mill towns that failed and ʾok lost now. At such times we were discouraged at the ˑspects for our river valley, for we wondered what ˑd become of vacant factories and of all those hol-niˑes that fill decadent Main Streets on Saturday of ˑhen, as we went downstream past the farms themˑ perhaˑ, so peaceful and beautiful, the images of rest waˑom our minds; and we felt that here, Finally, a future of the valley and that all the the north ˑn incident, an abortive experiment. that, whateˑs mouth, where Cambridge lies to vincial and th to the south, we began to feel will always suˑs, this valley will remain pro-way: that the v in the core of New England river's mouth in ˑe that we could see it this the amenities of th cialism are there at the quiet farms along with deep roots; that are apparent in the ˑes, wearing their prosperity or their hardships with equal grace; and that the banes of provincialism in this age of cosmopolitanism are visible in that lost, bewildered, defeated aspect of the upriver towns.

Bibliography

ADAMS, JAMES TRUSLOW, *New England in the Republic.* Boston: 1926.

—— *Revolutionary New England,* Boston: 1923.

—— *The Founding of New England.* Boston: 1921.

ALDEN, WILLIAM, *Physical Features of Central Massachusetts.* U.S. Geologic Survey.

ALLSTON, WASHINGTON, *Letters on Art and Poems* (ed. R. H. Dana, Jr.). Boston: 1854.

AMORY, THOMAS COFFIN, *William Blackstone.* Boston: 1877.

—— *William Blaxton.* Boston: 1886.

ANDREWS, CHARLES M., *Colonial Folkways.* New Haven: 1919.

—— *Fathers of New England.* New Haven: 1919.

BACON, O. N., *History of Natick.* Boston: 1856

BALLOU, ADIN, *History of Milford.* Boston: 1882.

BALLOU, HOSEA STARR, *William Blaxton.* Boston: 1931.

BISHOP, J. L., *History of American Manufactures.* Philadelphia: 1866.

BOAS, RALPH, *Cotton Mather, Keeper of the Puritan Conscience.* New York: 1928.

BOLTON, CHARLES K., *Real Founders of New England.* Boston: 1929.

BRIGGS, SAMUEL, *Essays, Humor and Poems of Nathaniel Ames.* Cleveland: 1891.

BRINTON, D. G., *American Hero Myths,* Philadelphia: 1882.

—— *The Myths of the New World.* Philadelphia: 1868.

343

CALHOUN, ARTHUR W., *A Social History of the American Family*. Cleveland: 1917.

CARRIER, LYMAN, *The Beginnings of Agriculture in America*. New York: 1923.

CAVERLY, ROBERT, *Life and Labors of John Eliot*. Lowell: 1881.

CHAMBERLAIN, DAVID, *Eliot of Massachusetts*. London: 1928.

CLAFLIN, MARY B., *Brampton Sketches*. New York: 1890.

CLARK, V. S., *History of Manufacture in the United States*. Washington: 1916.

COOK, ELIZABETH C., *Literary Influences in Colonial Newspapers*. New York: 1912.

CRANE, J. C., *Reverend William Blackstone*. Worcester: 1896.

CROCKER, G. G., *The Ferry and the Charles River Bridge*. Boston: 1899.

DE COSTA, B. F., *William Blackstone*. New York: 1880.

DUNIWAY, CLYDE A., *Freedom of the Press in Massachusetts*. New York: 1906.

DUNLAP, WILLIAM, *Diary*. Albany: 1929-1931.

—— *History of the Rise and Progress of the Arts of Design in the United States*. New York: 1834.

ELLIS, G. E., *The Indians of Eastern Massachusetts*. Boston: 1800.

FAŸ, BERNARD, *Franklin, the Apostle of Modern Times*. Boston: 1929.

FISHER, SYDNEY GEORGE, *Men, Women, and Manners in Colonial Times*. Philadelphia: 1900.

FISKE, JOHN, *Beginnings of New England*. Boston: 1899.

FLAGG, J. B., *Life and Letters of Washington Allston*. New York: 1892.

FRANKLIN, BENJAMIN, *Autobiography*. In *The Writings of Benjamin Franklin* (ed. Albert Henry Smyth). New York: 1907.

FRENCH, ALLEN, *Day of Concord and Lexington*. Boston: 1925.

——— *General Gage's Informers*. Ann Arbor: 1932.

——— *The First Year of the Revolution*. Boston: 1934.

FROTHINGHAM, RICHARD, *The Siege of Boston*. Boston: 1849.

GOODWIN, JOHN A., *The Pilgrim Republic*. Boston: 1888.

GORMAN, H. S., *A Victorian American*. New York: 1926.

GOZZALDI, MARY I., *Supplement and Index to the History of Cambridge*. Cambridge: 1930.

GREENE, SAMUEL A., *History of Medicine in Massachusetts*. Boston: 1881.

GREENSLET, FERRIS, *James Russell Lowell*. Boston: 1905.

HART, ALBERT BUSHNELL (Ed.), *Commonwealth History of Massachusetts*. New York: 1927-1928.

HIGGINSON, THOMAS WENTWORTH, *Old Cambridge*. New York: 1899.

HOLLIS, IRA N., *The Frigate Constitution*. Boston: 1901.

HOLMES, OLIVER WENDELL, *Complete Writings* (13 vol.). Boston: 1891.

HOWE, DAVID WAITE, *Puritan Republic*. Indianapolis: 1899.

HOWE, NATHANIEL, *A Century Sermon*. Andover: 1816.

HUBBARD, WILLIAM, *History of New England*. Boston: 1848.

HURD, DUANE H., *History of Middlesex County*. Philadelphia: 1890.

HUTCHINSON, THOMAS, *History of Massachusetts Bay*. Boston: 1795.

JACKSON, FRANCIS, *History of the Early Settlement of Newton*. Boston: 1854.

JACOBS, SARAH S., *The White Oak and Its Neighbors*. Boston: 1858.

JOHNSON, EDWARD, *Wonder Working Providence*. London: 1654.

JOSSELYN, JOHN, *New England Rarities*. London: 1672.

——— *Two Voyages to New England*. London: 1675.

LA FORGE, LAURENCE, *Geology of the Boston Area*. U.S. Geological Survey.

LEE, JAMES M., *History of American Journalism*. Boston: 1917.

LEVERMORE, C. H., *Forerunners and Competitors of the Pilgrims and Puritans*. Brooklyn: 1912.

LONGFELLOW, HENRY WADSWORTH, *Complete Poetical and Prose Works*. Boston: 1886.

LONGFELLOW, SAMUEL, *Life of Henry W. Longfellow*. Boston: 1891.

LOWELL, JAMES RUSSELL, *Works*. Boston: 1890-1892.

MACLEAR, ANNE B., *Early New England Towns*. Columbia University Studies in Economics, Vol. 29.

MANN, HERMAN, *Historical Annals of Dedham*. Dedham: 1847.

MASON, G. C., *Life and Works of Gilbert Stuart*. New York: 1879.

MATHER, COTTON, *Diary*. In Massachusetts Historical Society Collections. Boston: 1911-1912.

———— *Magnalia Christi Americana*. London: 1702.

———— *Wonders of the Invisible World*. London: 1693.

———— Cf. also his various sermons.

MATHER, SAMUEL, *Life of the Very Reverend and Learned Cotton Mather*. Boston: 1729.

MORISON, SAMUEL ELIOT, *Builders of the Bay Colony*. Boston: 1930.

———— *The Founding of Harvard College*. Cambridge: 1935.

———— *Harvard in the Seventeenth Century*. Cambridge: 1936.

MORSE, J. T., *Life and Letters of Oliver Wendell Holmes*. Boston: 1896.

MORTON, THOMAS, *New English Canaan*. Amsterdam: 1637.

MOTLEY, JOHN L., *Merry Mount*. Boston: 1849.

MURDOCK, HAROLD, *The Nineteenth of April, 1775*. Boston: 1925.

MURDOCK, HAROLD, *The British in Boston*. Cambridge: 1923.

MURDOCK, KENNETH B. (Ed.), *Selections from Cotton Mather*. New York: 1926.

NICHOLS, CHARLES L., *Notes on the Almanacs of Massachusetts*. Worcester: 1912.

NORTON, CHARLES ELIOT (Ed.), *Letters of James Russell Lowell*. New York: 1894.

PAIGE, LUCIUS R., *History of Cambridge*, Boston: 1877.

PARK, LAURENCE, *Gilbert Stuart*. New York: 1926.

PAYNE, GEORGE H., *History of Journalism in the United States*. New York: 1920.

SCUDDER, HORACE E., *James Russell Lowell*. Cambridge: 1901.

SMITH, FRANK, *History of Dedham*. Dedham: 1936.

SMITH, JOHN, *Advertisements for the Unexperienced Planters of New England*. London: 1631.

—— *Description of New England*. London: 1616.

—— *Works* (ed. Edward Arber). London: 1884.

SWEETSER, MOSES F., *Washington Allston*. Boston: 1879.

THOMAS, ISAIAH, *History of Printing in America* (2 Vols., 2nd ed.). Albany: 1874.

TURNER, FREDERICK J., *The Frontier in American History*. New York: 1920.

TAYLOR, EDWARD B., *Primitive Culture*. New York: 1877.

WARE, WILLIAM, *Lectures on Works and Genius of Allston*. Boston: 1852.

WEEDEN, W. B., *Economic and Social History of New England*. Boston: 1891.

WENDELL, BARRETT, *Cotton Mather, the Puritan Priest*. New York: 1891.

WHITLEY, WILLIAM T., *Gilbert Stuart*. Cambridge: 1932.

WILLOUGHBY, C. C., *Antiquities of the New England Indians*. Cambridge: 1935.

WILSON, WARREN, *The Evolution of the Country Community*. Chicago: 1923.

WINSOR, JUSTIN (Ed.), *Memorial History of Boston*. Boston: 1880-1881.

WINTHROP, JOHN, *History of New England*. (Winthrop's *Journals*, ed. James Savage). Boston: 1853.

—————— *Life and Letters* (ed. R. C. Winthrop). Boston: 1869.

WOOD, WILLIAM, *New England Prospect*. London: 1634.

WORTHINGTON, ERASTUS, *History of Dedham*. Boston: 1827.

—————— *John Eliot and the Indian Village*. Boston: 1828.

Collections of the Massachusetts Historical Society.
Proceedings of the Massachusetts Historical Society.
Publications of the Colonial Society of Massachusetts.
Proceedings of the Bostonian Society.
Notes and Queries.
Publications of the American Antiquarian Society.

American Historical Review.
Boston *Gazette*.
Boston *News-Leader*
Columbian Centinel.

Records of the Great and General Court.
Records of the Court of Assistants.
Records of the Middlesex County Courts.
The Massachusetts Archives.

Index

Index